Praise for *Humanize*

"*Humanize* offers practical content and insightful thinking that will help businesses make the deep changes needed to thrive in today's social world. "

—Mike Smith, author of *Matchpoint* and President of Forbes.com

"Companies need to be social, and worry less about doing social media. In this timely and important book, Grant and Notter provide a detailed model for making the humanization leap. Social media success is about people, not logos, and embedding that attitude in your company isn't easy. But armed with this book, you've got a fighting chance."

—Jay Baer, co-author of *The NOW Revolution: 7 Shifts to Make Your Business Faster, Smarter, and More Social*

"I like how-to. Which is why I like this book immensely. It gets beyond theory (which is interesting) to give you something you can actually act on (which is far more useful)! Think roadmap, not research. In other words, you won't finish reading this book and go, 'Now what...?'"

—Ann Handley, Chief Content Officer, MarketingProfs, and co-author of *Content Rules: How to Create Killer Blogs, Podcasts, Videos, Ebooks, Webinars (and More) That Engage Customers and Ignite Your Busines*

"*Humanize* is a deep dive on the impact of social media on leadership and the challenges of harnessing the power of engaged people. Wherever you are in the organization, this book helps you figure out what you need to change and dares you to make it happen. Stimulating and well done!"

—Mark Sanborn, New York Times Bestselling Author of *The Fred Factor*

"The days of controlling your message are dead. Born is the human organization where people buy from people, not companies. This is not another social media book. Notter and Grant dispel the notion that your leadership and your culture can continue to be self-centered and two-dimensional. With additional reading recommendations and worksheets, they'll have you well on your way to creating a sustainable shift inside and outside of your organization."

—Gini Dietrich, CEO, Arment Dietrich and founder, Spin Sucks Pro

"Our organizations have been modeled after mechanistic machines, where the human being is often treated as a cog. We know better. We know humans matter. It's time for a change. And this book illustrates how to be change agents as leaders, and for our organizations."

—Nilofer Merchant, author of *The New How: Creating Business Solutions Through Collaborative Strategy*

"In 2002, Malcolm Gladwell released *The Tipping Point*, and changed the way we looked at influence. In 2008, Seth Godin released *Tribes*, and showed us how small groups of people could take Gladwell's influence model and become leaders. Now, in 2011, Maddie Grant and Jamie Notter take these seminal books to their natural evolution. *Humanize: How People-Centric Organizations Succeed in a Social World* shows us how leadership and influence of your internal and external customer starts as all businesses start—with its people. This book strips away the myth of strong-arm leadership and offers solid, actionable paths that actually work. This is your compass for the direction your business needs to travel if you want to stay alive."

—Danny Brown, CEO of Bonsai Interactive Marketing, award-winning marketer and blogger at dannybrown.me, and author of *The Parables of Business*

"This is a systems leadership book hidden inside a social media book. We work with clients who encounter major challenges when we start helping them incorporate social media into their business practices, but those challenges are not solved with solely social media tactics and those hurdles are not cleared without digging deep inside the organization. By helping our clients figure out how to make their organizations more human, we get them on the path to success more rapidly. This book is an amazing first step and is a great tool for businesses as they venture into the social space. I can't wait to share it with our clients!"

—Shelly Kramer, CEO, V3 Integrated Marketing

"This book defines the new human quotient within organizations around the world. Large and small business alike should heed the call being screamed from the rooftops and shouted down the hallways. Maddie and Jamie make me want to be more human."

—Kyle Lacy, author of *Branding Yourself* and *Twitter Marketing for Dummies*

"Jamie Notter and Maddie Grant have produced a real rarity among management books: truly insightful thinking that is both brilliantly fresh and actionably disciplined. First, they comprehensively reframe the problem of leadership in organizations. Next, they draw out and organize the resulting insights into a system that hangs together of its own accord. Finally, they explain to any manager at any level what this means in a practical sense, and how to profitably adapt and act on it."

—Jim Stroup, DBA, author and management consultant

"Social media is not only changing how we communicate with key constituencies but it is challenging the very structure of our organizations. Historically, organizations have been structured to optimize efficiency for themselves, but not for their customers and markets. The open dialog organizations are now having with their markets is exposing how inefficiently those organizations work in the context of their larger ecosystems. Maddie Grant and Jamie Notter take a crack at pulling apart this puzzle and providing guidance in how to make concepts like trust and authenticity apply not only to people but to the organizations with which they interact."

—Rachel Happe, Co-Founder & Principal, The Community Roundtable

HUMANIZE

How People-Centric Organizations Succeed in a Social World

Jamie Notter
Maddie Grant

*To JP
Can't wait to talk mae! :)*

800 East 96th Street
Indianapolis, Indiana 46240 USA

Humanize: How People-Centric Organizations Succeed in a Social World

ISBN-13: 978-0-7897-4112-7
ISBN-10: 0-7897-4112-1

Library of Congress Cataloging-in-Publication data is on file.

Printed in the United States of America

Second Printing: December 2011

Trademarks

Warning and Disclaimer

Bulk Sales

Que Publishing offers excellent discounts on this book when ordered in quantity for bulk purchases or special sales. For more information, please contact

U.S. Corporate and Government Sales
1-800-382-3419
corpsales@pearsontechgroup.com

For sales outside of the U.S., please contact

International Sales
international@pearson.com

Editor-in-Chief
Greg Wiegand

Senior Acquisitions Editor
Katherine Bull

Development Editors
Ginny Bess Munroe
Leslie T. O'Neill

Managing Editor
Sandra Schroeder

Project Editor
Seth Kerney

Copy Editor
Geneil Breeze

Indexer
Cheryl Lenser

Proofreader
Apostrophe Editing Services, Inc.

Technical Editors
Maggie McGary
Joe Gerstandt
Brian Geyser
Chris Barger

Publishing Coordinator
Romny French

Interior Designers
Anne Jones

Cover Designer
Alan Clements

Compositor
Bronkella Publishing, Inc.

Que Biz-Tech Editorial Board
Michael Brito
Jason Falls
Rebecca Lieb
Simon Salt
Peter Shankman

CONTENTS AT A GLANCE

Visit http://www.humanizebook.com for access to a set of four downloadable worksheets that will help you turn the ideas in this book into concrete action. There is one worksheet for each of the four chapters on the elements of a human organization: Open (Chapter 6), Trustworthy (Chapter 7), Generative (Chapter 8), and Courageous (Chapter 9).

1	The Human Revolution	1
2	We Can't Go Back	11
3	We're Not Moving Forward	33
4	Challenges To Socializing Business	61
5	Social Organizations Are More Human	91
6	How to Be Open	115
7	How to Be Trustworthy	155
8	How to Be Generative	187
9	How to Be Courageous	219
10	What Now?	247
	Index	255

TABLE OF CONTENTS

1 The Human Revolution 1

    The World We Live in Today 2

    Tomorrow's World: Human Organizations 4

    How This Book Is Structured 6

    What's Different About This Book 9

2 We Can't Go Back 11

    Social Media by the Numbers 12

        Just the Beginning 14

    The Social Media Revolution in a Nutshell 16

        The Rise of Word of Mouth Marketing 18

        From Consumers to Producers 20

        Information Wants to Be Free 21

        Google Me, Baby 22

        It's Not Information Overload, It's Filter Failure ... 24

    From Conversation to Collaboration to Collective Action ... 25

        From Collective Action to [?]… 28

    So What? 29

    Must Read 31

3 We're Not Moving Forward 33

    Best Practices Versus Innovation 35

    Strategic Planning: The Comforting Lie of Predictability ... 38

        Strategic Planning Basics 39

        Pulling Back the Curtain on Strategic Planning ... 41

    Human Resource Management: We Are People, Not Spare Parts ... 46

        Why Does the Hiring Process Suck? 48

        Structure: Logical But Not Human 50

Leadership: Individuals Will Always Let Us Down 53

Is There Hope? 57

Must Read 59

4   Challenges to Socializing Business 61

Culture 64

What Is Culture Anyway? 66

Culture and Social Media 68

Risk 69

Authority and Control 71

Process 73

What Is Process Anyway? 75

Process and Social Media 76

Hierarchy 77

Silos and Communication 78

Measurement 80

Behavior 82

What Is Behavior Anyway? 84

Behavior and Social Media 85

Identity Management 85

Relationship Building 87

Knowledge Management 88

Now What? 89

5   Social Organizations Are More Human 91

The Machine World 92

Unplugging from the Matrix 95

A Trellis for Cultivating More Human Organizations 96

The Four Elements in the Real World 99

2008—The Motrin Moms Backlash 99

2009—United Breaks Guitars 101

2010—The Gap Logo Reversal 103

2010—The BP Oil Spill 104

2011—Etsy's Offensive Art Versus Censorship Debate 105

Open 106

Trustworthy 108

Generative 110

Courageous 112

Making It Happen 114

6   How To Be Open **115**

Open Culture: Decentralization 117

    Walking the Walk: Who Steps Up? 119

    Talking the Talk: Less Is More 125

    Thought: Cultural Assumptions 128

Open Process: Systems Thinking 131

    What Is Systems Thinking? 132

    Structural: Silos That Work 134

    Internal: Perpetual Motion 136

    External: Open Community 138

Open Behavior: Ownership 140

    Knowledge: Integrating Multiple Perspectives 142

    Skills: Tools for Action 146

Open For Business 150

Must Read 150

Get Started Today: Worksheet 151

7   How to Be Trustworthy **155**

Trustworthy Culture: Transparency 158

    Walking the Walk: Strategic Transparency 159

    Talking the Talk: The Power of Consistency 162

    Thought: Assumptions Behind a Culture of Transparency 165

Trustworthy Process: Truth 167

    Structural: Beyond Blowing Whistles 169

    Internal: Conflict Is a Good Thing 171

    External: Cultivating Truth in the Ecosystem 175

Trustworthy Behavior: Authenticity 178

    Knowledge: Know Thyself 179

    Skills: Equip for Exploration 181

Making New Meaning 183

Must Read 184

Get Started Today: Worksheet 184

8 How to Be Generative **187**

Generative Culture: Inclusion 190

Walking the Walk: An Infrastructure for Inclusion 192

Talking the Talk: Making Difference Visible 194

Thought: Assumptions Behind an Inclusive Culture 196

Generative Process: Collaboration 198

Collaborative Brand 200

Collaborative Strategy 203

Generative Behavior: Relationship Building 207

Interpersonal Relationship Building 208

Network Relationship Building 211

Accomplishing More, Better 216

Must Read 216

Get Started Today: Worksheet 217

9 How to Be Courageous **219**

Courageous Culture: Learning 223

Walking the Walk: The Power of Conversations and Failure .. 224

Talking the Talk: Actions Speak Louder 227

Cultural Assumptions: Free Your Mind 230

Courageous Process: Experimentation 232

Structural: Creating Space for Experimentation 233

Internal: Experimentation and Measurement 235

External: Shifting from Technology Experimentation to
Management Experimentation 237

Courageous Behavior: Personal Development 239

Make Time 242

Get Personal 242

Say Good-Bye 243

Just the Beginning 243

Must Read 244

Get Started Today: Worksheet 244

10   What Now? **247**

Social Media Challenges Are Organizational Challenges 248

How to Be the Catalyst for Change 251

Red Pill or Blue Pill? 252

Index **255**

About the Authors

Jamie Notter is vice president at Management Solutions Plus, Inc., in Rockville, Maryland, where he leads the consulting division. Clients call on him to solve tough problems, facilitate critical conversations, build internal capacity, and amplify leadership. Jamie has twenty years of experience in conflict resolution, diversity, and nonprofit and association management, including seven years running his own consulting practice. He is an accomplished speaker and author of three books. He has a master's degree in conflict resolution from George Mason University and a certificate in organization development from Georgetown. Jamie blogs on leadership at www.getmejamienotter.com.

Maddie Grant, CAE, is the chief social media strategist for SocialFish, a Washington, DC-based consulting firm that helps associations and nonprofits nationwide build community on the social web. Maddie draws from more than fifteen years of experience in marketing, communications, and international business operations to help organizations large and small build capacity for using social media to achieve business results. Maddie is also lead editor for SocialFishing, one of the most respected and visited blogs about social media for the association industry. Find Maddie at www.socialfish.org.

Dedication

To my parents, George and Sarah Notter.
Jamie Notter

To Lindy Dreyer, without whom this book could never have been written.
Maddie Grant

Acknowledgments

We couldn't have written this book without the support, encouragement, and extensive help of many people.

We are deeply grateful for the hard work put in by Christopher Barger, Joe Gerstandt, Brian Geyser, and Maggie McGary who served as external reviewers of the manuscript. Thank you for helping us write more clearly and authentically. We also got valuable advice from Jeff Hurt and Lindy Dreyer as we developed the online worksheets, from Jeff De Cagna on the topic of innovation, from MSP graphic designer Jon Benjamin on the design of the worksheets, and we thank Terry Brennan of Life Scenes Photography for our jacket and book website photos. Thank you also to Sterling Raphael at NFI Studios and Markku Allison at the American Institute of Architects whose stories informed the book. A special thank you also to Dave Sabol, who designed (and continues to help evolve) the website for this book.

A big thanks goes out to all the great people at Pearson/Que in making this book a reality: Katherine Bull, our amazing acquisitions editor who believed in us from day one; Ginny Bess Munroe, Romny French, Leslie O'Neill, Seth Kerney, Geneil Breeze, Alan Clements, Tammy Graham, Laura Robbins, and the whole team who worked hard keeping us on schedule and helping us to produce a really excellent book.

Jamie would especially like to thank Beth Palys of Management Solutions Plus, Inc., and the rest of the MSP team for giving us both the time and space to write this book. We know that we probably drove you all crazy as we disappeared into writing mode for days on end, and we are well aware of the extra effort you put in when we did. We are incredibly proud of our effort, but it wouldn't have been this good if we didn't have you covering for us.

Maddie sends a special heartfelt thanks to the smart and loving people in PVSM, with whom we were able to test ideas, overtly and surreptitiously, and whose continuing willingness to push back on and deepen our thinking is a testament to the amazing social business community we have all around us. Thank you also for all the past (and future) sharing you've done of our work and of your own, which will continue to inform our thoughts about humanizing organizations.

Thank you to our families for supporting us throughout the writing of this book, and thank you to all of our professional colleagues, especially our association industry community and friends, who helped us think through our ideas both in person and online over the last few years. This book is ultimately the result of many, many conversations with all of you, and we might not have had the guts to write it if it weren't for your ongoing support and encouragement and the exceptional quality of thinking in our online communities.

Humanizing our organizations is a collaborative effort. Thank you to all for being part of it.

We Want to Hear from You!

As the reader of this book, *you* are our most important critic and commentator. We value your opinion and want to know what we're doing right, what we could do better, what areas you'd like to see us publish in, and any other words of wisdom you're willing to pass our way.

As an editor-in-chief for Que Publishing, I welcome your comments. You can email or write me directly to let me know what you did or didn't like about this book—as well as what we can do to make our books better.

Please note that I cannot help you with technical problems related to the topic of this book. We do have a User Services group, however, where I will forward specific technical questions related to the book.

When you write, please be sure to include this book's title and author as well as your name, email address, and phone number. I will carefully review your comments and share them with the author and editors who worked on the book.

Email: feedback@quepublishing.com

Mail: Greg Wiegand
           Editor-in-Chief
           Que Publishing
           800 East 96th Street
           Indianapolis, IN 46240 USA

Reader Services

Visit our website and register this book at quepublishing.com/register for convenient access to any updates, downloads, or errata that might be available for this book.

1

The Human Revolution

Throughout human history, we have been dependent on machines to survive. Fate, it seems, is not without a sense of irony.
—Morpheus, in *The Matrix*, 1999

The Matrix movies, directed by the Wachowski brothers, tell an allegorical tale of a future where machines control the human race, creating for them an imaginary existence (the Matrix) that the humans perceive as real. This allows the machines to keep humans sedated to extract fuel from their bodies. The movies tell a story of revolution in which a small group of people, led by Keanu Reeves' character, Neo, is able to break free from the hypnotic clutches of the Matrix. They struggle to regain their autonomy and live more full, human lives. Like any good movie, the Matrix trilogy is rooted in a universal story—one of people seeking freedom, struggling to be fully human, and trying to escape oppressive control to create a better future for themselves.

The World We Live in Today

So how does this relate to you? Most of you reading this book are likely living in societies where oppressive controls are a thing of the past, right? Maybe a few centuries ago your brave ancestors rose up to throw off the shackles of an oppressive regime, but these days we don't particularly find ourselves struggling against oppression to regain our human dignity, do we? We can certainly relate to that story of *The Matrix* revolution in terms of our culture and history, but our everyday experiences, for the most part, would seem to have very little connection to a struggle to be fully human.

Or do they? Maybe you should think about that, the next time you are bored during a staff meeting. Or during that annual performance review, where once again you're reviewing issues with your direct report that haven't particularly been addressed in the last year. Or as you walk back to your office dejectedly after your boss has once again squashed your creative ideas because you didn't go through the proper channels. Or ask your colleague how she feels, after she complains to you that she has been crushed by the weight of layers of bureaucracy. Or talk to anyone who has seen opportunities pass his organization by because no one had the authority to act quickly or because the organization lacked any processes that would allow for deviance from the way things have always been done. Forget the science fiction of machines altering our brains to convince us that a virtual reality is actually happening. Take a look at our organizational lives, in which we routinely give up what is important to us, spending the overwhelming majority of our waking hours working in organizations that are more likely to inspire endless complaining and self-medication than truly fulfilling lives. We may not be locked in a literal struggle between life and death, but there is something disconcerting about the way so many of us plod forward in frustrating work environments. We tolerate a subpar existence, accepting that living a true and full human existence is actually a luxury, something we dream about, rather than a natural part of life to which we are entitled.

Perhaps it should not surprise us that we are here struggling to be more fully human within our organizational lives, because our organizations have for centuries been modeled after machines. Machines completely transformed our economy and our society. So it was only natural that we would look to them as we created the structures, processes, and behavioral expectations of our employees. We created organizations to be more productive, to grow as a society, so we wanted the same kind of efficiency and consistency that our machines provided for us. We organized into divisions, units, or components. We developed data-driven strategies. We reengineered our processes. We built companies with consistent brand messaging that measured outputs. We drive, direct, manage, order, measure, and process. There is no Matrix, but we certainly live in a machine world.

But over the last ten years, in an ironic twist of fate, a revolutionary breakthrough in technology—the Internet—has created a "glitch in the Matrix," so to speak. It is subtly (or not so subtly, depending on how much we're paying attention) shattering our perception of reality. As the Internet has become more central in our lives, we have begun to witness a revival of the importance of being human. Almost overnight, it seems, the world has become social, and the work world, too. Markets are conversations. Social media has enabled us to connect with individual people inside organizations and brands. We're leaping over corporate hurdles imposed by PR and marketing departments and the chain of command; customers are being heard in ways that ignore traditional channels. Content is being created that blurs the line between the "professionals" and the "amateurs." Rules are defied. People are demanding truth, honesty, transparency, and openness from the brands and organizations they deal with every day. The companies that are winning are those that are listening—and social media makes it easy to listen (though maybe not so easy to manage the work of listening and responding), so the rest have no excuse anymore. And why is all this so disruptive?

Because we like it. A lot.

We like being human. We like having the capacity to publish our own thoughts and to create things and share them with the people in our communities who actually matter to us. One of the reasons social media has grown so fast is that it taps into what we, as human beings, naturally love and need and want to do—create, share, connect, relate. So even though we don't know how these ever-changing technologies are going to play out or whether they will connect perfectly to our work world, we are diving right in and giving energy and attention to this new social world. We're watching as Twitter turns into a real-time news stream; we're amazed by the millions of people using Facebook every day; and we're trying to keep up with new social concepts like "engagement" and "influencers" and "gamification." But without knowing for sure what the business impact of these specific concepts will be, we're watching them unfold, we're personally excited by them, and we're ready to jump in and explore the newest social tool.

Our organizations, however, are not as enthusiastic. We see the potential that social media has for our organizations, because of the energy and attention social media attracts, but we are having a hard time trying to fit these new practices into our existing systems. We're drowning in tactics. We're arguing over who "owns" social media for our company. We mandate social media adoption, and then we're frustrated when our shiny new outposts on social media sites languish, unused and ignored. We're reading a lot of books about social media implementation, but the technology is moving faster than these books can be printed. The technologies we're trying to keep up with are not only developing faster, but they are also changing organically and unpredictably. What was the hottest site on the Web a year ago, with millions of people using it, just died almost overnight. A few individuals—bloggers, enthusiasts, and consultants—are just about able to keep up but not nearly enough to build the capacity we need for every organization to do the same. Ultimately, it's not (just) about writing better books about social media, or even printing them faster. There are some good books, and they hit the social media issues perfectly. What they do not address, however, is the deeper fabric of our organizations.

We are trying to force-fit social media technology—a technology that is unleashing a wave of creative energy that draws its strength by tapping into deeply human desires and aspirations—into organizations that have been built (and reinforced for decades) on an entirely mechanical model. We work in "systems," but we need to break down the doors and windows and let them become "ecosystems." We need to make human beings, not machine systems, into the core energy that drives growth. We are starting to realize that for our social media work to truly take off, we need more than smarter social media tactics and better social media implementation. The challenge here is not to do social media better. The challenge is to do our organizations better.

The challenge is to make our organizations more human.

This requires some different books (like this one), books that are not about tactics but about the deeper forces behind the disruptive changes we're seeing in a more social world. But more importantly, it requires more action. We need to unplug from how we traditionally have done things. We need to try new ways. We also need to stop doing other things at the same time. We have to take some chances. They can be calculated chances—we don't bet the farm, maybe—but we have to do things differently. That means giving up control. That means shifting authority. That means thinking about old issues from new perspectives, bringing in new voices. This is happening already around us, of course, because of the social web. People are finding ways to get things done without organizations, so this is actually the perfect opportunity to *not* do things like they have always been done. And we can talk about them and share what we are doing and learn from each other at a scale never seen before.

We need to follow the white rabbit, like in the movie. We need the red pill, the one that opens our eyes to the construct that is the world we live in, the one that unplugs us from the Matrix. (And yes, it might be gooey and messy when we do.)

We need to see the code to break it. This book will help.

Tomorrow's World: Human Organizations

We need organizations that are more human. We need to re-create our organizations so that the power and energy of being more human in our work life can be leveraged. This has the power not only to transform our individual experiences in the work world, but also to access untapped potential in our organizations.

That's what this book is about. We propose that the reason that we find it hard, in many instances, to truly take advantage of the opportunities created by social media is because our mechanistic business environment is not human enough. It's not built to allow for human qualities, as messy as they are—qualities like being open, trustworthy, generous, creative, courageous, loving, fallible, and fun. There's a lot of talk about these qualities, particularly emerging from social media circles. But talking about them is not the same as having them.

Because let's face it, our organizations still leave a lot to be desired. If you don't believe us, take a few minutes to walk around your office and pluck the various *Dilbert* cartoons off the cubicle walls to get a sense of what we've created. So many of our organizations are predictably bad. And the impact of the disengaged employees, turnover, and wasted productivity is unfortunately not as funny as those *Dilbert* cartoons. Part of our problem is our apparent inability to change the way we run our organizations. While we are all working on computers that would have seemed like science fiction only 40 or 50 years ago, we also work within cultures, structures, and processes that have not been noticeably innovated in more than a century. We are still mired in a machine-centric view of organizations, and we're paying a steep price.

And implementing social media is not the same thing as leading and managing organizations. This is not, in fact, a social media book. We dig into social media because it is relevant to the challenges we face in making our organizations more human. Social media is definitely here to stay and it has much to teach us. But social media is not going to get us out of our current mess on its own. Social media is shining a light on the root of our organizational problems. It has captured our attention and energy because it has quickly given us access at a broad, societal level to those elements of being human that we've been craving for the last few generations.

Creating human organizations requires more than social media. It requires new leadership. Ultimately, this is a leadership book, though not in the tradition of "individual leadership," where we provide executives and those who aspire to be executives a list of skills to develop to lead others. We lay ourselves bare here and tell you that those kinds of leadership skills are not enough to create human organizations. We need leadership that is accessible to everyone and that can develop the *whole system*'s capacity for growth. We believe leadership should be as unique as our Twitter streams—meaning that it should be cultivated in each of us through interactions and conversations and connections inside and outside our organizations, both in the center and at the periphery. This is leadership that leaves space for crowdsourced ideas, innovation, transparency as to what will work and what won't and why, courage to admit failures, and diversity of thought and experience. This is leadership that comes in the form of ownership and the ability to act. This is leadership that sparks and encourages turbo-charged, continuous learning. This is leadership in human organizations.

This book seeks to change our path, through all these things and more. Creating more human organizations is an imperative—the disruption brought about by the social web shows us that—and it is also incredibly achievable by all of us. When we talk about a human revolution, we do not imply that we need to come together to prepare for a generation of turmoil to achieve a new world order. Creating human organizations is simply a process of identifying the core elements of organization based on human principles, and then putting one foot in front of the other down that path. It may take a while, and like any valuable endeavor it will be hard work. But it is eminently doable, and doable by you and me, not just by people in positions of authority. Social media is showing us that, too. The amateurs are winning—and some of us are really pretty awesome. What we hope to achieve with this book is to provide a way for you—yes, you, at whatever level you are in your organization—to start making the changes necessary for your organization to become more human.

How This Book Is Structured

In the next three chapters, we set the scene and describe the big picture of the situation we're in now. Chapter 5 lays out the framework for taking action to become more human in our organizations, and Chapters 6 through 9 describe the four human elements we have identified as the most important and the ways they play out in three levels of organizational culture, processes and systems, and individual behavior. Most chapters include three "must read" resources for deeper learning on the topics we discuss. We also have developed four worksheets, one each to accompany Chapters 6 through 9, that help you assess your organization and figure out how to get started, no matter where in the system you are. The worksheets can be downloaded at www.humanizebook.com.

In Chapter 2, "We Can't Go Back," we take a big-picture snapshot of social media and how it is changing our popular culture, industry, and business. All this should be familiar to you already—you're living it just like we are. But if you have any lingering doubts about the power of social media, or still think it might be just a fad, we provide a practitioner's-eye-view of the deep cultural changes that are happening around us, backed up by some of the smart people who've paved the way in terms of our collective understanding of those changes.

Then in Chapter 3, "We're Not Moving Forward," we contrast the social media revolution with the relative stagnation in change and innovation in our organizations. We explain how a series of key assumptions and models for how organizations work have been breaking down over the past few decades—yet we seem unable to come up with viable alternatives. Our "systems," which have worked perfectly well in the past, are becoming ecosystems where things work differently, organically. But our management practices are not built to allow for that, and they're not adapting fast enough.

Chapters 2 and 3 ultimately present an intersection that sets the stage for an inevitable collision: Social media is changing the world around us radically, yet our organizations are not changing to accommodate this new reality. Chapter 4, "Challenges to Socializing Business," describes the challenges we face at this intersection. We have been hearing the cries of frustration from people who are trying to implement social media in our mechanistic organizations for some time now. In this chapter we break the challenges down at three different levels: organizational culture, internal process, and individual behavior.

All this sets the stage for Chapter 5, "Social Organizations Are More Human." We lay out a framework for actually addressing the conflicts and contradictions we are experiencing as mechanical organizations in a more social world. It's not a step-by-step model that you can copy into your organization. It's a framework that helps draw your attention to the areas that need work, inspiring you to come up with the answers that will help you create more people-centric organizations. The framework is organized around four key elements of being human—being open, trustworthy, generative, and courageous—that will help you create more people-centric organizations by making changes at the culture, process, and behavior levels.

Chapter 6, "How to Be Open"; Chapter 7, "How to Be Trustworthy"; Chapter 8, "How to Be Generative"; and Chapter 9, "How to Be Courageous," explore these human elements in greater detail. Each human element presents its own unique challenges and opportunities as you seek to change the way your organization operates. The framework we present is fleshed out as each chapter talks more specifically about the implications of being a more human organization in culture, process, and behavior:

- Being open translates to *decentralization* at the culture level, *systems thinking* at the process level, and *ownership* at the individual behavior level.

- Being trustworthy translates to *transparency* at the culture level, *truth* at the process level, and *authenticity* at the individual behavior level.

- Being generative translates to *inclusion* at the culture level, *collaboration* at the process level, and *relationship building* at the individual behavior level.

- Being courageous translates to *learning* at the culture level, *experimentation* at the process level, and *personal development* at the individual behavior level.

Our goal with this book is to facilitate action, so we provide guidance about making changes in all these contexts. Our discussion of culture in each chapter, for example, is broken down in terms of the "walk, talk, and thought" of culture creation and change.

- **Walk.** What organizations need to be actively doing to build a culture that is more open, trustworthy, generative, or courageous

- **Talk.** How organizations should actively communicate about their culture and what they are doing to change it

- **Thought.** How to address cultural assumptions that underlie "the way things are"

Similarly, at the level of organizational processes and systems, we look at the different challenges for each human element in addressing process at the structural, internal, and external levels:

- **Structural.** How to build capacity for being open, trustworthy, generative, and courageous by adjusting structure and the way work is organized

- **Internal.** Where certain internal processes and systems are getting in the way of being human

- **External.** What the human elements look like when the outside community or network is let in to participate

At the behavior level we explore the categories of knowledge and skills:

- **Knowledge.** What information any employee at any level should have access to, to be able to act in a more human way

- **Skills.** What interpersonal skills are specifically relevant to each human element

We present our four human elements in this way to enable you to find something, somewhere, you can hook into to get started doing the work of pushing your organization to be more human. There's a lot of meaty stuff in here, and you can't do it all at once. But in one or several of these subsections, you'll think, "OK. This is where I can find a chink in the armor. This is something I can talk to colleagues about. This is something I can look into today." The downloadable worksheets are designed the same way. They help you analyze and assess your organization and start comparing notes with other colleagues to develop an action plan for change.

Wherever you are in the organization, you can take steps toward creating a more human organization right away.

And of course, there is a certain amount of overlap between the chapters, too. Humans are not merely a collection of component parts. We are a rather magical combination of deep and complex layers of biology that somehow work together in such a way that we can walk around upright and sentient. Our human elements are the same—once you start honing in and thinking about one, you'll find areas of the others that connect. It makes sense to read this book with a notebook handy for making those connections and then revisiting them while reading later chapters. We have a logic for presenting the chapters in the order we do; though of course we have to practice what we preach and let go of control, knowing you'll read them in whatever order you want. Besides, the worksheets can be completed in any order, because we know that you may want to focus on one particular element that you already know your organization is ready to hone in on. Conversations are going on all over the social web about these four elements. Your customers or stakeholders may already be forcing you to pay attention to one or more of these areas, and this book will help to parse out what needs to be done.

We assume you're keen to start reading and to get to the meat. This brings us to an important point.

What's Different About This Book

Although we are both consultants, we tried hard to keep our framework from becoming a consultanty "model." It has no clever acronyms associated with it. (We actually really hate acronyms. There, we said it.) It's a simple, straightforward, common sense framework, broken down into manageable parts that you can use to help grow and nurture your organization within its particular ecosystem. The book is meant to simplify the many thoughts and conversations that may be swirling around your organization about becoming more human. It is a guide, and the resources and worksheets we've included will help.

Something else important to note—this book doesn't have a lot of stories. We include examples where relevant, of course, but we're a little tired of all those books that go on and on to illustrate their points. Storytelling is important, in general, to help readers identify with the theories raised in business books, but in this case, you know the story better than we do. You know the story because you're living it in your organization or business. We all are. And if that's not enough, there is also a whole Internet full of relevant stories. We're not here to Google that for you; we're here to help you just get cracking. Because the way we structured this book, looking at the four essential human elements of the social organization from a cultural, structural, and individual level, boils down to one simple fact: The buck stops with you.

There's no point in reading this if you don't want to get started making changes. If you're happy to stay plugged into the Matrix, that's totally fine; we won't waste more of your time. Organizations and businesses have mechanisms in place to *stop* progress, to stop themselves from evolving. Mainly because of an inherent fear of change and fear of losing control, they have an interest in maintaining the status quo. We feel strongly that such an approach is becoming increasingly less viable. Mark our words: If you think your organization is behind now, just spend a year or two treading water, and you'll see how much ground there is to make up. There's no time to waste. It's up to you, if you care about your organization, to help it not only survive this transition but to also flourish.

And you're not alone. We can all help each other—on the social web, everyone's watching. Follow the white rabbit. Let's go.

2

We Can't Go Back

"When we change the way we communicate, we change society."
—Clay Shirky, *Here Comes Everybody: The Power of Organizing Without Organizations*

If you are reading this book, you already know that social media is not a fad. You are already aware that the impact social media is having on business is deep and pervasive. You have probably read some of the seminal books that explain why the rise of social media has created such a fundamental disruption in the way we traditionally communicate, and therefore in the way we do business— books like Charlene Li and Josh Bernoff's Groundswell, *Clay Shirky's* Here Comes Everybody, *and Don Tapscott and Anthony D. Williams'* Wikinomics. *And you picked up this book because you realize that the changes that need to happen in how we run our businesses, so we can flourish in this social world, go far deeper than just using social technologies and tools in tactical ways.*

But that doesn't mean we should gloss over our coverage of the social media revolution. It's not enough to declare victory for social media and move on. Some of what has been written in the past five to ten years focused on the exponential growth of social media. Other analyses zero in on how it has changed the way we communicate or do marketing. Others focus on mass collaboration, or the role of social media in the political landscape. It is all important, but what we want to do in this chapter is connect the dots among these insights so we can all get on the same page as we move forward. It's not about whether social media is here to stay. It's about what has been driving social media's success more fundamentally. It's about what threads weave together all that has been written about social media's growth in the last ten years. The first step in understanding the revolution is unpacking the numbers.

Social Media by the Numbers

First, a basic definition: *Social media* can be described most simply as any website or application that enables individuals to create and share content that others can view, share, and/or modify. Many kinds of social media tools and sites are on the Internet: blogs and microblogs, social networks, forums, wikis, photo and video sharing sites, podcasts, virtual communities, group sites, collaboration or crowdsourcing sites, bookmarking sites, and so on. All of them have in common that a user can respond in some way to another user. So, yes, even email counts as a social technology. Originally designed and perceived to be used primarily for social interactions, social media today is commonly used by all kinds of businesses—business to business (B2B), business to consumer (B2C), nonprofit, for-profit, government agencies, big brands, and small business owners—in various tactical ways to achieve business goals.

The growth of social media use is staggering. Here is where it stands as of early 2011.

Facebook, arguably the poster child for social media, has more than 500 million active users. According to Facebook's statistics page, these users share more than 30 billion pieces of content, such as links to news articles and blogs, notes, photos, events, videos, and so on in a month. The average individual user has 130 friends; is connected to 80 community pages, groups, and events; and creates 90 pieces of content each month. 200 million people use mobile devices to access Facebook, and more than 2 million websites have integrated with Facebook. All of this has been accomplished in less than seven years—Facebook was founded in February 2004.

Twitter, once labeled a potential Facebook killer (though it seems the two social media giants will be content to share the space, at least for a while) has seen equally amazing growth. Twitter doesn't share official statistics, but its CEO, Evan Williams, is on record[1] as stating that the microblogging platform had 175 million user accounts and would hit 200 million by the end of 2010. That would make it the fifth largest country in the world, but even more amazing is the fact that 50% of its accounts were created in one year (2010). What we do know for sure is that Twitter reported its 20 billionth *tweet* (or 140-character message) in September 2010,[2] with 5 billion tweets coming in only 2 months. No matter how you slice it, that's a lot of tweeting.

LinkedIn, the more business-focused social network, hit the 100 million mark in early 2011, with members in more than 200 countries, including representatives from every single Fortune 500 company.[3]

YouTube, the video-sharing site where people watch two billion videos a day, is the second largest search engine site in the world (now of course owned by the first largest, Google). In fact, every minute, 24 hours of video is uploaded to YouTube.[4]

Wikipedia, the online encyclopedia written, edited, and managed by users, is a veritable dinosaur in the social media world. It was founded in 2001 (did we even have the Internet back then?!) and has managed to become one of the world's largest reference websites. In June 2011, they were welcoming 400 million unique visitors per month. More than 91,000 active contributors worked on more than 17,000,000 articles in more than 270 languages—3,654,382 articles in English alone.[5]

Contrary to popular belief, social media is not the exclusive domain of young people. A Pew Internet report on *Generations Online in 2010*[6] states that "while the youngest and oldest cohorts may differ, certain key Internet activities are becoming more uniformly popular across all age groups. These include

- Sending and receiving email

- Performing searches

1. Verna, Paul. "Inside Twitter's '100 Million New Members' Number." Web log post. The EMarketer Blog. 13 Dec. 2010. Web. 28 Jan. 2011. <http://www.emarketer.com/blog/index.php/twitters-100-million-member-number/>.

2. Ostrow, Adam. "Twitter Hits 20 Billion Tweets." Mashable. 31 July 2010. Web. 28 Jan. 2011. <http://mashable.com/2010/07/31/twitter-hits-20-billion-tweets/>.

3. "About Us." LinkedIn Press Center. Web. 28 Jan. 2011. <http://press.linkedin.com/about/>.

4. "YouTube Fact Sheet." YouTube. Web. 28 Jan. 2011. <http://www.youtube.com/t/fact_sheet>.

5. "Wikipedia: About." Wikipedia, the Free Encyclopedia. 9 Jun. 2011. Web. <http://en.wikipedia.org/wiki/Wikipedia:About>.

6. Zickuhr, Kathryn. "Generations Online in 2010." Pew Research Center's Internet & American Life Project. 16 Dec. 2010. Web. 28 Jan. 2011. <http://www.pewinternet.org/Reports/2010/Generations-2010/Overview.aspx>.

- Seeking health information

- Getting news

- Buying products

- Making travel reservations or purchases

- Doing online banking

- Looking for religious information

- Rating products, services, or people

- Making online charitable donations

- Downloading podcasts

Even in areas still dominated by Millennials, older generations are making notable gains. Some of the areas that have seen the fastest rate of growth in recent years include older adults' participation in communication and entertainment activities online, especially in using social network sites such as Facebook." The report notes that the fastest growth in Internet usage comes from users age 74 or older.

The bottom line is that your customers, your stakeholders, your kids, your parents and grandparents, your friends, and likely everyone you know is active in social media nowadays. Let's face it, if members of Congress and your local police are on Twitter, you know social media has become mainstream.

Just the Beginning

Becoming mainstream, however, is not an endpoint for social media. There are over 2 billion Internet users today, representing 30% of the world's population. In North America, that penetration rate is higher, at 78% (272 million people). Here's the most important point, however—by the time you read this, *all the numbers we just quoted will have grown exponentially*. Look at Table 2.1; the penultimate column on the right shows growth over the last eleven years (2000–2011). At the absolute minimum, every world region has more than doubled its population's Internet usage in ten years, with Latin America, the Middle East, and Africa each growing more than tenfold.

Table 2.1   World Internet Users and Population Stats, Internet World Stats - Usage and Population Statistics, 9 June 2011, http://www.internetworld stats.com/stats.htm

World Regions	Population (2011 Est.)	Internet Users Dec. 31, 2001	Internet Users March 31, 2011	Penetration (% of Population	Growth 2000–2011	Users % of Table
Africa	1,037,524,058	4,514,400	118,609,620	11.4%	2,527.4%	5.7%
Asia	3,879,740,877	114,304,000	922,329,554	23.8%	706.9%	44.0%
Europe	816,426,346	105,096,093	476,213, 935	58.3%	353.1%	22.7%
Middle East	216,258,843	3,284,800	68,553,666	31.7%	1,987.0%	3.3%
North America	347,394,870	108,096,800	272,066,000	78.3%	151.7%	13.0%
Latin America/ Caribbean	597,283,165	18,068,919	215,939,400	36.2%	1,037.4%	10.3%
Oceania/ Australia	35,426,995	7,620,480	21,293,830	60.1%	179.4%	1.0%
World Total	6,930,055,154	360,985,492	2,095,006,005	30.2%	480.4%	100.0%

Usage and Population Statistics, 9 June 2011, http://www.internetworldstats.com/stats.htm

This growth will accelerate as more people access the Internet via mobile devices. This is a particularly important trend globally, and one that (unlike some of the statistics we mentioned) cuts across the division between the developed and developing world. According to the International Telecommunication Union,

> While high-speed Internet is still out of reach for many people in low-income countries, mobile telephony is becoming ubiquitous, with access to mobile networks now available to over 90% of the global population. ITU's new data indicate that among the estimated 5.3 billion mobile subscriptions by the end of 2010, 3.8 billion will be in the developing world. That's 71% of the subscriptions in the developing world.[7]

The reason for this, of course, is that the mobile market in many developed countries is hitting (or surpassing) the saturation mark. Across all developed countries, subscription growth has slowed considerably, gaining only 1.6% between 2009 and 2010, but that is because they have hit the point where new subscriptions are going to people who already have subscriptions. Those countries are now averaging more

---

7. Acharya, Sanjay. "ITU Estimates Two Billion People Online by End 2010." ITU Newsroom. 19 Oct. 2010. Web. 28 Jan. 2011. <http://www.itu.int/net/pressoffice/press_releases/2010/39.aspx>.

than one subscription per inhabitant (1.16 to be exact).[8] In short, *everyone has a mobile phone*. Gartner estimates that by 2011, more than 85% of handsets shipped globally will include a browser and advises that "in mature markets, the mobile Web, along with associated Web adaptation tools, will be a leading technology for B2C mobile applications through 2012, and should be part of every organization's B2C technology portfolio."[9]

We're not sharing these stats on mobile usage just to get the attention of the mobile app developers. It is a critical trend to understand when gauging the reach and impact of social media growth. As impressive as the social media usage statistics have been to this point, all of that growth relied primarily on the development of high-speed Internet, which has been growing but is limited by poorer infrastructure in the developing world. When you add the capacity to start using, modifying, or creating social tools in a mobile setting, we have the potential for this revolution to grow exponentially. Again.

Social media has become a permanent fixture of the Internet, just as the Internet has become a permanent fixture in commerce. Specific tools will come and go, and even the dominance we see today of tools like Facebook and Twitter is not guaranteed to last. As we write this, the question and answer site Quora seems to be at a tipping point, but by the time you read this, it could be anywhere from completely nonexistent to the app that killed Wikipedia. That is because the driving force behind social media is not the technology or the look, feel, or capacity of the specific tools. As we explain in the following section, the driving force behind social media is that it taps into the driving forces behind what it means to be human.

It's not the "media" that is important—it's the "social."

The Social Media Revolution in a Nutshell

Now that social media has gone mainstream, we can feel a bit more comfortable referring to it as a revolution. Like any revolution, of course, the early leaders may not have been universally accepted at the time they first started delivering their message, but looking back we can see how impressive their foresight really was. In 1999, for instance, Christopher Locke, Rick Levine, Doc Searls, and David Weinberger issued their now famous *Cluetrain Manifesto*.[10] It contains 95 clear and simple theses that make the early case for the profound impact social media was having on business and the human community at large. Thesis #1 is simply,

---

8. Acharya, Sanjay. "ITU Estimates Two Billion People Online by End 2010." ITU Newsroom. 19 Oct. 2010. Web. 28 Jan. 2011. <http://www.itu.int/net/pressoffice/press_releases/2010/39.aspx>; for more statistics on mobile, see mobithinking.

9. "Gartner Outlines 10 Mobile Technologies to Watch in 2010 and 2011." Gartner Inc. 24 Mar. 2010. Web. 28 Jan. 2011. <http://www.gartner.com/it/page.jsp?id=1328113>.

"Markets are conversations." Thesis #18 continues by saying that "companies that don't realize their markets are now networked person-to-person, getting smarter as a result and deeply joined in conversation are missing their best opportunity." They were giving voice to an idea that had been percolating around the Internet as the ability for users to connect directly to each other was growing: the idea that the center of gravity was shifting away from centralized bodies like companies and "the media" and toward the decentralized masses.

Almost ten years later, Josh Bernoff and Charlene Li called this movement the *groundswell*: "a social trend in which people use technologies to get the things they need from each other, rather than from traditional institutions like corporations."[11] They painted a picture of the world where business executives might become afraid, because the things they thought they controlled are now being accomplished by their "markets" directly.

> Your company's customers are talking about your brand right now [...], probably in ways you haven't approved. Your support representatives' conversations with customers will show up on YouTube, and so will your TV commercials, intercut with sarcastic commentary. If your CEO has any hair left, he or she is going to tear it out and then ask for your help in taming this torrent of people expressing themselves.[12]

For decades, we've taken for granted that it was the company's role to create and deliver value (in the form of products, services, and so on) to its market. It created, owned, and managed its "brand" from the comfort of headquarters, and its main challenge was responding to competitive threats or better understanding the market to make the brand messaging more effective. Traditionally, a company could rely on its PR department to push out a press release with its carefully crafted, yet bland statements. It could have its media spokesperson be the contact for media inquiries. It could plan marketing campaigns with a reasonable expectation of the outcomes. But now, overnight it seemed, people could not only say negative things in public ways, but build groups and followings all about those negative things. People could ignore the marketing and advertising messages and insist on using social networks to get the answers they needed, or even access to other employees of the company. Now the groundswell presented a new threat: The market itself was wresting back some control, and as Bernoff and Li pointed out, company CEOs tended to react by asking how to get the control back.

---

10. Levine, Rick, Christopher Locke, Doc Searls, and David Weinberger. "The Cluetrain Manifesto - 95 Theses." The Cluetrain Manifesto. 1999. Web. 28 Jan. 2011. <http://cluetrain.com/book/95-theses.html>.

11. Li, Charlene, and Josh Bernoff. Groundswell: Winning in a World Transformed by Social Technologies, Boston, MA: Harvard Business, 2008. 9.

12. Groundswell, 9.

Sorry, CEOs. You are not going to get the control back. Now that the masses have tasted the power, they expect it as a matter of course. They are going to wield their power first and ask questions later, and that will help this movement gain even more momentum. That's what a "groundswell" is. You can't stop it. Your only hope is to understand it well enough—really tune in on what drives it—so you can try to harmonize with its energy and force. If you're really good, you can thrive in it. But if your goal is to control, spin, and manage it (which is what marketing PR, sales, and customer service functions tend to do), then you're out of luck. The social media revolution erupted first in marketing circles because it was the first area where the reality of social media simply could not be ignored.

The Rise of Word of Mouth Marketing

Jackie Huba and Ben McConnell wrote *Creating Customer Evangelists* in 2003 and *Citizen Marketers* in 2007. Both books are about empowering customers to share the love—via online word of mouth—about a brand or product through deepening relationships between companies and their audiences. These books, among others, brought the idea of word of mouth marketing more into the mainstream. Their basic points are similar to those made in *Groundswell*, where the people in the market end up exerting more power directly. Consumers using social media facilitate a more rapid dissemination of grass-roots opinions about products, services, and companies than in the past. Word of mouth is no longer the relatively slow phenomenon of an individual telling a small circle of friends who might then tell some of their friends.

> With citizen-created content, people are the message because their role as publishers or broadcasters hoists them above the boundaries that one-way media communicators have erected around themselves. Citizen marketers and online-content creators with substantial audiences and dynamic authority rely and thus interact with their audiences. They work in the public piazzas where other people write, work, and play, too. They are not the balcony standers of one-way media, concealed behind walls of organizational privacy. Participation is their medium and their platform. [13]

Huba and McConnell were writing about the then-growing use of blogs, online forums, and all kinds of rating and reviewing sites where consumers could talk about products and services and begin to affect (positively or negatively) not only the buying decisions of their friends, but also those of complete strangers.

---

13. McConnell, Ben, and Jackie Huba. Citizen Marketers: When People Are the Message. Chicago, IL: Kaplan Pub., 2007. 30.

Consumer-facing businesses quickly began to pay attention. According to *McKinsey Quarterly* in April 2010, word of mouth (WOM) has become the primary factor behind 20%–50% of all purchasing decisions. This is partially because consumers are growing weary of contrived, traditional marketing messages, something that the *Cluetrain Manifesto* predicted years ago (Thesis #15): "In just a few more years, the current, homogenized 'voice' of business—the sound of mission statements and brochures—will seem as contrived and artificial as the language of the 18th century French court." Messages in word of mouth marketing are more authentic and more human, and the influence of WOM is growing:

> Its influence is greatest when consumers are buying a product for the first time or when products are relatively expensive, factors that tend to make people conduct more research, seek more opinions, and deliberate longer than they otherwise would. And its influence will probably grow: The digital revolution has amplified and accelerated its reach to the point where word of mouth is no longer an act of intimate, one-on-one communication.[14]

The concept of word of mouth marketing quickly became part of the marketing lexicon. In 2004, you knew it was on the way to being mainstream when a professional association was created to represent this new field. One of the first things the new Word of Mouth Marketing Association (WOMMA) did was to create a code of ethics, which took a stance against what they called deceptive and stealth marketing practices. The code calls for honesty and openness in all WOM marketing, requiring full disclosure for anyone doing word of mouth. The essence of the WOMMA Code comes down to its Honesty ROI:

- Honesty of Relationship: You say who you're speaking for.

- Honesty of Opinion: You say what you believe.

- Honesty of Identity: You never lie about who you are.

Not only have we lost control, but now marketing needs to be honest and authentic? What is the world coming to?! Social media wasn't just becoming popular, it was shaking up the status quo, and it was doing it in some interesting ways. What used to be closed and controlled was now open and decentralized. What used to be contrived, was now authentic. Social media wasn't growing like gangbusters simply because Mark Zuckerberg built a better widget. It was growing because as human beings we all have a deep connection to openness and authenticity. We all want power to be closer to us and trust to be present in our relationships. It's part of being human. Now, thanks to social media, it was becoming part of business.

---

14. Bughin, Jacques, Jonathan Doogan, and Ole Jorgen Vetvik. "A New Way to Measure Word-of-mouth Marketing." McKinsey Quarterly. Apr. 2010. Web. 28 Jan. 2011. <https://www.mckinseyquarterly.com/A_new_way_to_measure_word-of-mouth_marketing_2567>.

From Consumers to Producers

Meanwhile, as more and more people took to the Web to write, comment, share, opine, rant, and otherwise talk about the things they cared about including brands and companies), we began to see the impact of the social media revolution growing beyond merely marketing goods and services. More than just enabling consumers to share opinions, social media delivered the powerful capacity for individuals to create and distribute content more broadly than ever before.

The Internet grew, initially, as a publishing vehicle, and in the beginning it shared the basic rules of content creation that traditional media had developed: That is, content was created, controlled, and broadcast out to the masses by a small group of professionals. Early on, few people had the resources or knowledge to put content online, so it was left to the professionals and the organizations to create. Social media began to change this. In 2005, a Pew Internet research study called *Teen Content Creators and Consumers*[15] pointed out that more than half of online teenagers were deemed to be "content creators" on the Internet. Each one of the teen creators (12 million of them at the time) had done one or more of the following activities online:

- Create a blog

- Work on a personal web page

- Create or work on a web page for school, a friend, or an organization

- Share original content such as artwork, photos, stories, or videos online

- Remix content found online into a new creation

These findings proved to be the tip of the iceberg in terms of our sociological and cultural understanding of how people's online habits were changing. The creation and sharing of content, generally assumed to be the realm of early adopters and younger generations, was becoming more and more mainstream as every demographic began to spend more time online.

Consider blogging, which is one of the most popular ways for individuals to create and share content online. Blogs became popular around 1999, the year Evan Williams launched Blogger.com and Brad Fitzpatrick founded LiveJournal. The growth was staggering. Political blogs, tech blogs, and gossip blogs like Gawker catapulted the medium for user-generated content into the mainstream, and in 2004 the word "blog" was Merriam Webster's Word of the Year. By 2009, Technorati estimated that more than 200 million blogs existed worldwide.

---

15. Lenhart, Amanda, and Mary Madden. "Teen Content Creators and Consumers | Pew Research Center's Internet & American Life Project." Pew Research Center's Internet & American Life Project. 2 Nov. 2005. Web. 28 Jan. 2011. <http://www.pewinternet.org/Reports/2005/Teen-Content-Creators-and-Consumers.aspx>.

From writing blogs to sharing photographs on sites such as Flickr to uploading millions of videos on YouTube, social media gave Internet users the means to become content producers in ways never before imagined. As Clay Shirky points out in his 2010 book, *Cognitive Surplus*, many different websites now have a magical "publish now" button on them, giving everyone the ability to do what only a scarce few could accomplish before social media: become a published author.

> Yes, there is such a button. Publishing used to be something we had to ask permission to do; the people whose permission we had to ask were publishers. Not anymore. Publishers still perform other functions in selecting, editing, and marketing work…, but they no longer form the barrier between private and public writing.[16]

This concept applies beyond the written word. Photographers, musicians, and filmmakers could now publish and share their works on sites such as Flickr, MySpace, and YouTube, and suddenly access to content was radically transformed, much like it was back in the 1500s with the advent of movable type and the printing press. This, of course, gives amateurs a lot more power relative to the existing professionals (why buy stock photos when you can find what you need on Flickr for free?) leading to Andrew Keen's infamous diatribe against the *Cult of the Amateur: How Today's Internet is Killing Our Culture* in June 2007, in which he lamented the pervasiveness of "user-generated nonsense" that he saw as swamping the opinion of experts.

Information Wants to Be Free

Shirky agrees, actually, that when it's easier for anyone to publish anything, we see a decline in the average quality of what's being published, but it also enables greater experimentation with form, and that benefit outweighs the average loss in quality. The blogs, online communities, and other content-sharing sites that developed over the last few years are new forms that enable a different kind of information than we had available to us in the old system. The same thing happened when newspapers, novels, and scientific journals emerged following the invention of the printing press. Yes, the printing press enabled a bunch of bad stuff to be created (compared to the Bible or the classics, which were the only books being reproduced before the press), but the new forms that were created helped to advance science, literature, and society in ways that hadn't been imagined. The same dynamic is at play today with social media. Now that the consumers of content have become broadly the producers of content, the opportunities for advancement are shifting and growing, though they typically challenge the status quo in often uncomfortable ways.

---

16. Shirky, Clay. Cognitive Surplus: Creativity and Generosity in a Connected Age. New York: Penguin, 2010. Print. 46.

For example, Jeff Howe argues in *Crowdsourcing* (published in 2009) that before social media, experts trafficked in the acquisition and interpretation of exclusive information. Only lawyers knew the arcane details of our legal system, only journalists had the sources that would reveal the news, and only politicians had access to classified information or the mechanics of government. But the Internet busted open those closed systems on which the experts relied for their monopoly.

> The architecture of the Internet conspires against closed systems. A network, by definition, is composed of a multitude of nodes so that information multiplies rapidly and effortlessly. The architecture of a network flattens all hierarchies. ... On the Web, restricting information is harder—more difficult—than distributing it broadly. Simply put, the people are empowered with enough knowledge to peek behind the Wizard's curtain; the amateurs are able to use the Web to acquire as much information as the professionals.[17]

The result of this is the idea that "information wants to be free." Information wants to be free because closed organizations that might traditionally have been the gatekeepers of specialized information can no longer keep up with the rate of content creation. Information that takes too long to come out publicly will be superseded by the latest news relevant to that topic—and this cycle feeds itself, where the volume of information available will feed any prior content and move discussions along faster than it can be published on paper. And by "latest news," we mean latest online news. Just look at what is happening, as we speak, to the newspaper industry. In 2000, at its peak, the newspaper industry earned $48.67 billion in print advertising. By 2009 that number drops, like a burning car off a cliff, to $27.56 billion—a loss of 44% of its revenue in less than a decade.[18]

Google Me, Baby

Of course we can't talk about social media without talking about the phenomenon that makes all of the Internet work: online search. The first major breakthrough of the Internet was the ability to store a seemingly incomprehensible amount of information online, but that would have been worthless without the second breakthrough, exemplified by Google, which is the ability to find just what you are looking for in approximately 0.11 seconds. Whether it's specialized, niche *information* (or just the very latest) or specialized, niche *products*, the key to finding them is

---

17. Howe, Jeff. Crowdsourcing: Why the Power of the Crowd Is Driving the Future of Business. New York: Crown Business, 2008. 40.

18. "Advertising Expenditures - Newspaper Association of America: Advancing Newspaper Media for the 21st Century." Newspaper Association of America: Advancing Newspaper Media for the 21st Century. Mar. 2010. Web. 31 Jan. 2011. <http://www.naa.org/TrendsandNumbers/Advertising-Expenditures.aspx>.

online search. Search has become ubiquitous. According to the same Pew Internet *Generations 2010* study we mentioned at the beginning of this chapter, search is the number one online activity for all generations after email—87% of U.S. adults online use search engines. (It does not appear, however, that the Pew study takes into account social network search—meaning searching for keywords directly on Facebook, LinkedIn, or Twitter, for example, so the numbers are likely to be even larger.) If information is everywhere and search is how we find it, the next step in that progression is finding conversational information through social networks and, in the case of Twitter specifically, real-time search.

In a *New York Times* article titled "Finding Political News Online, the Young Pass It On,"[19] Brian Stelter quoted a college student who said, "If the news is that important, it will find me." In just a couple of years, that quote has become part of the lore of social media, encapsulating in just a few words how a whole generation now expects to receive relevant information through their online networks. Stelter was writing about the 2008 Obama campaign, which energized voters under the age of 30 in unprecedented numbers.[20] "According to interviews and recent surveys, younger voters tend to be not just consumers of news and current events but conduits as well—sending out e-mailed links and videos to friends and their social networks. And in turn, they rely on friends and online connections for news to come to them. In essence, they are replacing the professional filter—reading *The Washington Post*, clicking on CNN.com —with a social one." So now, relevance, the holy grail of search engine optimization, has become more and more networked, meaning that search results are tied to information filtered through an individual's social connections.

With this backdrop in mind, where people (especially younger generations) use search to find information through their social networks and receive news as it happens through those same networks, we've seen the rise of real-time search as a crucial development in the spread of social media. When events can be reported much faster on Twitter than traditional media outlets can keep up with them, those traditional news sources become less and less relevant, and it's another nail in the coffin of broadcast communications. This has to be extrapolated to any business trying to reach an audience—if most of that audience expect information to find them, that means they will not come to you unless they are specifically looking (hence the importance of search). Social media is forcing every kind of business to rethink how to get its messages out.

---

19. Stelter, Brian. "Finding Political News Online, the Young Pass It On." New York Times. 27 Mar. 2008. Web. 28 Jan. 2011. <http://www.nytimes.com/2008/03/27/us/politics/27voters.html?_r=1>.

20. Keeter, Scott, Juliana Horowitz, and Alec Tyson. "Young Voters in the 2008 Election." Pew Research Center. 12 Nov. 2008. Web. 28 Jan. 2011. <http://pewresearch.org/pubs/1031/young-voters-in-the-2008-election>.

It's Not Information Overload, It's Filter Failure

When Clay Shirky famously said "it's not information overload, it's filter failure" at the Web 2.0 Expo in New York in September 2008,[21] he was talking about how our traditional systems for managing the information we have access to have been completely blown out of the water by social media. According to Shirky, we've always had more books in the world than we could possibly read—so it's not actually an issue of too much information. But in a society where we spend hours and hours of every day online, and more and more information in all its forms comes to us, we need better filters. The volume of information has not actually increased, Shirky argued, but the systems that limit how much we can process are no longer working—like a river overflowing a dam.

Enter the "content curator," a term coined by marketing blogger and author, Rohit Bhargava. Bhargava posted his *Manifesto For The Content Curator: The Next Big Social Media Job of the Future?*[22] almost exactly a year after Shirky's appearance in New York. In it, he notes that algorithmic search engines such as Google, bookmarking sites such as Digg and Delicious, and blog aggregation sites such as Alltop are perhaps not enough to truly filter the best and most relevant content for us. Maybe a person with curating skills could do this better. Our challenge is not creating content—we need people who can make sense of it all and bring the best content forward. Organizations themselves, Bhargava predicts, will invest in content curation, recognizing the power in their hands if they can connect customers with just the right content. The result is a "new dialogue based on valued content rather than just brand created marketing messages."

Since this manifesto, curation and filtering has become a hot topic in social media. Online platforms have emerged that purport to do this, and discussions continue about curation as a skill set. Curation sits alongside other identified emerging skill sets for businesses that want to build community online to reach their constituents, stakeholders, and customers better through social interaction: listening online, the art of conversation (not a comfortable or traditional skill for employees), social etiquette, facilitating and mediating, and collaboration.[23]

21. "Web 2.0 Expo NY: Clay Shirky, It's Not Information Overload. It's Filter Failure. - Web2Expo - Blip.tv." Web2Expo on Blip.tv. 19 Sept. 2009. Web. 31 Jan. 2011. <http://web2expo.blip.tv/file/1277460>.

22. Bhargava, Rohit. "Manifesto For The Content Curator: The Next Big Social Media Job of the Future?" Influential Marketing Blog. 30 Sept. 2009. Web. 28 Jan. 2011. <http://www.influentialmarketing-blog.com/weblog/2009/09/manifesto-for-the-content-curator-the-next-big-social-media-job-of-the-future-.html>.

23. Dreyer, Lindy, and Maddie Grant. Open Community: A Little Book of Big Ideas for Associations Navigating the Social Web. Madison, WI: Omnipress, 2010. 59.

So the social media revolution continues to double back and revolutionize itself. The consumers of information, entertainment, and media suddenly became the producers, and no sooner did we embrace that idea than we needed to figure out ways to use social media to aid us in our consumption once again. This is another important theme in the social media revolution—the system grows, multiplies, divides, and expands organically. One breakthrough generates both new solutions and new problems that simply spur the generation of new breakthroughs. No wonder we don't have control any more. The revolution is alive.

From Conversation to Collaboration to Collective Action

So far we have seen how social media facilitated some radical shifts in marketing, content creation and sharing, and finding and filtering the vast amounts of information that drive today's economy. Few, if any, businesses are exempt from this transformation. But the depth of this change has impact beyond simply communication and content and into the areas of collaboration and collective action.

Consumers (or the group Clay Shirky often refers to as the "people formerly known as the audience") not only communicate directly with each other, they also are starting to do things together as a result. A full chapter in Tapscott and Williams' *Wikinomics* is devoted to "the Prosumers"[24] and looks at how companies like Lego and BMW have embraced their communities of enthusiasts and incorporated them into their research and development processes. People come together online to create communities based on their enthusiasm for particular products or brands, and companies can welcome this and actually leverage it. It's not about controlling these groups—they formed online usually without the help (or interference) from the company in question. But the companies can engage with and learn from these self-formed communities.

> Companies are discovering that "lead users"—people who stretch the limits of existing technology and often create their own product proto-types in the process—often develop modifications and extensions to products that will eventually appeal to mainstream markets. In other words, lead users serve as a beacon for where the mainstream market is headed. Companies that learn how to tap the insights of lead users can gain competitive advantage.[25]

---

24. Tapscott, Don, and Anthony D. Williams. Wikinomics: How Mass Collaboration Changes Everything. New York: Portfolio, 2006. 124-150.

25. Tapscott, Don, and Anthony D. Williams. Wikinomics: How Mass Collaboration Changes Everything. New York: Portfolio, 2006. 128.\

Communities of enthusiasts for particular products is one thing. Collaboration that advances an entire industry or champions social good is quite another. Clay Shirky makes the same point that Tapscott and Williams made about the power of new forms, but in this case applied to collective action, rather than just publishing content.

> Our electronic networks are enabling novel forms of collective action, enabling the creation of collaborative groups that are larger and more distributed than at any other time in history. The scope of work that can be done by noninstitutional groups is a profound challenge to the status quo. The collapse of transaction costs makes it easier for people to get together—so much easier, in fact, that it is changing the world.[26]

For Shirky, Tapscott, and Williams, the collaborative aspect of social media in the business world is deeply disruptive to traditional business structures. Obviously, too, the power of "noninstitutional groups" can extend beyond business.

Consider the current plight of trade associations and professional societies, for example, who have recently been dealing with an identity crisis of sorts. The IRS defines an association as "a group of people banded together for a specific purpose." Back in the old days (that is, a few years ago), that definition made sense to the tax agency because the act of banding together (filing articles of incorporation, electing a Board of Directors, setting up a bank account, deciding on policies and action plans) was difficult enough to limit this activity. We can see now how the social Web might put a bit of a wrench in the works, as banding together for a specific purpose can happen instantly and on a large scale with very little cost.

The association industry has centuries of tradition (the first recorded association was the Chamber of Commerce of the state of New York, formalized by 20 merchant members in 1768) and a large presence in this country. In 2009, there were close to 91,000 professional and trade associations in the United States and more than 1.2 million philanthropic or charitable organizations.[27] But if it is so easy to form groups around what people care about, why would anyone pay dues to these institutions? What happens to the traditional value proposition—usually education, networking, advocacy, and so on—when people can get what they need or achieve certain collective goals cheaper and faster without you, using social technologies? The smarter organizations in the association community are adapting to these new ways of communicating with their members, advancing their industries, and achieving their missions, but it requires a lot of attention and effort.

---

26. Shirky, Clay. Here Comes Everybody: The Power of Organizing without Organizations. New York: Penguin, 2008. 48.

27. "Associations FAQ - Advocacy- ASAE." ASAE - The Center for Association Leadership. Web. 28 Jan. 2011. <http://www.asaecenter.org/Advocacy/contentASAEOnly.cfm?ItemNumber=16341>.

For advocacy organizations and charitable nonprofits in particular, the advent of social media has resulted in an explosion of collective efforts toward social good, fueled by the power of social networks in connecting people with interest in particular causes and also by taking advantage of mobile technology to reach people in the third world who might not otherwise have had access to the Internet. More than $30 million was raised for Haiti through the Red Cross in ten days in January 2010, and 42% of that was donated either by email, on the Web, or via text message. There are thousands of other examples of nonprofits using social media to advance their causes, such as

- Powerful online projects led by one individual, such as Invisible People, a video blog (vlog) project where Mark Horvath "makes the invisible visible" by talking to homeless people all across the United States; Dan Savage's "It Gets Better" campaign benefiting LGBT youth; and GiveMN.org, who raised $10 million in one day for Minnesota nonprofits (Give to the Max Day).[28]

- Aggregation sites, where users can select projects to support from a national database, like CitizenEffect.org, Kiva.org, and DonorsChoose.org.

- Corporate social good campaigns like Pepsi Refresh and American Express's Small Business Saturday.

- International collaborative projects such as CrisisCamp, which is "a global network of hybrid barcamp/hackathon events which bring together people and communities who innovate crisis response and global development through technology tools, expertise and problem solving,"[29] and Ushaidi, a nonprofit technology company that provides open source data visualization and mapping software.

The nonprofit industry is finding ever-amazing ways to harness the power of technology and online collective action, but nonprofits, like every other business, have to compete for the attention of their audience. Many are currently debating the value of "slacktivism," defined by the Urban Dictionary as "the act of participating in obviously pointless activities as an expedient alternative to actually expending effort to fix a problem." These include campaigns in which people are encouraged to "like" a Facebook page, or change their status or avatar in support of a good cause. In other words, campaigns which may or may not raise awareness of a cause,

28. Kanter, Beth. "How Minnesota's 'Networked Nonprofits' Raised over $10M in 1 Day! | Beth's Blog." Beth Kanter's Blog. 10 Dec. 2010. Web. 28 Jan. 2011. <http://www.bethkanter.org/mn-give-2/>.

29. "About CrisisCommons." CrisisCommons. 6 Mar. 2010. Web. 28 Jan. 2011. <http://crisiscommons.org/about/>.

and may or may not lead to more donations or volunteering on behalf of those causes.

From Collective Action to [?]...

It's becoming harder and harder to keep up. The social media revolution has gone through so many cycles, it is difficult to even recognize what has been revolutionized. It all seems new. In a few short years, the debates about control or marketing or content are being supplanted by discussions of literal revolutions driven by social media in Tunisia and Egypt. For-profits and nonprofits now occupy the same spaces, and the cutting edge conversations are less about markets and now actively discussing the idea of community.

Co-author Maddie Grant has already published a book with Lindy Dreyer that explores the idea of Open Community:

> **Open Community (noun):** A diverse group of people, bonded by a common interest in an industry and an organization, who care enough to contribute and cooperate online for the good of the group.[30]

Although the book was written specifically for the association industry, it is applicable to any business that seeks to understand how certain aspects of this new Open Community will impact their survival. Alongside developing the new skill sets for becoming "social organizations" that we mentioned previously, businesses must accept that social media has created online ecosystems around them. People are talking about them in several different social spaces (Facebook, Twitter, LinkedIn, their own blogs, private community groups, and so on), and each of those spaces has a culture, language, rules, and etiquette that is unique. Social media has created influencers among people traditionally outside an organization's database of members or donors or customers. These are people whose activities and opinions can have tangible, measurable financial effects (good or bad); people on the periphery but who have social capital (i.e., trust) among their own networks.

Some of these influencers are what Beth Kanter in *The Networked Nonprofit* describes as "free agents":

> Millennials, with their passion for causes and fluency with social media, are also part of a powerful new force for social change called *free agents*. Free agents are individuals working outside of organizations to organize, mobilize, raise funds, and communicate with constituents. In the old paradigm, organizations could dismiss free agents as amateurs not worthy of their time and attention. And without the connectedness

---

30. Dreyer, Lindy, and Maddie Grant. Open Community: a Little Book of Big Ideas for Associations Navigating the Social Web. Madison, WI: Omnipress, 2010. 17.

of social media they might have been able to afford to ignore them. But not any more, not with the power of an entire social movement in the palm of an individual's hand.[31]

We used to hold back, but not any more. We used to wait for the institutions to take action and solve problems, but now we do it ourselves. We learn, we connect, we try new things, and suddenly we have formed communities where we had never imagined we could. The social media revolution is so much more than Facebook friends and putting your homemade movie up on YouTube. It has actually unleashed a broader wave of courageousness that is changing societies, not just companies. It has energized our learning and increased our capacity to experiment. It is legitimately a revolution.

So What?

In April 2009, Jeremiah Owyang identified what he called five eras of the social web, which he described as not sequential but overlapping:[32]

1. **Era of social relationships.** In the mid-1990s, social networks (bulletin boards, forums) started growing in popularity, so people started signing up for online accounts and connecting with their friends to share information. Websites also existed but were fairly distinct and separate from the social network activity.

2. **Era of social functionality.** This exists today, where the act of "friending" is just the beginning, because it allows you to use those lists of friends in what Owyang calls "social interactive applications" and widgets. The social networks, though, are all distinct, so we each have ended up with siloed and inconsistent lists of contacts, friends, followers, and so on.

3. **Era of social colonization.** By late 2009, Owyang predicted that technologies like OpenID and Facebook Connect would begin to break down the barriers between social networks. This is happening to some extent, and it does allow individuals to start integrating their online experiences. Now the lines between the networks and other websites are starting to blur.

---

31. Kanter, Beth, and Allison H. Fine. The Networked Nonprofit: Connecting with Social Media to Drive Change. San Francisco: Jossey-Bass, 2010. 15–16.

32. Owyang, Jeremiah. "The Future of the Social Web: In Five Eras « Web Strategy by Jeremiah Owyang | Social Media, Web Marketing." Web Strategy By Jeremiah Owyang: Web Marketing, Social Media. 27 Apr. 2009. Web. 28 Jan. 2011. <http://www.web-strategist.com/blog/2009/04/27/future-of-the-social-web/>.

4. **Era of social context**. Owyang believed 2010 would be the year when sites would begin to recognize personal identities and social relationships, which would allow these sites to deliver customized online experiences. Social networks now become the base of operations for online experiences.

5. **Era of social commerce**. In the near future, Owyang believes social networks will be more powerful than corporate websites or CRM (customer relationship management) systems. "Brands will serve community interests and grow based on community advocacy as users continue to drive innovation in this direction."[33]

This is where we are today. Social commerce. Where social media is not just integrated into our daily personal lives, but also in the way we conduct business. But we have to remember that this is not merely an issue of integration. When we think about social commerce, we cannot fall back into the safe challenge of figuring out how to use the social media tools most effectively within our organizations. It's not about the tools.

It's really about the underlying drivers of the social media revolution, to which we have been alluding throughout this chapter. The "groundswell" taught us that we do not have as much control as we thought we did, and that the system is much more *open* and decentralized. The rise of word of mouth marketing showed us how important it is to be *trustworthy* and authentic. Content was revolutionized as the consumers became producers, which then required a revolution to the second power as we figured out how to curate. This revealed the *generative* power of social media. And now the revolution is taking us into the realm of collective action and the power of community that brings forth a new generation of *courageous* actors.

Although the social media revolution is based in technology, it is the very organic and human elements of being open, trustworthy, generative, and courageous that provided its transformative power.

But turning back to our question of "so what," how does all this apply to you, in your organization, with the details of your market, and your employees, and your organizational culture? The business literature is replete with books that document the social media revolution, and they usually mention case studies of forward-thinking companies and organizations such as Zappos, Dell, the Red Cross, Starbucks, Best Buy, Netflix, and a few others. But as inspiring as those stories are, you probably don't work at any of those organizations. And why is it that those

---

33. Tsai, Jessica. "Social Media: The Five Year Forecast." CRM Magazine. DestinationCRM.com. 27 Apr. 2009. Web. 28 Jan. 2011. <http://www.destinationcrm.com/Articles/CRM-News/Daily-News/Social-Media-The-Five-Year-Forecast-53635.aspx>.

stories come up over and over again? They are certainly not the only companies doing social media. We've already established that it is ubiquitous. So why aren't we seeing a lot more examples of successful evolution and innovation through the incorporation of social media practices?

That is the question we tackle in the next chapter. Our organizations are not stepping up to the challenge that the social media revolution has presented us. And it's not because we can't handle the technology. It gets into the way our organizations were built and their apparent inability to thrive off the human elements driving social media.

Must Read

There are hundreds of books on social media, but we chose these three for this chapter's "must read" list because they most clearly provide the basics and the history, including case studies, of the trends and themes we discussed in this chapter.

Kanter, Beth, and Allison H. Fine. *The Networked Nonprofit: Connecting with Social Media to Drive Change*. San Francisco: Jossey-Bass, 2010.

Li, Charlene, and Josh Bernoff. *Groundswell: Winning in a World Transformed by Social Technologies*. Boston, MA: Harvard Business, 2008.

Shirky, Clay. *Here Comes Everybody: The Power of Organizing Without Organizations*. New York: Penguin, 2008.

3

We're Not Moving Forward

"You can't shuffle your way on to the next S-curve. You have to leap. You have to vault over your preconceived notions, over everyone else's best practices, over the advice of all the experts, and over your own doubts."

—*Gary Hamel,* **The Future of Management**

In Chapter 2, "We Can't Go Back," we looked at the state of social media and the reasons why society (and the business world specifically) will never look the same. The next logical step would be to dig a little deeper into how the business world is coping with this radical change. How are businesses changing some of their core processes to adapt to this social world? How are companies integrating not only the tools of social media, but also the underlying principles and values of social media into their cultures and behaviors?

In short, they aren't. Sure, the business world has jumped on the social media band-wagon and now everybody has a Facebook page, but beyond the cosmetic changes, are they really embracing the revolution? We don't see it. We see organizations struggle even at the tactical level, because the way social media has evolved is so foreign to most organizational structures, processes, and cultures. Yes, some are tak-ing the ball and running with social media, but we still rarely see any that use this opportunity to actively question the way they do things. For all the public rhetoric about the social media revolution, we are still left mostly with an armada of organi-zations that seem content to keep chugging along, adapting to these technological advances at a pace that is comfortable to them. As our chapter titles imply, there may be no going back to the way it was before social media, but we don't seem to be moving forward either.

So what is keeping us stuck in this limbo? Two words: best practices. When it comes to our organizations, we love our best practices. We love our benchmarking and our competitive analysis. We love that feeling we get when we don't reinvent the wheel. We like our case studies and our white papers and our army of consultants who can go out there and figure out what the best practices are so we don't have to.

There is just one problem. Best practices are evil.

We know this sounds impossible. The argument in favor of best practices is strong. In any industry, you have many different people all working on the same kinds of things, so why wouldn't you take the time to analyze the different ways of doing things and identify the ones that were consistently more effective than others, and then replicate them? It's almost a Darwinist survival of the fittest approach—if we weed out the less-effective practices and replicate only the best ones, then we can dramatically increase the performance of the industry or the organization over both the short and long term. And think of the efficiency! By relying on best prac-tices, we get to take advantage of all the time and effort people before us put into perfecting their practices, and then take up where they left off. No more "reinvent-ing the wheel."

Search for "best practices" in Amazon, and you'll find more than 13,000 books to read across almost as many industries and topic areas, each one offering that tempt-ing promise of being able to catapult you to that next level. The business commu-nity is flat-out in love with best practices, which is why you may need a minute to let the following statement sink in: Best practices are killing us.

If you don't believe it, go back and re-read Chapter 2. The social media revolution was not built on the copying of best practices. If anything, social media takes some of the best practices in media, marketing, and learning and turns them on their head, achieving astonishing results in the process. Consider Twitter. It was origi-nally set up as a means for people in one organization to communicate with each other via text messaging. Had the founders of Twitter focused exclusively on best practices for text messaging, or intra-organizational communications, Twitter would never have been transformed into the incredible social network that it is, with millions of messages exchanged daily and, given what we have seen in Iran, Tunisia, and Egypt, arguably the power to topple dictatorships and fuel revolutions. There are no best practices to tell you how to do that.

Now, we know what you are thinking. Best practices can't be all bad. We have all lived through moments where we saw what someone else was doing and used that knowledge to our own advantage, so how can they be evil? True, observing your environment and learning from it is a good thing. But remember that you must always adapt what you observe to fit your own context. In simple systems, this is easy, but the more complex things become, the more work you have to do to adapt the best practices to your context. That is the real problem now. With the speed of the social media revolution, the context is changing faster than we can adapt our best practices. The harder we try to find answers to our problems by looking backward, the more and more we fall behind. Our love affair with best practices is dragging us down, and we need a new approach. At the center of this new approach is innovation.

Best Practices Versus Innovation

Innovation has an inherent distaste for best practices because it is about new solutions, not copying existing solutions. Definitions of innovation vary by guru, but they revolve around two words: change and new. Innovation implies change and doing things differently, but it has to achieve some new level of performance, or create some kind of new value. It is not enough just to be different; it has to be better. It is about creation, not copying. Although it is often applied to new product development, we have to be careful to not relegate innovation to the arena of inventing the next hot product. You will certainly find innovation to be central in organizations that are consistently ahead of the market in their product development, but innovation is much more broadly applicable than that. You can innovate internal governance, or manufacturing processes, or knowledge management. Anywhere you are creating a new level of value and performance, you can be innovating.

Innovation and best practices are different at their very core. Innovation's logic understands that systems by their nature are constantly generating new problems (and new solutions) all the time. In fact, as soon as you solve a particular problem, the solution then becomes a part of the status quo, which is part of a dynamic, evolving system, thus the solution starts to generate new problems of its own. That is why best practices are killing us. By the time you adopt a solution that was generated in the past, it is less likely to be applicable in your current situation.

You can certainly solve individual problems by looking back, but if we don't innovate, the problems simply grow in complexity and number to the point where we start to lose the ability to grow and regenerate faster than we are deteriorating. This is true of biological systems, social systems, and organizations alike. As innovation expert C. K. Prahalad points out in his *Harvard Business Review* article "Best Practices Get You Only So Far," best practices and benchmarking "may allow enterprises to catch up with competitors, but it won't turn them into market leaders. Organizations become winners by spotting big opportunities and inventing next practices."

Innovation values a future focus, creativity, and the discipline of experimentation, where answers come through learning, rather than pure imitation. Where else have we seen that? Social media. We have seen plenty of technological innovation in the past hundred years, but the speed of change has never been quite like this, and it is the centrality of innovation in social media that is driving it. Although it is amazing that the Internet can move from initial creation to 50 million users in only 4 years back in the 1990s (it took radio 38 years to accomplish the same feat several decades earlier), Facebook added 200 million users in just 9 months in this century.[1] Facebook routinely makes substantial changes to its platform and then sees what happens, each time weathering complaints from a vocal minority of users. This kind of evolution does not take place because the people involved study what other companies have done and imitate them. We didn't get to where we are in social media because of best practices. That kind of change has been driven by ruthless innovation.

Let's get back to the business world. Despite the amazing model that social media provides in the business world, we still seem to value best practices far more than we value innovation. The fields of management and leadership and the disciplines of human resources, diversity and inclusion, and organization development sometimes give lip service to innovation and its value, but in the end they fall squarely in the best practices camp. They value consistency and efficiency, formulas, and benchmarking studies over prototypes, experimentation, risk, and creativity. The result? Our organizations have used essentially the same management technologies for the past 100 years. The business world has changed rapidly in nearly every aspect, except in the way we run our businesses.

It is high time we start applying the principles of innovation to the way we run our organizations. Innovation is not just about creating new products (or new social networks, for that matter). It is about change, creation, and new pathways, so it is just as applicable to management and the way we run our organizations as it is to

---

1. Qualman, Erik. "Statistics Show Social Media Is Bigger Than You Think | Socialnomics – Social Media Blog." Socialnomics. 11 Aug. 2009. Web. 31 Jan. 2011. <http://socialnomics.net/2009/08/11/statistics-show-social-media-is-bigger-than-you-think/>.

products or social media. Management, after all, is really just a tool—a technology we use to help run our organizations. Unfortunately, our track record with management innovation in the last century has been dismal.

In *The Future of Management*, Gary Hamel recounts the not so impressive history of management innovation. He points out that if we could magically transport a U.S. executive back from the early 1960s to today's world, he (more likely a "he" back then) would no doubt marvel at the amazing changes that have taken place in the last 50 years. From technology to population growth to the evolution of social norms, we can imagine he would be overwhelmed by the change he would face, but if he needed a break—some place he could go that would be comforting and remind him of his home—we could simply make him an executive in one of today's organizations. He would actually be able to relax a little by facilitating a strategic planning meeting or conducting a performance review—*because those processes have not changed substantially in 50 years.*[2]

You could certainly respond with the "if it's not broken don't try to fix it" argument. After all, not all innovations are good things (just look at Enron's "innovative" accounting practices!). Maybe our management technologies are still working just fine, so that's why we haven't changed them?

We don't buy it. This is one of the central arguments of this book. Our organizations are staying alive (and even growing) *despite* our management practices, not *because* of them, and that run won't last forever. The growth of social media simply shined a glaring light on this situation because the radical success of social media was accomplished by abandoning what has become standard in most organizations. We are never ones to advocate change simply for change's sake. We don't argue for innovation because we think it is cool, or we wish we could all be Apple or Google. We need management innovation because that is the weak link in our collective chain right now. As long as we cling to our management technology that was invented decades or centuries ago, we will be squandering the opportunities that this new, social world presents.

Of course, part of the problem is that our organizations have, in fact, been succeeding despite antiquated management technology. We don't feel the pain enough to make a shift. Take the traditional media establishment, for example. *Advertising Age* reported back in September 2007 that "old world media" was starting to be in trouble.[3] A mainstream market research firm reported that ad sales were on the decline for two quarters in a row, and that hadn't happened in more than 6 years. The article suggested that although this was as a result of the early indications of a recession, there were still opportunities in online advertising, which was something that

---

2. Hamel, Gary. The Future of Management. Boston, MA: Harvard Business School, 2007. 6.

the traditional market research report did not study. It was 2007 and the market research firm was not including online advertising in the research! Only when things started to get bad, did they begin to study the alternatives. This is a typical pattern. We change only when the pain is great enough to motivate us to make the change.

This pattern is deadly. When the pain has become measurably bad, the effort required to make the appropriate change is, in fact, much greater than it would have been had changes been made just a little bit earlier. When you wait too long, you end up needing to reverse the trend, rather than just bend it. So it may be counter-intuitive, but it is much easier to make the changes you need to make when things are still going well. This allows you to jump over to the next S-curve without the long transition time of reinventing yourself. Legacy media (and legacy airlines and any other company that gets "legacy" put in front of them) will learn this the hard way. So one of the main lessons leaders in organizations can learn from social media is this: Change now, even if things aren't crumbling yet.

That is precisely our point of view as we look at the way we run our organizations in today's social world. We don't care that we cannot yet see back-to-back quarters of decline to tell us that we have a problem with the way we are doing things. We can see the cracks in the foundation. We can see the logical reasons why, in the coming years, these practices are going to fail us. Now is the time to change them.

To make our case, we go straight to the heart of the matter and challenge three basic building blocks of modern management: *strategic planning*, *human resources management*, and *leadership*. Each area is well established. They are veritable pillars of the management establishment, complete with ample support from academics and practitioners in the management world. But like all of our management best practices, they are killing us. We take them for granted, and cling to them even, while the social media world runs circles around our organizations. That is pre-cisely why we take a closer look at each one and expose them as myths. These best practices are holding us back in ways that might have been okay a few decades ago, but in today's digital age we simply can't afford to accept these twentieth century ideas as truth.

Strategic Planning: The Comforting Lie of Predictability

The concept of strategy is thousands of years old, and of course it is important for organizations. But we do think you need a better understanding of what it means

---

3. Creamer, Matthew. "Old-World Media Start to Feel the Pain - Advertising Age - News." Advertising Age. 17 Sept. 2007. Web. 31 Jan. 2011. <http://adage.com/article?article_id=120490>.

and how we do the work of strategy in organizations. The earliest applications of strategy were in the military realm. The essence of military strategy was a focus on the big picture, rather than the details of tactics. Strategy is about how to win the war, whereas tactics are about how to manage the troops or wield the weapons to win each battle. In addition to the big picture view, strategy also implied a certain future focus. The moves you made today were designed to achieve an outcome some time in the future based on a decent understanding of the big picture.

For organizations, strategy has the same big-picture and future-focus implications. Organizations with strategies make intentional choices about where to put their attention or their resources to be successful in their particular marketplace (in theory, anyway). Apple is famous for its emphasis on both design and simplicity as a strategy for growing market share in the personal computer market. Nintendo, realizing it was not competing with the technological advances of both Sony (Playstation) and Microsoft (XBox), changed the game (literally) by introducing its radically new *Wii* gaming system, which made use of physical interaction among players. Southwest Airlines abandoned many of the elements of traditional airline strategy (such as hub-and-spoke routes, assigned seating, different classes, and the puzzling norm that airline employees should never have fun) and as a result has become one of the few (if not the only) U.S. airline in recent years to post an annual profit.

These companies made intentional choices about their overall direction based on their broad understanding of the market and what would be successful, and subsequently committed significant resources based on those strategies that resulted in success. That is strategy in action. Success also requires effective tactical implementation, of course, but it is not the implementation of Apple or Southwest or Nintendo that is written about in our business school textbooks. It is the brilliance of the strategy that sets these companies apart.

Of course it is much easier to identify brilliant strategic moves when looking backward. We love to recount the strategic brilliance of our corporate heroes when we are standing at the end of the timeline, marveling at their foresight, creativity, and courage to create new products, enter new markets, and think outside the box. But we need more than inspiration to succeed. As compelling as our retrospective success stories are, the more difficult (and pressing) challenge is creating successful strategies at the beginning of the story, when we don't yet know how our strategies are going to play out or how our competitors or customers are going to react. Fortunately, we have a "best practice" for that: strategic planning.

Strategic Planning Basics

Strategic planning is one of the most well-defended best practices in management history. Developed in earnest about 100 years ago, its popularity has waxed and waned, yet it is still ubiquitous in today's organizations. Large corporations actually devote entire departments to their strategic planning processes, but you can still find some kind of strategic planning process going on in nearly every company, mom and pop shop, nonprofit charity, trade association, or government agency around. We are to the point where strategic planning rarely needs to be actively "defended." It is simply declared "a critical management process for creating and sustaining effective organizations."[4]

Not so fast.

Let's take a closer look. We start with a simple definition of strategic planning:

> Strategic planning is a formalized process within an organization for making decisions about direction and resource allocation to improve the chances for future organizational success, resulting in a plan that includes measurable goals and action steps.

We don't think this is the best definition of strategic planning ever, but it does cover the basics of how strategic planning is generally practiced today:

- It is formalized; it is practiced through authorized organizational processes.
- It is about decisions and making choices, particularly about resources.
- It is about the future, and its aim is the success of the enterprise.
- It absolutely is about a plan, and it expects metrics, goals, and action steps.

This rational and somewhat mechanical approach to strategy making was born out of a movement pioneered by Frederick Taylor in the early 1900s called *scientific management.* Taylor and his colleagues looked at the way people did their work, hoping that analysis would help them find ways to do it better, or faster, or less expensively. He studied how men shoveled coal and how machine tools were cut and devised ways to eliminate unwanted or wasted motion to make the work more efficient. At the time, it was actually revolutionary to apply abstract analysis to things like manufacturing or manual labor, and it led to some stunning results. We started analyzing and perfecting all kinds of industrial practices, to the point where our manufacturing output per labor hour in this country increased 500% in only seven decades.[5]

---

4. Gallery, Michael E., and Susan Waters. "The Development of Consensus Guidelines for Strategic Planning in Associations - Publications and Resources - ASAE." Journal of Association Leadership (2008). ASAE - The Center for Association Leadership. Summer 2008. Web. 31 Jan. 2011. <http://www.asaecenter.org/Resources/JALArticleDetail.cfm?ItemNumber=35736>.

5. Hamel, The Future of Management. 13.

So it seemed only natural that we could apply that kind of thinking to the business challenge of devising effective strategy. In the 1950s, U.S. corporations used strategic planning processes to produce annual operating budgets that reflected strategic choices. A few decades later, they were using strategic planning processes to determine a portfolio approach to growth, or analyzing markets for competitive advantage. This was the time when larger companies were establishing entire planning departments whose job was to design and implement processes that would produce effective strategic plans for the organization.

But even without planning departments, nearly all organizations have implemented strategic planning processes. Who hasn't been forced to do at least a rudimentary SWOT analysis (Strengths, Weaknesses, Opportunities, and Threats), a bedrock practice in strategic planning? Or your company might have hired futurists to conduct research studies and environmental scans to guide planning processes. Or your company might have engaged people both inside and outside the organization in large-scale "scenario planning" processes, making choices based on ongoing discussions of multiple futures. An entire industry of consultants emerged to help us with vision statements, values statements, mission statements, purpose statements, planning by objective, competitive analyses, integration, alignment, champions...the list goes on.

Strategic planning is so globally accepted as a best practice, it is probably the only process that has the unlikely (and somewhat puzzling) distinction of being favored and defended both by Fortune 500 companies in the United States and the Communist leaders of the former Soviet Union. Strategic planning's status as a best practice seems unassailable. And beyond its ubiquitous presence, there is a solid logic to strategic planning. After all, in the absence of strategy and planning, an organization's activities would seem to be random, and success would thus be attributable to chance. How depressing would that be? All this time we have been elevating our brilliant business strategists to hero status, only to discover that their success all came down to dumb luck. No, that can't be right, we tell ourselves. Logic assures us that through strategic planning we can apply the intelligence and insight of our leaders and managers to the broader success of the enterprise. If we take the time to do it right, we will generate a plan that can guide everyone in our system in a coordinated way to achieve the results we have chosen.

Pulling Back the Curtain on Strategic Planning

No. We have to stop falling for the siren's song of the strategic planners. Remember, that the communists were the poster children for this logic, and look where it got them. Despite its compelling logic and ubiquitous adoption, strategic planning, in fact, works a lot better in theory than it does in practice. Notice that the famous strategic success stories like Apple, Southwest Airlines, and Nintendo rarely, if ever, make reference to strategic planning processes. We love brilliant strategy, but we have not seen compelling evidence that there really is a connection between brilliant strategy and the "best practice" of strategic planning.

In fact, there is plenty of evidence that life simply doesn't work the way strategic planning wants it to work. Let's start with the notion of success and failure. Strategic planning assures us that we will be more successful if we engage in strategic planning, right? That sounds nice, but when you start observing the universe more carefully, you actually see a lot more failure than success. Paul Ormerod has studied both biological systems and the business world, and he has identified a unifying similarity between the two: failure. Of all the species that have ever lived on this planet, only 0.01% of them are alive today, and businesses don't have a much better record: Only 19% of the world's largest industrial companies in 1912 survived more than 80 years, and today 10% of American companies disappear each year. Numbers like that might make you think twice about the value of strategic planning. Ormerod agrees. He argues that an executive implementing a strategic planning process has more similarity to a biological creature going through random mutations than he or she would to some kind of all powerful "rational economic man" that is controlling outcomes. In an interview in *Harvard Business Review*,[6] Ormerod argued that companies should

> ...embrace the inherent randomness that drives success and failure and that no amount of cleverness or information can overcome. The companies that are most able to explore and innovate—something akin to random mutation—and then rapidly and flexibly adapt when an innovation succeeds or fails, will do best.

We are comforted by the thought that we can control our own destiny through good strategic planning, but life simply doesn't work that way.

And it's not just the theoretical economists who study biology that point out the failure of strategic planning. Henry Mintzberg got his Ph.D. from MIT in 1968 and teaches at the business school at McGill University in Montreal, Canada. He has published about 150 articles and 15 books, and he won two McKinsey prizes for articles he wrote in *Harvard Business Review*. If anyone were qualified to champion the virtues of strategic planning as a best practice, it would be Mintzberg, but in fact he chose the opposite path.

Nearly two decades ago, Mintzberg published *The Rise and Fall of Strategic Planning*, which exposes some of the basic fallacies underlying strategic planning theory and practice. He spent years researching it both among his colleagues in academia and among leaders and managers in the businesses that were using strategic

---

6. Morse, Gardiner. "Set Up to Fail." Harvard Business Review, Case Studies, Articles, Books. June 2007. Web. 31 Jan. 2011. http://hbr.org/2007/06/set-up-to-fail/ar/1.

planning, and his conclusion is clear: Strategic planning doesn't work. According to Mintzberg, there are three fundamental problems with strategic planning: (1) you can't predict the future, (2) you can't separate thought from action, and (3) you can't script the formation of strategy. Let's dig into these a little bit.

You Can't Predict the Future

First, strategic planning is based on the assumption that you can truly predetermine outcomes in this world. It is predicated on the notion that we can sit here, at point A in time, and devise a plan to get us through to point B in the future, knowing enough about how the future is going to play out to make the correct strategic choices today. It's a comforting thought, actually. We want the world to be predictable. We want to rationally analyze the world and figure out ahead of time how things are going to work out. That's what makes the plans work—we choose a path and then the world stays stable enough as it plays out so that our envisioned chain of cause and effect can unfold just as we predicted. Hmmm. How convenient.

This is why the most common metaphor in strategic planning is that of the road map. We start by envisioning our destination—the endpoint of our vision, and then we work hard to draw up a map of our operating environment in enough detail so we can pick the appropriate routes. Though we may stray off course at times, we can always return to the map to regain our bearings and adjust our heading to reach our destination.

Sorry, but that whole story is a lie. The map metaphor has two fatal flaws. First, it assumes that our vision—the endpoint—is static and won't change. That makes sense to us here at point A, but over time, the results that we need and want are going to shift. They always do, because at every point after point A, the world is a new place. Of course our needs are going to change (yet our map stays the same). Second, the map metaphor assumes that we can accurately predict or forecast what will happen in the future. Your plan makes sense only if you can look into the future and accurately predict how it is going to play out. If you're wrong, and in the future your competitors or other stakeholders move in a direction you did not anticipate, you typically end up with a plan that must be radically altered or abandoned altogether (these plans have been called "credenzaware"—plans sitting in nice binders on the credenza in your office that are rarely consulted because they arc out of date the moment they are printed).

Researchers are on our side on this one, concluding (according to Mintzberg) that long-range forecasting is "notoriously inaccurate." We know it is comforting to think that we can clearly see enough about the future to devise effective plans, but it does not work.

You Can't Separate Thought from Action

The second fallacy of strategic planning is the idea that strategy is somehow detached and separate from its implementation. We really like this assumption, if for no other reason than it gives those top executives an important job for a few months out of each year as they develop the strategic plan. This is where our illustrious leaders head off to their strategy retreats to develop their carefully laid plan that is then distributed to the worker bees for flawless execution.

Besides being overtly paternalistic, this approach is flawed because separating the thinking from the action like that is artificial. Again, it is a comforting thought to be able to temporarily wall yourself off from world at that luxurious retreat so you can do that important strategic thinking that will guide your organization for the next two to five years. But in reality, you need strategic thinking woven into your implementation all the time. Strategic planning ignores that fact.

Consider the SWOT analysis, for example. It is hard to imagine anyone in today's business world that has not gone through this process. You and your colleagues are sitting in a conference room, or at an offsite retreat, and a number of facilitators are at the ready, colorful markers in hand, ready to write down on chart paper the list of your organization's Strengths and Weaknesses. The result is typically a bland list of characteristics that the people in the room like (strengths) or don't like (weaknesses), though you frequently will find the same characteristic on both lists. That is our favorite, when we identify one of our strengths as also a weakness. It is a valid point at one level, but why do we never stop and question this process when it happens? If you can have the same thing on both lists, then what is the point of coming up with the lists?

The problem here lies in how the process has been designed to identify strengths and weaknesses through abstract thought alone. It is done as a brainstorming exercise, hoping that by identifying a long list of strengths and weaknesses, we will suddenly be able to see the situation more clearly. Broadening our thinking is fine, but what it also does is pull us out of any kind of context as we devise our lists. That is why we end up with the same characteristic on both lists—because we are free to think about them within any context we please. But the critical truth here is that strengths and weaknesses *only matter within a specific context*. Being seven feet tall is a strength if you play basketball, but a weakness if you are a jockey. And the context is continuously changing. So your competitive strength when it comes to the computerized systems you put in place to track customers and sales last year, could easily become a weakness down the road when the cloud-based services become more robust and flexible. But strategic planning, quite frankly, does not like that kind of complexity. It upsets the process and gets in the way with the ultimate end goal of strategic planning, which is to create a plan. So the facilitator will typically brush over your objections and continue filling out the sheets labeled "strengths" and "weaknesses," so he can get to the next part of the process.

This will get you a plan, but it will not build the strategic capacity of your organization because strategic choices must always be made within a context, and strategy and action are always integrated, not detached.

You Can't Script the Formation of Strategy

The third core fault with strategic planning is its formalization. Our formalized and usually excruciatingly boring processes are what Mintzberg calls strategic planning's "grand fallacy."[7] Be honest: When was the last time you got excited about a strategic planning session? These meetings are typically boring for participants, or they are primarily a recycling of previous conversations, or they fail to generate any progress on strategy because there were not enough data available.[8] The minute we start to formalize the process of strategic planning and force people to come up with strategy based on our preconceived rules, we begin to suck the life out of the work of strategy. It may make sense to the planner to rigidly formalize the planning and strategy making process, but it rarely does for the people who are forced to do it. And frankly, it isn't supported by the research. There is no research that supports the idea that elaborate planning processes work any better than the messy, informal processes that have also been used to create strategy.[9]

The main problem with formalization is that it cuts out important parts of what is needed to create effective strategies. Pressed for time, planners design strategy processes that contain a bias toward what we call *convergent thinking*. As you script a strategy process, you have to take the participants through certain steps, and you obviously have to finish step A before you can progress to step B. That means we are not allowed to get stuck on part A, or the whole process gets thrown off. So the process has built-in mechanisms that force us through a phase, even if we are not ready. "I know you've identified some confusing and overlapping lists of strengths and weaknesses, but please pick five that we will work on in the next part of the process." We are forced to converge our thinking, narrow down, and rule out.

In doing so, we end up closing our eyes to what is happening in our system, when that is precisely what we need to generate strategic foresight. We avoid the confusing and uncomfortable state of not knowing, when that is often where real strategic insight emerges. We block out the nonrational when we all know from experience that emotion and intuition can be powerful strategic guides.

---

7. Mintzberg, Henry. The Rise and Fall of Strategic Planning. New York: Prentice Hall, 1994. 814.

8. Mintzberg, The Rise and Fall of Strategic Planning. 817.

9. Mintzberg, The Rise and Fall of Strategic Planning. 821.

So when you ask strategic planners if good strategy is informed by a clear vision, they will say yes. If you suggest to them that strategies must be "living" and nimble, able to respond to challenges as they arise, they will surely agree. And if you argue that your people, your customers and even your market are often characterized by nonrational influences, they will be on your side. But when you point out that the way they script the strategy-making process actually makes it much harder for your organization to do any of these things, they will be in denial, explaining that you don't understand their proprietary process.

No, dear strategic planners, we are pretty sure that it's you who do not understand. Blinded by precedent and (limited) logic, you are now constantly defending strategic planning processes with circular arguments, and frankly it's getting boring and frustrating. Strategic planning is deeply flawed in its need for predictability, its artificial separation of thought, action, and context, and its dependence on deductive and ordered processes. So as much as we love strategy and our glorious examples of strategic brilliance, the well-established best practice we have for producing strategic results turns out to be seriously flawed. Strategic planning is a perfect example of how best practices in the area of organizational management and leadership are not taking us to the next level.

Human Resource Management: We Are People, Not Spare Parts

Like strategic planning, human resource management is a best practice with good intentions but not so great results. The theory is something we can all stand behind: that people are different from machines or equipment, therefore they need to be managed differently. That wasn't always the case, particularly in the twentieth century when our work became more mechanized. Even Frederick Taylor's early work took an obviously mechanical view of human resources: He literally measured how people shoveled coal to make the coal-shoveling process more efficient.

But eventually we realized that people are not machines. So the field of human resources management developed to perfect the ways we recruit, hire, retain, motivate, and organize the people in our organizations. We even have a fairly long list of HR specialties now:[10]

- Workforce planning

- Recruitment (sometimes separated into attraction and selection)

- Induction, orientation, and onboarding

---

10. "Human Resource Management." Wikipedia, the Free Encyclopedia. 20 Jan. 2011. Web. 31 Jan. 2011. <http://en.wikipedia.org/wiki/Human_resource_management>.

- Skills management

- Training and development

- Personnel administration

- Compensation in wage or salary

- Time management

- Travel management

- Payroll

- Employee benefits administration

- Personnel cost planning

- Performance appraisal

- Labor relations

Again, these specialties all have the same goal in mind (at least in theory): creating better organizations by managing all the people with maximum efficiency and effectiveness. It is a mixture of both tactical management and strategic leadership (according to the HR professionals anyway), where organizations can put their "people first" in ways ranging from providing extensive training to employees to supporting self-managed teams to extensive sharing of financial and performance information throughout the organization.[11] Other strategic approaches to human resources emphasize a contingency approach, where the specific human resource practices vary depending on the strategy of the organization, its life cycle, or the particulars of its industry.

Still, for all the talk of strategic human resource management, the function in many organizations is still viewed as administrative. From "Dilbert" cartoons to the television show *The Office*, HR is an easy target for satire in our culture, being portrayed as anything from pure evil to completely irrelevant. Of course just because we think it is irrelevant doesn't mean we stop doing it. Although you probably need at least 20 employees or so before you start having a dedicated human resource staff, even tiny organizations copy the activities of HR professionals in managing their people. In this way, HR suffers a similarly ironic fate to strategic planning: It is mocked widely, yet practiced ubiquitously.

Like strategic planning, we mock human resources because the field simply does not live up to its promise. Again, it means well. This is not an issue of intention or even levels of effort, and yes, as with strategic planning, we know there are organizations

---

11. Pfeffer, Jeffrey. The Human Equation: Building Profits by Putting People First. Boston: Harvard Business School, 1998. 64.

that have invested significant resources in human resource management programs and have done a good job at developing competent and successful organizations. We just don't think there is a definitive cause-effect relationship there. Like many of our organizational best practices, we succeed *despite* our actions, not necessarily *because* of them. This becomes apparent when we start to have more honest conversations about these practices, just like we did above with strategic planning. In the human resource management field, you start to see the dysfunction just by looking at two staples of HR: the hiring process and organizational structures.

Why Does the Hiring Process Suck?

Consider the hiring process. We have all been through it. You see the job announcement, and you send in a cover letter and resume—two to three pages designed to provide your prospective employer with enough information to decide to commit likely hundreds of thousands of salary dollars to you (millions at higher levels) over the span of your employment. At least, they will use those two to three pages to do the first round of sorting where only the individuals with the best resumes will be called in to sit down with a hiring manager (and perhaps a few other employees) for an in-person interview.

If you are lucky enough to be in this group, you will prepare by reading about the company, so you can come in and impress your potential boss with good answers to the standard questions about what excites you, where you perform well, what your challenges have been, and what kinds of specific things you have accomplished in your previous jobs. Depending on your performance in those interviews (and maybe on the reports from the references that you chose), you may get the job. Congratulations.

At one level, the process just described (which is grossly generalized, we admit) seems logical. When hiring someone, it makes sense to take a look at her history, as documented in a resume, which includes references to educational programs or previous job experiences that have some shared meaning among you, your colleagues, and the candidate. Knowing a person got a Ph.D. at Harvard won't tell you everything about her, necessarily, but it can certainly help in your evaluation related to the job opening.

The in-person interview provides a new and richer set of data about the individual, which includes not only the person's thought process and oral communication skills, but also the opportunity to probe through conversation to identify elements of the individual that will (or won't) fit with the particular job for which the person is applying or with your organizational culture. When the boss or hiring manager finally makes that decision about who to hire, it certainly feels like the process used was adequate. It may not necessarily be guaranteed to have identified the absolute best person in the world for the job, but it certainly moved you in the right direction. Certainly one would argue that picking a random resume out of the pool of applicants as a method for hiring would eventually lead to poorer job performance and higher turnover in your organization, right?

Not so fast. It turns out that a lot of research indicates our hiring process is hardly better than picking a name out of a hat. Fred Mills is a human resources consultant with decades of experience working in and consulting to U.S. federal government agencies in the human resources function, and in his book *A Civil Disservice*, he provides a much harsher assessment of the basic hiring process used in most federal agencies:

> What passes for applicant evaluation and assessment in many agencies is still rudimentary at best: an often cursory, uninformed initial review of voluminous paper applications and rote submissions; followed by an unstructured, unguided, informal interview by a lone selecting official; after which HR effectively executes a lifetime contract.[12]

Does this sound familiar? As harsh as his analysis is, it is hard to argue that it is not accurate. We need to be more honest about what we know and don't know about how to hire people. Like strategic planning, we take comfort in the processes that have been handed to us, but that doesn't mean they are effective. Mills does go on to suggest that the private sector does a much better job than the federal government in this area, where human resources functions actually apply rigor to the hiring process by using substantive job evaluation and competency definitions and professionally designed and validated assessment instruments, not to mention better-trained interviewers. Yes, these better practices exist, but we're not convinced that they are universally practiced in the private sector either.

But even if they were, is there evidence that these more rigorous hiring practices actually bring in people who have a positive impact on organizational performance? Jeffrey Pfeffer and Robert Sutton argue that the evidence is not clear on that front either. They have found that the best predictor of job performance (documented in research) is general intelligence, as measured by the IQ test. They don't necessarily like that fact (IQ is only one narrow measure of intelligence after all), but they did find it to be the "most powerful predictor of job performance across studies."

But this "most powerful" predictor rarely correlates with performance by more than 0.4, which leaves 84% of the variation in performance unexplained.[13] In other words, every other factor we might use to predict job performance ends up leaving more than 84% of variation in job performance unexplained.

---

12. Mills, Fred. Civil Disservice: Federal Employment Culture and the Challenge of Genuine Reform. iUniverse, 2010. 75.

13. Pfeffer, Jeffrey, and Robert I. Sutton. Hard Facts, Dangerous Half-truths, and Total Nonsense: Profiting from Evidence-based Management. Boston, MA: Harvard Business School, 2006. 91.

Are you still feeling confident about your hiring process? Well before you scrap it and move to the IQ test, you should also know that the problem is then compounded by the fact that individual performance naturally varies over time. Sometimes we are on our game, and sometimes we are not. So even our wildly imperfect methods of resume review and one-off interviews are going to be even less predictive of future job performance than we thought, because we have no way of knowing if our candidates are having a good day or a bad day when we do our evaluation. The way around that problem would be to rely on multiple measurements, or larger samples, yet Pfeffer and Sutton point out that this insight is typically ignored, as hiring decisions are mostly based on a single test, work sample, or interview.[14]

We recognize that we are all doing the best we can. We are never going to come up with a simple process that guarantees the future job performance of a human being. Of course, Mintzberg probably could have told us that, based on the fallacy of predetermination that strategic planners tend to miss. So we gather data because it probably increases our odds compared to literally picking someone randomly off the street. Reviewing resumes and conducting interviews are not evil.

But we need a more honest assessment of what we are doing, rather than doing it simply because it has been done like that before, or there is a trained professional insisting we do it that way now. Let's start from a more honest place: We don't know the best way to hire people or to ensure that we have the people we need when we need them. This may feel disconcerting. We know it would be more comforting to follow a scripted list of steps that will get us from the vacancy to the perfect hire. But that is part of the big lie that are "best practices." If we can give up this need for security and comfort, and be more honest about what we know and don't know, then we might actually be able to discover some new practices.

Structure: Logical But Not Human

Like our hiring practices, the basics of organizational structure are rarely called into question in our organizations. If you have more than a handful of staff people in your organization, then you have an organizational chart. You probably even have written job descriptions for the different positions on the chart, or at the very least an informal shared understanding of who does what. The bigger your organization gets, the more substantial your organizational chart becomes. Departments will form, where several people will claim a shared professional identity based on the fact that they do similar work to others in the department. These are typically drawn vertically on your chart. Once several departments are drawn in, you now start to see a conglomeration of individuals at the top of these departmental columns, and presto, you have given birth to the management team.

---

14. Pfeffer and Sutton. Hard Facts. 91.

There is perhaps no more deeply ingrained management best practice today than structure, and like the other best practices we've been discussing, there is an obvious logic to it. Division of labor makes sense; people have expertise in different areas. It makes sense to put all the accountants in one department and have them do, well, accounting work. And from an overall coordination perspective, it is important that the different departments don't get too inwardly focused on their own expertise, so it also makes sense to create that management layer to coordinate and make strategic decisions. These basic structural rules have been in operation in a variety of contexts for thousands of years.

We have certainly tweaked the basic structure over the years. The science behind organizational structure grew (as did many of these best practices) during the early years of the twentieth century. Famed sociologist Max Weber wrote extensively about the ideal bureaucracy, and since his time we have developed improved structural solutions, like the functional or divisional structures we described and the more modern "matrix" structures, where reporting relationships can overlap across divisions or functions. Despite the tweaks, however, the basic model has not changed much in about 100 years, and at one level, who can blame us? Our collective productivity has skyrocketed over that time, and we accomplished this feat using fairly rigid, hierarchical structures. As with our other best practices, though, we think it is dangerous to draw the conclusion that there has been a cause and effect relationship between our structures and our collective productivity. There is surely some relationship but not a simple cause and effect. And even if there were a more stringent cause-effect relationship over the last 100 years, we still might be past the apex of our S-curve beginning a downward track that will take great effort to reverse unless we consider new structural solutions now.

And we have examples we can study. W. L. Gore & Associates is the company that makes Gore-Tex®, an innovative fabric that many consumers know as part of their weather-proof clothing. An engineering company at its heart, Gore developed a large number of products and materials that have been extremely successful and have dominated the particular market segments, from dental floss to guitar strings.[15] The company's founder, William Gore, built the organization to be different from most organizations very intentionally. He wanted to create an organization built on the assumption that human beings were self-motivated problem solvers who found meaning in their work.[16] Although not necessarily a revolutionary idea, it turns out that when you put it into practice, it challenges the very heart of our "best practices" around organizational structure.

---

15. Hamel. The Future of Management. 85.

16. Hamel. The Future of Management. 86.

W. L. Gore & Associates is not completely without hierarchy. The organization has a CEO, divisions, and product-focused business units, each of which has an individual identified as the head of the unit. But below this top level, the organization flattens out nearly completely, and organizational charts simply don't exist. According to management innovation expert Gary Hamel,

> Bill Gore conceived of the company as a "lattice" rather than a ladder-like hierarchy. In theory, a lattice-based architecture connects every individual in the organization to everyone else. Lines of communication are direct—person to person and team to team. In a hierarchy, responsibilities are more up and down than they are lateral. A lattice, on the other hand, implies multiple nodes on the same level; a dense network of interpersonal connections where information can flow in all directions, unfiltered by an intermediary. In a lattice, you serve your peers, rather than a boss, and you don't have to work "through channels" to collaborate with your colleagues.[17]

How does this play out in real life? There are no titles like executive, manager, or vice president. The only title used consistently is "leader" (about 10% of employees have that on their business cards), but it is not a title that the senior leaders give to the junior leaders—it is a title that is given to you when people actually want to follow you. According to one Gore leader, "If you call a meeting, and people show up, you're a leader."[18] Employees don't have "bosses," but they do have sponsors—individuals who help a newer employee maneuver the lattice and settle with a team that is a good fit. Teams do not have to accept new members into the fold, and individuals can choose a new sponsor if they want desire. And job assignments are effectively negotiated among peers, rather than delivered from those above you in the hierarchy.

You may have a task suggested to you, but you have the authority as an employee to reject the task. This brings in a new level of commitment when you actually do say yes to a task. (And obviously you will be evaluated on the contributions you make, so saying no to every task doesn't provide much job security.) Does W. L. Gore & Associates have the solution to our hierarchical structure problem? We don't know. But it is a good place to start exploring—not only because of the huge success Gore has achieved as a company, but also because their management innovations are starting to address some of the core flaws in our existing best practices.

Just like strategic planning, our rigid hierarchical structures suffer from the fallacy of separating thought from action. We design our perfect organizational structures in the abstract, devoid of context (just like we assess our strategic strengths and

---

17. Hamel. The Future of Management. 87.

18. Hamel. The Future of Management. 88.

weaknesses out of context). W. L. Gore & Associates has actually designed a way to structure the organization where the thinking and the action happen more at the same time. The title of leader in the organization is not based on the assessment of an expert in organizational design—it is based on the assessment of the leader's peers, based on real-time actions and results. You get the title of leader based on what you are doing in the system at that time, and you can just as easily have that title removed if the direction you take suddenly has few followers.

Traditional organizational structure assumes that you can design the most efficient and effective structure in the abstract. It assumes you can write up the perfect job descriptions and then find the right people to fill them and implement the vision of whatever "architect" designed the system. Gore's approach is to let the design unfold based on the insight and learning of the people in the system itself.

When it comes to human resource management, we think experiments like W. L. Gore & Associates' more dynamic structure will provide more inspiration than the rigid and tired best practices on which we have been relying for decades. If we can give up our need for the comfort of the familiar and structured processes, we can discover ways to run our organizations that get us the same kind of results we have been seeing with social media.

But our best practices are not limited only to structured processes. If we are serious about challenging the status quo and creating more powerful organizations, we need to take on the big picture ideas too. Like leadership.

Leadership: Individuals Will Always Let Us Down

Leadership is not a best practice like the others investigated in this chapter. The disciplines of strategic planning and human resources are more specific and, frankly, easier to define and "practice" than leadership. The idea of leadership in the business world is more like a philosophy or an ideology, rather than a business practice. On top of that, leadership is also a big business. The large sums that companies spend on leadership development or leadership training and speakers end up putting pressure on how leadership thought leaders frame their ideas. If you want to stand out in the marketplace, you're better off with your unique contribution to the leadership conversation. Integration and synthesis don't sell. The result has been a field of leadership replete with distinctively different (and sometimes contradictory) definitions of leadership. There simply is no consensus on how to define leadership, let alone clarity on how to recognize or expand the practice of exemplary leadership in organizations.

Still, there is plenty of good stuff out there on leadership, even if it's a bit messy and overlapping, and there's no doubt our organizations need it. For example, James Kouzes and Barry Posner have written several well-respected books on leadership.

In their 1980s bestseller *The Leadership Challenge* they identified five "fundamental practices of exemplary leadership":

- Challenge the process.
- Inspire a shared vision.
- Enable others to act.
- Model the way.
- Encourage the heart.

These were based in fairly extensive research, and in 2010 (after another couple of decades of research), they expanded their five fundamental practices into ten enduring truths:

- You make a difference.
- Credibility is the foundation of leadership.
- Values drive commitment.
- Focusing on the future sets leaders apart.
- You can't do it alone.
- Trust rules.
- Challenge is the crucible for greatness.
- You either lead by example or you don't lead at all.
- The best leaders are the best learners.
- Leadership is an affair of the heart.

This sounds almost like a list of best practices. And we would agree there are plenty of important points made in this list, that are also backed up by others in the leadership field. Stephen M. R. Covey presents a thorough case for the power (and speed) of trust for leaders, for example.[19] But what about the "level five leadership" that Jim Collins writes about in *Good to Great?* Collins argues that the best leaders have a blend of "personal humility and professional will." Where does that fit into Kouzes and Posner's list? In *Primal Leadership*, Daniel Goleman, Richard Boyatzis, and Annie McKee argue that the elements of emotional intelligence are at the heart of leadership. Ronald Heifetz's model of "adaptive leadership" adds an interesting twist by distinguishing the skills leaders need to deal with more simple problems (that respond to authoritative solutions) versus more complex problems that

---

19. Covey, Stephen M. R., and Rebecca R. Merrill. The Speed of Trust: the One Thing That Changes Everything. New York: Free, 2006.

require the authority to partner with those not in authority to jointly solve the problem. Can we synthesize these good ideas into Kouzes and Posner's ten truths? Maybe, but there's still the issue of the other 10,000 books on leadership that have good advice about how to be a better leader.

There are simply too many good ideas about how to behave as a leader in an organization to come up with one grand "theory of everything" for leadership. Perhaps the best we can do is organize the many different leadership models into a smaller number of schools of thought. There may not be a single list of best practices for leadership, but we can at least divide them into some buckets where the different authors and models can be put together.

Leadership author Jim Stroup suggests there are four basic schools of thought in the leadership literature, organized around the basic competencies that each school advocates for individual leaders:

- Ability to deal with change
- Rally others behind a goal
- Adhere to a moral compass
- Self-knowledge

But this doesn't feel much better than Kouzes and Posner's ten enduring truths. We can see that dealing with change is indeed an important challenge for leaders in organizations, but when do you accept and cope with change, and when do you push for change? And isn't adhering to the status quo in the middle of a naturally changing environment actually a form of change?

Each one of these schools of thought has some valid contributions to what we need in our leaders, but they are each simultaneously frustrating because they leave too many questions unanswered. Yes, we need to rally others behind a goal, but doesn't that draw our attention too much to what the leaders say the goals are, rather than what results we are achieving for the enterprise? Yes, adhering to a moral compass makes sense, but isn't that true for everyone, not just leaders? Yes, the process of adult development requires us to know ourselves, but how do we know if we've gone too far, doing too much navel-gazing while our organization is faltering?

Stroup asks these same questions,[20] because his bottom line is similar to ours. All these schools of thought (thus most of the leadership books that are out there) place an undue emphasis on the individual leader. The field of leadership seems much more concerned with the individual leader than with the idea of leadership. The centuries-old debate about whether leaders are "born" or "made" attributes the

---

20. Stroup, Jim. Managing Leadership: Toward a New and Usable Understanding of What Leadership Really Is—and How to Manage It. iUniverse, 2004. 20.

essence of leadership to something inside an individual, regardless of whether it got there via nature or nurture. The business of leadership has been fueled by leadership training programs designed to give individuals the edge they need to become leaders. Leadership, in short, is about individual leaders.

This fits with our need for best practices, of course, but it also reveals their flaws. As we stated previously, each valid point about leadership starts to break down when you think in real terms about how to implement the ideas. By focusing on leadership as an individual capacity, each school of thought *fails to consider the context—* the organization or community somehow being "led" by these individual leaders. Too much responsibility is placed on the leader, and too little on the organization and its owners. This leads to a separation of the leader from the organization that she was presumably appointed to lead. Her policies and decisions are evaluated based on her personal characteristics of creativity and courage, rather than on the more mundane standards of the organization, its purpose, and its operating circumstances.[21]

Are you starting to sense a pattern here? The best practices in strategic planning argue that we can step back and identify our organizational strengths and weaknesses in the abstract, out of context. The best practices in human resources argue that we can design the perfect job description or the ideal organizational structure and then implement those regardless of context. Now the best practices in leadership tell us that we can identify the enduring truths about individual leadership behavior that any of us can follow to be better leaders, in any context. All these best practices have some truth in them, but they are ultimately misleading.

In the case of leadership, the problem is in the detachment of the individual leader from his or her organizational context. All our leadership competency models do this. There is a certain logic to these models. We all have experiences of what we would call good leaders and bad leaders, so it would stand to reason that we can identify the characteristics and develop them in individuals to get "better" leadership. But that same compelling (but false) logic exists with strategic planning. We have experienced strengths and weaknesses in our past experiences in organizations, so shouldn't we be able to sit around the table at the offsite retreat and list them as part of strategic planning?

No, because the strengths don't make sense out of context, and the application of the strength will change the system in ways that may change how other strengths and weaknesses come into play, and over time our needs will shift, throwing all our calculations off. Although we want to be able to simply list our strengths and weaknesses at the retreat, the way the world works actually gets in the way.

---

21. Stroup. Managing Leadership. 20.

The same is true with leadership. While each new leadership scholar can present a truly compelling story about the importance of trust, or credibility, or passion, or adaptability, the true application of these ideas (in the "best practice" sense) will elude us because the model is context-less. This separation of the leader from the community being led is false and one of the primary reasons why no coherent, synthesized understanding of leadership can be developed. The never-ending debates about which competencies are at the core, or which skills or concepts are the real "truths," cannot be resolved because they are all being evaluated out of context. In the same way that a strength could also be a weakness in a SWOT exercise, a good leader in one kind of organization could be ineffective in another.

To move forward we need a different approach to leadership—one that understands individual competencies but does not revolve around them. We don't need new best practices, but we need a much better conversation about what leadership is and how we collectively make it happen. This rest of this book intends to advance that conversation, and we build on others who have started taking a different approach. Peter Senge, for example, defined leadership as "the capacity within the human community to shape its future." Think about it. Leadership is a capacity within a system, not only a skill possessed by an individual.

When leadership, more broadly understood, is present in your organization, then you have a shot at creating a future that is at least somewhat more to your liking. We've all been in organizations where leadership is lacking. For those organizations, the future simply happens to them, and the odds for success go down. Can we build leadership capacity by increasing the skill levels of people in authority positions? Of course, but that's not the essence of leadership. When we can move past our need for individually focused best practices in leadership, we can start to change the conversation and build more powerful organizations.

Is There Hope?

We're presenting here a bleak picture of today's management environment. The best practices that we are counting on in strategic planning, human resources, and leadership have been shown to have some serious flaws. In Chapter 2, we documented the revolutionary change that social media has brought to the business world, and now we point out that the bedrock practices we have in organizations for dealing with this kind of change are all broken. Do we have any hope?

Yes, there is hope. When you look at the failings of the three best practices we examined in this chapter, you begin to see a pattern in their underlying problems. Strategic planning's failure is linked to three different disconnects with reality. First, it assumes you can accurately predict the future when in fact the complexity of reality unfolding makes forecasting nearly impossible. Second, it separates the thinking from the action and isolates the thinking in one part of the organization. And third, the way it formalizes its process actually robs it of power, because it pushes out divergent, open-ended, and creative thinking. Interestingly, the two human resource practices we investigated also fell victim to these core problems. The hiring process ran into the problem of predictability, and our common approaches to organizational structure typically fail due to a similar separation of thought and action. Even our critique of leadership is based on the way it detaches the individual leader from his or her organizational context. Putting it all together, we see three global failures when it comes to organizational management best practices:

- Misunderstanding cause and effect

- Overseparation into component parts

- Rigid formalization of process

Although cause and effect does exist in the world, we take the concept too far when it comes to organizations, ignoring the inherent complexity of our organizational systems. Similarly, our organizations are obviously made up of component parts, but we are so focused on the parts we lose sight of how they work together sometimes, and while formal processes are not evil by themselves, the way we apply them rigidly in our organizations leads to the failures we cited previously.

But here's the thing. There is a context where being hyperfocused on cause and effect, having excessive detail about component parts, and designing rigid processes are all actually highly valuable: *the engineering, production, and use of machines.* Although few of today's organizational leaders know the details of Frederick Taylor's work, they live it on a daily basis because his mechanical approach to designing efficiency and managing people has been deeply infused in all of the best practices that have been developed in the past 100 years. We run our organizations like machines, and that's why our best practices are letting us down.

The explosive growth of social media, on the other hand, is most decidedly not based on a mechanical model. The way it engages consumers in the market as producers, changes faster and more unpredictably than our traditional structures can keep up, and abandons traditional ideas of control look more like organic, natural ecosystems than what happens in an internal combustion engine.

Scary? Maybe. But this gives us hope.

As we argue in the remainder of this book, the lessons from social media can actually be applied to the way we run our organizations in ways that can overcome the best practice shortcomings described in this chapter. Social media is changing the business world from the outside in; we need to change our traditional business practices from the inside out to evolve and keep pace with the changing times. In the next chapter, Chapter 4, "Challenges to Socializing Business," we illustrate what we're talking about in more concrete detail. We look at the business process challenges we all facing when we try to incorporate social media into our daily work—when social media integration actually bumps heads with these traditional business processes. In Chapter 5, "Social Organizations Are More Human," we provide a model for how to fix this, and in the four chapters that follow it we get practical about how anyone in an organization can start implementing these ideas.

Must Read

As indicated in the quote that leads off this chapter, we need to make a leap. Many books that can help you figure out just how to do that, but these three made our "must read" list for this chapter. Hamel's *Future of Management* is foundational because he connects a deep knowledge of innovation to an equally deep understanding of the status quo view of management. Pfeffer and Sutton's *Hard Facts, Dangerous Half-truths, and Total Nonsense* is equally valuable because it breaks down the logical and research-based faults in many of today's "best practices" in management. We also wanted to include one book on leadership because it is such an important concept in understanding organizations, so we chose Stroup's *Managing Leadership*—not because it is the one book that has all the answers, but because it is one of the best that challenges the mostly untested assumption that leadership is effectively an individual pursuit.

Hamel, Gary. *The Future of Management.* Boston, MA: Harvard Business School, 2007.

Pfeffer, Jeffrey, and Robert I. Sutton. *Hard Facts, Dangerous Half-truths, and Total Nonsense: Profiting from Evidence-based Management.* Boston, MA: Harvard Business School, 2006.

Stroup, Jim. *Managing Leadership: Toward a New and Usable Understanding of What Leadership Really Is—And How to Manage It.* iUniverse, 2004.

4

Challenges to Socializing Business

The key issue is whether or not you believe software alone is sufficient to engineer fundamental business change. In some cases, perhaps it can; but in general, simply grafting new tools and systems onto existing business culture and practices is unlikely to result in the change we are looking to achieve.
—Lee Bryant, Dachis Group

We seem to be at a difficult intersection in the history of organizations. We have two trends, each dangerously unaware of the other, moving swiftly down their respective paths, heading for a collision.

On one path is social media. In Chapter 2, "We Can't Go Back," we identified the deep ways that social media shifts both commerce and society at large. Our collective capacity to create, share, connect, and collaborate has exploded, and we value these activities so much that marketplace behaviors are generated that are sometimes at odds with our traditional understanding of how business works. Consumers have much more control than they used to, and massive decentralization has led to the ability to develop new markets in the "long tail."

Where producing and distributing content used to be a primary challenge for organizations, we are now trying to figure out how best to help customers curate or make sense of content. It's a new world, and it seems clear that we are not going back to the way it was. It is now up to our organizations to adapt to this radically different reality.

Unfortunately, the trend that is moving down the intersecting path is our organizations' collective inability to innovate. Just when we need to adapt the most, we realize adaptation is our biggest weakness. In Chapter 3, "We're Not Moving Forward," we clearly demonstrate that our organizations have a profound lack of capacity when it comes to management innovation. The management practices widely used today—regardless of industry, tax status, size, or location—were frequently developed 50 or 100 years ago. In some cases, despite mountains of evidence against them or compelling case studies of alternatives, our organizations plow ahead using their traditional processes. From strategic planning to human resources to leadership, it somehow seems to require more effort, more evidence, and more time than ever to successfully change the way things are run.

The inevitable collision of these two trends is already starting to happen. Social media in 2011 is certainly now considered mainstream, and fewer and fewer organizations are actively resisting it. When McCarran International Airport in Las Vegas, Nevada, is posting signs encouraging you to follow them on Twitter and "like" them on Facebook, you know social media is not on the fringe any more. But just because it is mainstream, does not mean it has been easy. More often than not, companies that adopt social media have a tough time with the transition. For many businesses and organizations starting out with using social media, the experience and the experimentation can be overwhelming. There are so many tools, all of which change constantly. Only early adopters seem to have an intuitive sense of how they work and how to keep abreast of the changes, and these people (social media consultants, enthusiasts, perhaps younger employees who are comfortable online) are the ones who seem to live social media 24/7. It's frustrating trying to figure it all out if you actually have to get some of your "real" work done. This leads many (like, we are guessing, McCarran International Airport) to simply leap into implementing the more popular tools, with little understanding of how to best use those tools.

Other businesses take a more strategic approach and make their tactical (tool) decisions based on a strategic understanding of where their customers and other stakeholders are (and are likely to be) actually engaged in social media. For both the tactics and the strategy, we're beginning to see a more advanced pool of resources for integrating social media communications more deeply into business practice. The number of resources to help your business begin to integrate social media management is more limited than those available to support your tools, but they are out there. So you have help.

But it's obviously not enough, because even the companies that take the time to understand how social media best fits into their current and evolving business strategies encounter challenges in making it work. It turns out that social media not only presents a challenge to the way we do marketing or public relations, it is also challenging the way we run our whole organization. If you've gotten into these tools at all, you've probably noticed that they are not implemented in the same way as many other initiatives within your organization. Several different departments (IT, marketing, public relations, sales) are all claiming ownership of the social media work. You're not sure who's supposed to tweet or blog, and suddenly people outside your organization are saying things your staff used to say. Plus, there's the tug of war between the enthusiasts who can't wait to do more and try more experiments, and the skeptics who want to see some return on investment (ROI). Not to mention having to justify all this activity to the C-suite, who perhaps remain unconvinced. Even as you're learning the intricacies and nuances of the tools, the complexity of organizational implementation can be overwhelming.

The big problem with "overwhelming" is that it translates into inaction. It translates to slow, and that's a problem for social media (and the rest of your organization, for that matter). Social media is fast, and it doesn't wait for you. Yes, you have to figure things out, but you have to do it as a parallel process to the implementation. While you are learning the tools, you also need to figure out the organizational implications for social media. But as we saw in Chapter 3, we don't seem to be too skilled at figuring out organizational implications of anything and are more comfortable sticking with practices that our grandparents grew up with. This is the collision of the two trends we are talking about. The collision results in continued stress, inaction, and frequently botched social media implementations.

In our work over the past 3 years with organizations beginning to implement social media practices, we have noticed that all the challenges and hurdles faced today tend to fall into one of three categories: organizational culture, internal process or structure, and individual behavior.

- The lack of an open, accommodating, friendly culture (for example) is perhaps the easiest "excuse" for failing to implement social media campaigns or experiments. Unless you work at a startup, your organizational culture will be older than social media. So it is easy to find incompatibilities between what needs to be done with social media and the underlying rules and values that guide decisions and behavior in your organization.

- "Process" refers to all the internal processes and procedures, structures, and systems that make our enterprises run. They, too, were designed before social media, so they can throw wrenches into the works as well.

- Regardless of those higher level constructs, the simple fact remains that "the way we've always done it" consists of individual behaviors and behavior expectations that get in the way of our social media efforts.

In the rest of this chapter, we break down each of these three areas and talk about opportunities for change.

Culture

Organizational culture can be a frustrating paradox. On one hand, it is frequently depicted as some type of secret weapon, or answer to our prayers. Look around the business literature, and you will find countless authors who point to culture as the linchpin for success, or the next level, or true transformation. A December 2010 survey of large corporations in Europe identified organizational culture as a key driver of customer satisfaction, and a focus for driving success in 2011.[1] In Jim Collins' extensive "Good to Great" research, he identified six areas that distinguish the truly great companies from the merely good ones, and one is a "culture of discipline." The most recent poster child for the value of organizational culture is Tony Hsieh and Zappos, a remarkably successful company that, according to one Strategy + Business article, "has a belief that the right culture with the right values will always produce the best organizational performance."[2]

On the other hand, organizational culture is simultaneously depicted as a frustrating mystery. Even though a good culture is obviously the key to keeping your best employees and the only way you can become a "great" company, organizational culture is rarely clearly defined, even among the experts. The definitions we do find are fairly slippery, such as "the way we do things here," which makes it difficult to figure out exactly how one creates a powerful culture or changes a bad one. Culture change tends to be on those lists of things we would like to get to if we only had time, and even when it makes it to our list, we're not always clear who drives the culture change, who defines what the best culture really is, or how we measure our change efforts. It's almost as if culture is some kind of sentient being that senses when we are trying to change it and can mobilize to stop our efforts in ways we are not allowed to fully grasp.

---

1. "Survey: Organizational Culture as a Key Driver of Customer Satisfaction." Call Center International. 23 Dec. 2010. Web. 1 Feb. 2011. <http://www.call-center-international.com/News/Research/385/16032/Survey-Organizational-culture-as-a-key-driver-of-customer-satisfaction.html>.

2. Richards, Dick. "At Zappos, Culture Pays." Strategy Business: International Business Strategy News Articles and Award-winning Analysis. 24 Aug. 2010. Web. 01 Feb. 2011. <http://www.strategy-business.com/article/10311?pg=2>.

This paradox is magnified by the challenges brought about by social technologies. Here are some examples we hear all the time:

- The staff in my department is really into social media, but we're always having to justify what we're doing to the higher-ups. They just don't get it.

- We can't control what people might say about us or our industry on our blog. What if it's negative? What if it's wrong? How do we know who should respond and in what way?

- There are people in my office who are gung ho about starting social media initiatives, but I think we don't have a strategy. I want to know more about why this is important for me, or for my department, or for my company as a whole.

- How do we respond if someone wants to know more than we want to share about our company?

- We have some smart younger folks in our company who we'd love to start managing social media for us because they find it easy and they're tech savvy—but we're not sure we can trust them to act professionally.

- I'd love to have our CEO write a blog. I think it would be good for our brand visibility, but he refuses.

- Someone's using our logo for an unofficial fan group. I know this is a good thing, but my boss wants me to send a cease and desist letter. What do I do?

- This blogger has a huge following. How do we make sure she doesn't say anything bad about us? How do we get her on our side?

These are the prototypical examples of the inaction around the intersection of social media and our inability to innovate organizationally. We see opportunities in social media, and we see potential to meet our business objectives using these tools, but something holds us back. Sometimes it's the higher-ups who "don't get it." Sometimes it is our organization's fear of taking risks. Sometimes it is our organization's obsession with controlling everything, even though it is obvious we now live in a social media world where control has been dispersed. Whatever the reason, the result is the same: We are too slow or we don't take action, and we end up missing opportunities. The fault seems to reside in the culture. We have a culture that doesn't like to take risks, or wants to control too much, or has an unrealistic view of what leadership in our industry really means. These elements of our culture are getting in the way of the tremendous opportunity social media presents right now, so we need to start a culture change program, pronto.

Or do we?

As mentioned previously, the only thing harder to understand than organizational culture are the culture change initiatives that have been forced upon us over the years. To truly make sense of this dilemma, we first need a better understanding of organizational culture.

What Is Culture Anyway?

The main problem with our definitions of organizational culture is that they over-simplify a complex concept. Einstein's famous quote applies here: "Everything should be made as simple as possible, but no simpler." Culture is often defined as something you can only connect to with your intuition, like the underlying values in an organization, or it is defined in terms of objective behavior: the way we do things here. Those definitions are close, but oversimplified. As a result, our efforts to change the culture are oversimplified or misguided.

There simply isn't a one sentence definition of culture—not one that is useful, any-way. One anthropological definition of culture (from Dictionary.com) describes it as "the sum total of ways of living built up by a group of human beings and trans-mitted from one generation to another." That is great, except that we now need another, clearer definition of what "the sum total of ways of living" really means. The same is true for any of the pithy, one-sentence definitions of organizational culture you find in the business literature. They don't help because they don't pro-vide enough of an understanding of what culture is to actually help you do things differently or better in your work environment.

But we can't abandon definitions altogether; otherwise, we will be equally helpless when we try to make the workplace better or, as is our focus in this book, help our organizations take advantage of social media. So instead of providing an overarch-ing definition of what culture is, we put our attention to defining it at three differ-ent levels in an organization: walk, talk, and thought. In every organization, the culture exists simultaneously at each of these three levels.

The "walk" part of our culture is understood, partially, in the way we do things: the actions, structures, processes, buildings, furniture, equipment, and other tangible elements that are a part of who we are and what we do. A lot of organizations do similar things, but they often do them differently based on their different cultures. Whether everyone has their own office with doors that close or sit all together in open cubicles is an element of your culture. Whether the men in your office wear dark blue suits with red ties every day or jeans and mock turtlenecks is part of your culture. How many hours people spend in the office is part of your culture. How you conduct staff meetings is part of your culture: Do you hold staff meetings vir-tually or in the office? Who develops the agenda? Who is allowed to have input on the agenda? Are you allowed to ask a question at the staff meeting if you don't have "director" in your title? The list goes on.

This part of your culture is frequently measured or described in terms of behavior (the way we do things around here). If a stranger steps inside your organization, he will be able to observe the "walk" part of your culture and begin to draw conclusions about it, but it does not provide enough information to gain a true understanding of the organization's culture. For example, when someone comes in for a job interview, he has presumably learned a lot about your organization before coming in for the interview, and he may be able to glean a small amount of knowledge by looking around the place and making observations during the interview process. But when it comes time for that part of the interview where the hiring manager says, "So, do you have any questions for us," the candidate frequently leads with something like "Tell me about the culture around here." He wants to look past the tangible elements such as behavior, dress code, and office decor to understand the second level of organizational culture—what the people in the system actually say about the culture.

Culture is understood simultaneously by what we do, and what we say we do. That is the "talk" element of organizational culture. This part of our culture is found in what we say we're all about and what we value. It is found in written policies that tell employees how they can and cannot act. It is found in marketing messages, websites, and brochures that tell the world who we are and why we exist. It is found in mission statements and strategy documents. It is found in the orientation process we have for new hires, and it is found in our exit interviews. It is found in the answer that the hiring manager gives to the candidate who asks what the culture is like at this organization. We might say we have a customer service culture, or that we value innovation, or efficiency, or creativity, or industry expertise. Our behaviors may be critical, but to understand culture, we also have to look at our words.

Of course, the words and the behaviors don't always match. If you do get that job, you may remember what the hiring manager said about the culture, and 6 months or a year down the road you may look around and notice some inconsistencies. The culture isn't always what we say it is. That is not an indication, necessarily, of a weak or "incorrect" culture. It is simply part of the human condition. We always struggle to walk the talk. Systems are complex, so we should not expect that we have the capacity to simply declare our culture to be a certain way and have it always work out like that.

The third level of culture is the deepest, and usually the hardest one for us to understand. It is a set of shared, but unspoken, assumptions about the best way to do things. We call this the "thought" level of culture. It starts with the thinking of the founders of an organization, but it develops over time through a shared learning process. What makes this level of culture hard to grasp is the fact that the thoughts and assumptions are unspoken. They are taken for granted, in fact. Both the thoughts that we think are good about our culture and the ones we think don't work rarely get vocalized. They are simply a part of "how we do things around here," even if we can't articulate them clearly. For example, many organizations claim in the "talk" part of their culture that they value customer service. You'll see it in the "walk" as well. Even though they have a small staff, they answer every call by the second ring and rarely let it go to voice mail. They commit to responding to customer or client emails and messages within 24 hours. They are responsive to customers.

Over time, however, an assumption became baked into that organization: Reacting to the customer is the driver of success. The foundation of business growth is the ability to react and react quickly. The potential problem with this underlying assumption is that it can drive out the ability to be proactive. As the company grows, the ability to stay on top of all the customer demands may wane, even with more staff. Even a stable customer base may end up responding to the superb customer service by demanding more of it. Suddenly the organization cannot keep up with demand, but because this element of the culture is unspoken, they frequently won't be able to see what the problem is.

That last point highlights two important elements of culture that must be understood if you are going to try to change them. First, cultures are inherently stable. Because they are built upon thoughts and assumptions that are taken for granted, cultures are hard to change. In fact, not only are they difficult to change, we also *want* them to be difficult to change because in a complex and shifting world, we value having something we can count on. The fact that I don't have to figure out how things are done on an ongoing basis is actually comforting to me. Good or bad, the culture being the way it is allows me to direct my attention elsewhere so I can get work done. Second, organizational culture impacts organizational performance differently depending on the life cycle of the organization. What works for a startup may not work for a more mature organization. As organizations grow, the elements of the culture that got them to that point may not be the ones that enable their continued growth in the future.

Culture and Social Media

Think back to the questions at the beginning of this section. These are real questions we hear all the time from people who are struggling with how their organization can leverage social media, and they reflect an underlying conflict between key elements of their organization's culture and the way social media happens today. What if people say negative things? What if staff doesn't act professionally? Why can't that passionate group of followers use our logo? Why don't the higher-ups get it? How do we control the bloggers out there? What if they ask questions we don't want to answer?

These kinds of questions emerge during social media implementation, so we often experience them as tactical stumbling blocks, but in fact they are shining a light on

deeper issues of culture. Of course much of culture is unspoken, so it is often difficult to identify these issues, but until we understand how our organizational cultures are often incompatible with the principles behind social media, we are
destined for failure. We see three areas where cultures typically clash with social
media implementation: risk, authority, and control.

Risk

Taking risks is simply about moving forward even though there is the potential of a
negative outcome. All organizations face risk, but obviously there is a huge range of
potential negative outcomes, so the larger the potential negative outcome we are
willing to endure, the more risk we will take. An organization's orientation toward
risk is a part of its culture. It is uncommon for much of the explicit conversation
about culture (the talk) to be focused on risk, except in companies (often startups)
that focus on innovation. In most organizations, the risk orientation must be teased
out through observation of organizational behavior and an exploration of the
assumptions that drive that behavior. How often are we asked to "run it by legal"?
How many sign-offs do we need to get before we do something differently? What
happened the last time the organization encountered an unexpected negative outcome? Were people punished for their mistakes, or was it embraced as a learning
opportunity? These are all indications about an organization's cultural comfort with
risk.

Organizations that thrive on risk are rare, and this is particularly true in established
organizations. The longer the organization has been around, it seems, the more
there is at stake, thus the lower the tolerance for risk. As organizations grow in size
or governance complexity, tolerance for risk also seems to go down. With more
people involved, more individuals feel they are putting a piece of themselves or
their career on the line, which is a natural incentive to avoid risk. Many nonprofit
organizations face this dilemma when ultimate decision making authority rests in a
Board of Directors who have the responsibility of representing the community that
they are serving. Board members typically serve limited terms, so there is a tendency to not want to be the ones minding the store when it goes out of business.
The natural tendency is to choose less risky paths, the result being "let's do it the
way we've always done it."

So it may be a broad generalization (with plenty of exceptions, we know), but most
organizations could be characterized as risk averse. This poses a challenge, of course,
to social media implementation because it is new (so we are less sure of what the
outcome will be) and because it is decentralized, thus less within the control of the
people in the organization who make the decisions. Moving forward into an area
where you are less sure of the outcome and have less control is, by definition, risky.
So if your organization has a risk-averse culture, social media will activate the

defense mechanisms. Even if you've been monitoring the community's conversation about your brand or product and you can identify opportunities for engaging and building up brand loyalty, increasing trust, improving word of mouth marketing, and improving customer service response, when you make the case, you'll get stopped with the "what if somebody says something bad" questions. Okay, it's probably a stretch that you could make a legitimate case for all that, but even if you could, a risk-averse culture would rise up to at least delay your efforts because it feels too risky.

Even if you are able to get a few experiments in social media authorized, a risk-averse culture will remain suspicious of the efforts in many cases. Leaders frequently put a disproportionate amount of attention on negative outcomes, even if they are small. For example, that one customer who does, in fact, say something negative on the blog, or the online community that does not attain a critical mass of participants in its first 3 months. These small bits of data end up being magnified in the evaluation of social media efforts, resulting in a further slow-down of the activities—which in today's environment, can completely kill an initiative.

Not all cultures respond that way, of course. Leslie White is a risk management consultant and speaks frequently to organizations about social media. In one recent engagement, she made a presentation to the Board of Directors of a spiritually focused nonprofit organization. Interestingly, as they explored the ins and outs of how they could use social media to build community and enhance their mission, Leslie noticed that not once did they ask any version of the "What if somebody says something bad about us?" question. They just started digging into the tools and how they could work. It was noticeably refreshing for Leslie, though she points out in her blog that this group was not simply oblivious to the risk:

> Building community is risky stuff but to this board, the risks are not a barrier to their goal. But many other organizations see online communities as very risky. So why do people have such different perceptions of these risks? Because human feelings and emotions play a significant role in decision making. Some fear the power of a community, while others embrace it.[3]

This connection between culture and fear is critical when it comes to risk, as we explore in more detail in later chapters.

3. White, Leslie T. "Community, Social Media and Risk Perceptions—SocialFish." SocialFish Association Social Media. 2 Dec. 2010. Web. 03 Apr. 2011. http://www.socialfish.org/2010/12/community-social-media-and-risk-perceptions.html.

Authority and Control

The "command and control" organizational culture is typically described these days as somewhat old school. It is the preferred style of the Silent Generation, nearly all of whom have retired from the workforce, and it is a hallmark of the old manufacturing economy of the 1950s. But this is one of those examples where what we preach and what we practice are quite different. At least some elements of command and control culture can be found in nearly every organization today. Exceptions like W. L. Gore notwithstanding, how many organizations can you think of that do not have a clear organizational hierarchy? From large corporations to small businesses with less than ten employees, you are bound to find an organizational chart with some boxes higher than other boxes and a host of supervisor-subordinate relationships. It doesn't even seem to bother us that we use the word "subordinate." Some organizations may be more rigid than others, but nearly all of them share some assumptions that decision making authority is centralized, and control is valued and a perk that expands as you move up the organizational chart. These assumptions run so deep we sometimes don't even recognize them. That is what allows us to take the public stand that command and control is outdated, while still working in cultures that are infused with the command and control approach.

Social media, however, was born out of a culture that was almost diametrically opposed from command and control. Its basis of power is the distributed end user, rather than the centralized author of the software. The users are the people who wrote Wikipedia. The users are the ones who create the hashtags on Twitter. This simply doesn't make sense in command and control cultures, which is why your boss might ask you how to "register" the Twitter hashtag for your brand or conference.

This is also why your organization may be having a tough time swallowing the fact that it cannot control or own what is said about it in social media spaces. After all, the command and control hierarchy created a marketing department with the responsibility to create and enforce the proper branding messages about the company. Now industry bloggers and even customers can produce and distribute (quite easily) messages that deviate from the official message. A command and control culture may revert to what it knows: Try to bring those voices in house. See if we can get that blogger on our side. Have marketing post comments on the blog that provide the approved messaging. Maybe even get lawyers involved. These strategies tend to backfire. Social media has the power to elude central control, so it uses it.

The challenges of a command and control culture extend internally to the organization as well, when it comes to social media. Relationships in social media are made person to person, not person to company. That means participation in social media is more effective when more and more people can do it. In command and control cultures, this can be difficult. Waiting for approval or allowing only a small number of approved people to participate creates bottlenecks and delays that are unacceptable in the social media culture. It can kill a social media initiative quickly.

This reflects the "control" part of command and control culture, and it revolves around the idea of "boundaries." All organizations have boundaries. The very act of creating an organization sets it apart from the rest of the people in the system. It creates the important categories of "in" and "out." It also creates a new set of relationships between the organization and its stakeholder groups, like customers, members, suppliers, and so on. An organization's orientation toward control, then, focuses on the boundaries between these different groups and what information or people can easily move across the boundary lines—who is in and who is out, or what information gets shared and what information does not.

Cultures that highly value control have more strongly reinforced boundaries and opaque walls to protect information. When the senior management team goes off-site for a retreat, no one knows what they talked about. Different departments might develop their own, separate information sharing systems, and the systems might not even be compatible (even though they are part of the same organization). The lines are drawn more clearly, and the consequences for crossing the lines are generally well known.

For example, we spoke with a manager in a large organization who told a story about one of his direct reports, who was relatively new in the organization and, being in his twenties, among one of the younger employees in the organization. The manager and the young employee were talking in the office when one of the division vice presidents walked past them. The younger employee recognized the vice president and stopped her as she was walking by to ask her a question about something work related. According to the manager, this behavior was shocking to nearly everyone who witnessed the event. He may have been exaggerating, but the scene was depicted as one replete with wide eyes and gasps of shock and horror. Exaggeration or not, it was clear that it was deemed culturally inappropriate for this junior employee to stop a vice president in the hall and ask her a question. This particular company has a culture that values control highly, so the act of crossing a clear boundary without going through the proper steps (contacting the vice president's scheduler, requesting a meeting, waiting for the appropriate time, showing up in the vice president's office, and *then* asking the question) was a violation of cultural norms.

Not all organizational cultures value control that highly, of course, but those that do are more likely to be resistant to social media. The company in question, in fact, only began allowing employees to access social media sites like Facebook from their work computers in the middle of 2010 and have engaged very little as a company in social media. When boundaries are strongly reinforced and information is tightly controlled, some of the basic premises of social media—like the users becoming producers of content—will be difficult to absorb. It simply makes less sense to let younger employees represent the company in social media, or to allow commenters to say whatever they want on our blog. Social media is built on the concept of authenticity, which requires a certain amount of transparency—showing the world who you really are. Cultures that value control highly tend to bristle at the idea of transparency, because control of information is viewed as a source of power. We dig deeper into the concepts of transparency and authenticity in Chapter 7, "How to Be Trustworthy."

Clearly the way that many organizations' cultures approach risk, authority, and control gets in the way of social media implementation. Before we start getting practical about how to change that, however, let's explore the other two levels of process and behavior.

Process

It can be difficult to wrap our heads around the concept of organizational culture sometimes, but the part of "the way we do things around here" that is more tangible and easy to describe is the collection of processes, systems, structures, and operating guidelines that make our organizations run. In fact, it may be a bit too easy, because it has led to the development of an entire field of "business process reengineering" specialists advancing a Taylor-esque view of management, that keeps us squarely anchored in the early 1900s.

As we saw in Chapter 3 with Frederick Taylor's scientific analysis of work practices and even earlier from Adam Smith, business processes were initially analyzed in the context of manufacturing processes, so the popular discussion of processes in the management world has a decidedly mechanical feel to it. But it applies well beyond mechanical processes, extending into how we communicate with each other, make decisions, learn, are rewarded, market and sell, manage reputations, and even build communities.

In our organizations, we have created specific structures, rules, processes, and procedures in all these areas to more clearly define how we do things. The value of defining things, of course, is in making our work more efficient and effective. This becomes particularly important in larger enterprises, where the costs of wasted time and effort can be deadly for an organization. But even small organizations invest in clarifying structure and process to maximize their efforts. The alternative—allowing everyone in the system to invent and reinvent their own way of doing things as they go along—rarely keeps you ahead of the competition.

As we mentioned in Chapter 3, however, our track record in innovating our management practices in organizations is less than impressive, which means the processes that are prevalent in organizations today—our best practices—might not have evolved much in the past few decades. As noted at the beginning of this chapter, this creates the conditions for a collision between aging best practices and the new demands of a socially connected economy. The more we learn about how to do social media most effectively, the more frequently we become stymied by our dependence on existing business processes in our organizations. This conflict shows up in complaints and questions like the following:

- I don't know enough about what other social media initiatives are going on in my company.
- The PR department insists that we clear every tweet and Facebook post through them first. We can't work like this.
- Marketing wants to own our social media activities, but we think it should be under IT.
- No one's keeping track of all the social sites where we have a presence.
- We look bad because we sent out conflicting information from different departments.
- Our social media director just keeps demanding more content from us. Isn't that *her* job?
- There's an issue percolating on some blogs, and it's getting worse—but by the time we figure out what to do internally, and the right people approve our response, it's too late to respond and the damage has been done.
- I just heard of Quora and I want to start answering questions about our industry. Can I just go for it? Whom do I ask?
- I'm the social media director for a large organization where few departments want to talk to me because they think I'm just going to add more to their plates.
- We have no idea how to measure success. Is there some rule as to how many Facebook followers we need?
- I wish all of us who do social media for our individual departments could get together and talk about what we're doing.
- My coworker started a LinkedIn group but we already had one. What do we do now?
- I'm in charge of our brand monitoring and I use some good tools, but it's really hard to be the only one. What if I got hit by a bus?

- The education department got really annoyed that we responded to a post asking about the date of our conference. That made no sense! We knew the answer; we should be able to respond!

- How do we figure out how to staff our social media work? Should it be a team? A director level position? An intern?

We hear these questions at the organizations that already think social media is a good idea! They have the buy-in from the top of the organization, and they released the resources—both money and staff time—to do the work of social media, even to the point of hiring a social media team in some cases. Yet they are continuously thwarted in their efforts because the organization's existing business processes were designed before the advent of social media and turn out to be incompatible. Sounds like a case for business process reengineering, right?

Not so fast.

Let's take a closer look at what lies at the foundation of this process-social media train wreck before we suggest a solution.

What Is Process Anyway?

Like culture, business process has developed an academic definition (by Harvard Business School author and consultant Thomas Davenport) that ends up being a little too high level for practical application:

> A process is thus a specific ordering of work activities across time and space, with a beginning and an end, and clearly defined inputs and outputs: a structure for action. ... Processes are the structure by which an organization does what is necessary to produce value for its customers."[4]

We understand where Davenport is coming from, but as we are not talking exclusively about process reengineering, we're going to try a different approach. At a practical level, our organizational processes are simply the collection of rules, instructions, and shared understanding of how we do the work of the organization. An organization that is completely without process is simply a group of people performing tasks randomly without regard to what the others are doing. The minute they start thinking about it ahead of time, and agreeing who will do what when, they have added process to the mix.

---

4. Thomas Davenport. Process Innovation: Reengineering Work Through Information Technology. Harvard Business School Press, Boston, 1993, as cited in Wikipedia.

So the typical notion of a business process—a description of work flow and responsibilities within a team accomplishing a specific task, for instance—is really just one piece of the process puzzle. We believe an organizational process covers any situation where the organization puts thought ahead of time into how the work gets done. So in addition to the who-does-what-when processes, it also includes how the organization is structured, what kinds of external systems it brings in to help with the work (technology systems, communication systems), and all the relevant documentation, policies, instructions, and guidelines.

Organizational processes fall along a broad continuum of formality. In small organizations, process can be almost completely intuitive. There is little need to write down or document formal processes, because for the most part people just get together and get the work done. At most, it might call for an occasional staff meeting to clarify some sticking points. In larger organizations there can be an entire library of procedure manuals covering just about any component of anyone's job. There may even be departments created to enforce compliance with organizational policies and processes.

Whether formal, all processes share a common goal: Help the organization to be more effective and efficient. Certainly the who-does-what-when processes emphasize the efficiency aspect more, but that is not all of it. The reason we spend the time thinking about how to organize our work is because we want to be more effective. We may lose sight of that sometimes, particularly if we end up stuck in a large organization's bureaucracy, but processes are all ultimately designed with effectiveness in mind. Whether they work that way or not is another story.

By understanding process more broadly as a shared understanding of how the work gets done, we can identify a few different categories of process (which sometimes overlap):

- **Structural.** Departments and their relationships to each other, reporting authority and lines of supervision, decision making authority, roles and responsibilities, job descriptions.

- **Internal.** Internal communications and memos, staff meetings, planning processes, email use, "open door" policies, work flow, administrative processes, human resources, evaluation, and rewards.

- **External.** Sales and marketing, PR, community building, partnerships and alliances, technology, and communication systems.

Process and Social Media

If our organizational processes are founded in logic and, certainly, the good intention of creating better, more effective, and more efficient organizations, then why is social media having so much trouble with them? Why are opportunities for meeting customer needs on Twitter left to languish while we wait for departmental approval of our message? Why do entire social media initiatives stay on hold while we figure out how to connect them to the metrics in our strategic plan? Why do valued members of our stakeholder community flee from our social media outposts in droves while we wait for our product departments to supply us with useful content?

The short answer is simple: As logical as our organizational playbook has been over the last several decades, it simply wasn't written with the world of social media in mind. Our decision trees and contingency plans and operations manuals are failing us because the world has changed faster than our core processes. Social media is built on principles that are fundamentally at odds with the principles that have gone into the creation of most organizational processes. It wasn't necessarily intentional, but the incompatibility between our current processes and the needs of effective social media are glaring. In our work, we have noticed three areas of particularly acute incompatibility: hierarchy, silos/communication, and measurement.

Hierarchy

Hierarchy is the process equivalent of the command and control culture that we discussed previously. Hierarchies are natural. It simply means that people or things within a system are ranked one above another. We have seen it in all societies, families, and organizations throughout the ages. The way we define those power relationships is an organizational process because it involves forethought about how best to get things done. Command and control cultures, for instance, assume that there will be chaos if we allow all the workers in an organization to each make their own decisions about organizational resources, so we create a formal organizational hierarchy that gives the power for those decisions to people who have been anointed as managers, directors, vice presidents, and the like.

Other organizational hierarchies are less formal. For example, many organizations give certain departments or functions a higher status compared to others, for a variety of reasons. The human resources department frequently ends up with lower status and complains about not having a "seat at the table" when it comes to strategic management of the organization. The unofficial hierarchy can vary wildly from organization to organization, but make no mistake, it is there.

As we discussed previously, command and control cultures emphasize the centralization of authority, and that can be problematic for social media initiatives that are typically decentralized in nature. At the process level, the way we design and enforce hierarchies in our organizations can cause similar problems. Hierarchies parse out control, which means some people get to decide and others don't. This is not inherently a problem, actually, but with this decision making authority written into our operating procedures comes responsibility. The people who are deciding become responsible. This, too, is not by definition a problem—there is nothing wrong with responsibility—but it creates a problems when those who are burdened with responsibility start doing everything themselves and feel like they must internalize (own) the information that is needed to make the decisions.

Bill George, professor of management practice at Harvard Business School, sees an even bigger problem:

> The biggest threat presented by social networks is to middle managers, who may become obsolete when they are no longer needed to convey messages up and down the organization. The key to success in the social networking era is to empower the people who do the actual work—designing products, manufacturing them, creating marketing innovations, or selling services—to step up and lead without a hierarchy.[5]

It is not necessarily intentional, but hierarchies push us to limit who we involve, who we talk to, and who helps us understand what to do. This is why the marketing department and PR department might launch competing social media initiatives, neither of which particularly include those involved with product design. Although all of these departments operate within a wildly interconnected system, our way of organizing—our process—prevents us from engaging the whole system in solving our problems. It's not only that collaboration is inhibited (we'll get to that in a minute). Our ability to even understand the impact we have on different parts of the system is inhibited. So the content that we send to our new social media outpost makes perfect sense to us in the marketing department, but we don't realize that it creates confusion or is annoying to people in other departments.

Silos and Communication

Perhaps the most common process problem in organizations these days (regardless of the level of social media adoption) is communication. Hardly any organizations would argue that they are completely free of communication problems. As the sophistication and reach of our communication technology grows ever more quickly (remember when the fax machine seemed ridiculously futuristic?), the problem only seems to get worse. We all complain of our inability to communicate effectively within the confines of our own organization, let alone out to customers or stakeholder groups.

---

5. George, Bill. "How Social Networking Has Changed Business - Bill George - HBS Faculty - Harvard Business Review." Business Management Ideas - Harvard Business Review Blogs. 23 Dec. 2010. Web. 01 Feb. 2011. <http://blogs.hbr.org/hbsfaculty/2010/12/how-social-networking-has-chan.html>.

In terms of social media, though, one of the biggest communication stumbling blocks can actually be traced back to an element of organizational structure that nearly everyone takes for granted: departments, divisions, and units. There is an obvious logic to dividing organizations into component parts. Bringing people together who work on similar things or share similar expertise allows them to collaborate and be productive in ways that would be difficult if they were dispersed. It's a classic example of a process solution designed with effectiveness in mind. It makes sense that your marketing department is staffed with people who all have expertise in marketing.

Of course we all are also familiar with the downside of this organizational structure, which goes by the pejorative term *organizational silos*. When those organizational divisions become too rigid and separate, they end up operating too independently, even competitively. Suddenly the value we derived by deepening our level of expertise in functional domains is overshadowed by the dysfunction created by our inability to communicate across departmental lines. The silo structure (and a host of processes that are designed to support the structure) too often results in diminished communication and collaboration.

This is where it becomes a problem for social media. Social media lives and dies on its ability to communicate and collaborate effectively. That is in part the definition of "social." In any community, social media is effective when its members can quickly come together and collaborate. They create and share social objects and communicate to build a network of strong and weak ties that keep the community active. If they can't get together to collaborate like that, the community and any social media initiatives within it suffer.

True collaboration is more than just "getting the right approvals." According to social media marketer and blogger Beth Harte:

> Being successful at social media internally takes more than appropriate approvals, especially if you want to be successful long term. It takes internal business, communication and political skills as well as all sorts of "-logical" skills (sociological, psychological, anthropological, ethnological, etc.). You may think "it's just a blog," but to others it might be a threat, a challenge, a narcissism vehicle, a new experience, a window into their department, etc.[6]

The true collaboration we mean may, in contrast, seem somewhat "micro." For instance, when someone comments on a blog post, and the author builds on that comment in the subsequent post, that is micro-collaboration; but it is precisely

---

6. Harte, Beth. "Social Media from the Inside Out." The Harte of Marketing. 21 Jan. 2011. Web. 01 Feb. 2011. <http://www.theharteofmarketing.com/2011/01/social-media.html>.

through this small-scale coming together and creating together that the power of social media has grown.

If you want your organization to actively support a social media initiative that tries to support that kind of micro-collaboration among its community members, then you need that same kind of collaboration internally. It requires a high volume of small interactions that cut across traditional lines, and you will never be able to help that happen through a centralized, one-department program. You need diversity. You need a strong flow of interaction. You need micro-collaboration baked into your organizational process and structure.

The problem, interestingly enough, is that organizational silos were designed, in part, with the specific intent of eliminating that kind of micro-collaboration. Those cross-boundary joint projects lead to the inconsistency and inefficiency that we tried to weed out of the organization when we first started organizing people into departments. You didn't want the product developer writing the copy for the promotional brochure—that was the marketing department's job, because copy writing expertise was something you specifically hired for in the marketing department. If everyone spends time communicating frequently with people from other departments, then overall efficiency would certainly diminish. When we stray outside our expertise, we end up duplicating effort and not producing the best results, right?

Maybe not.

The generative nature of social media says it may not be that simple. If your product lineup is broad, then your customer base is broad, so tapping into communities that are forming in that customer base requires social media outposts that can facilitate a broad array of connections between content and community members. This means many different departments in your organization will share information, hopefully in a coordinated way, and that just might require internal communication and collaboration across departments that your silo structure did away with decades ago. The silo structure makes sense when production and distribution are centralized and controlled from the top—which may be the case, still, when it comes to physical products. But it's not true when it comes to idea generation, communication, and data gathering among employees and customers. That's why your silos make it difficult, if not impossible, for social media efforts to thrive.

Measurement

There is a maxim in business: What gets measured gets done. We actually think this is a horrible maxim, and we explain more about that in later chapters, but when it comes to the best practices in organizational process, that maxim clearly reflects the popular view. Whether it is the reengineering focus on measurable inputs and outputs or the ever-present demand for SMART goals in our strategic planning process (the M is for Measurable), most organizations bake measurement into many of their processes.

There is nothing inherently wrong with measurement. It is simply a tool we use as we go about achieving our goals. The trick is in how we use it, of course, and the traditional ways measurement is integrated into our business processes can generate serious friction with social media initiatives. Although social media is often perceived as on the "soft" side of business, being about relationships and community, it also brings with it a whole host of measurements that are the lifeblood of the harder aspects of business. As soon as your company sets up social media outposts, you can instantly track the number of friends, followers, connections, or subscribers and correlate that with hits, page views, unique visitors, bounce rates, discussions, and more. Depending on how much time you have, you can generate a mountain of graphs, charts, and trend analyses of your social media data.

Before you fire up that Excel spreadsheet, however, be sure you can answer an important question: How does any of that data connect to your business goals? We aren't suggesting that they don't necessarily, but the connection is not always clear. Social media metrics make it easy to track the growth of social media, but you run the risk of becoming too circular about it. (We have to increase our efforts in social media to show that our social media has increased.) It is much harder to draw cause and effect inferences that connect social media and business growth. Because social media is so new, your business is not going to have a process set up for this. We just don't have a place in our measurement model to put the social media statistics. We can generate lots of data and reports, but not too much insight or clarity. Our systems were not designed to incorporate these new data.

Over time, we have built systems to analyze the connection between advertising in traditional media, for instance, and generating more sales; so now our executives might even have an intuitive sense about what to invest and how to quickly read the reports and draw conclusions. We simply don't have similar systems set up for social media. This results in battles between departments about the value of spending time or money on social media, when what we really need is collaborative work toward developing new measurement systems and processes, so we can figure out what works.

A crop of new social tools (or rather, improving back-end analytics for various existing social media management and monitoring tools) can help you collect data, and some new books help us learn how to measure social media activity against business objectives (we particularly recommend Olivier Blanchard's *Social Media ROI*), but these resources and tools can help only if there is also a collaborative internal process where we can know what objectives are to be met and how to share information between the social media marketing people and the data crunchers. Somehow we're not there yet.

It is clear that we do not understand how to measure social media in a way that is relevant to the business, and because we (mistakenly) believe the maxim that if we can't measure it then it doesn't matter, we end up with the problem identified at the beginning of the chapter: lack of action. We freeze. We hold off on implementing social media. We even hold off on experimenting with it. Without a metrics process in place, we are afraid to do anything, which of course makes it impossible to learn. Without our measurement process, we don't know how to prove to the higher-ups that our social media outposts connect to this year's strategic plan, so we never get the go-ahead to invest in it. Even worse, they give you the go-ahead to start creating the online spaces, but not the time to nurture and develop them.

Those who are on the social media side end up focusing on their own (sometimes circular) measurement processes, also afraid to try experiments that might shed light on how the social media work impacts business objectives. They don't want to try something that might prove their efforts wrong, so they, just like that management team that "doesn't get it," end up inactive and not learning.

You can see how the deck is stacked against social media in our organizations. Both the prevalent cultures and our standard organizational processes are derailing our attempts to take advantage of the power of social media. Unfortunately, the problems don't stop there. They go straight down to the most basic level of individual behavior in our organizations.

Behavior

We keep this final section on individual behavior short, because we talk a lot more about the human elements that need to become integrated into our organizations in the rest of this book, and much of these ideas stem from individual people connecting with individual people. But let's just make the point here that it is sometimes comforting to stay at the 30,000 foot level and talk only about why our organizational cultures and processes are getting in the way of social media. It is fairly easy to make culture and process the villains. This is particularly useful for the army of consultants out there ready to swoop in and defeat these villains with their mighty models and proprietary processes. In the end, however, nothing changes unless behavior changes. Pick your cliché here: A journey begins with a single step, change starts at home, be the change you want to see, and so on. Unless we figure out ways to change people's behaviors, our grand ideas about how to change the processes or the cultures won't work. Our favorite cliché, actually, is "if you do what you always did, you'll get what you always got." So behavior is important.

The trick is in determining how important. Sometimes, when it comes to change, the bigger challenge is in the process or the culture. Our people may understand the basic business behaviors involved; they just need to change them in the context of new processes or moving toward a different culture. We know how to have meetings, for example, but we may have to change who attends the meetings or when we have them. With social media, the behavior part seems to be at least equally as important as the culture and process elements. Social media, however, poses challenges to some basic business behaviors. This is what we hear from the people in organizations who are struggling with social media adoption:

- How do I friend regular customers, without sharing too much of my personal stuff?

- My boss doesn't get that when I'm interacting online with people, that's good for work. If they know me, they will keep coming back.

- I don't know enough about the big picture. Why is this particular initiative important? What are we trying to achieve?

- I want to be able to respond to someone online, on behalf of my organization, but I'm not sure if that's okay.

- Check out this Facebook discussion. This could get a little ugly, but I don't know who to tell about it.

- We need a community manager for our private site, but we don't have anyone on staff who really knows how to nurture a community.

- How do I get people to come back to our Facebook page, after they have "liked" it?

- I'm not sure if any of this stuff is working. I was told to set it up and keep track of it, but I think there should be a better way to report our activity than just meaningless numbers.

- Am I expected to essentially be on-call 24/7? Social media doesn't stop at 5 p.m. when I clock out.

- What do I do if a bunch of my members/customers are arguing online? Should I step in?

- I would be much more comfortable using social media on behalf of my company if they would write up some policies so I know what's expected of me.

- I would be much more comfortable letting my staff get started with social media activities if we had policies in place that they had to abide by.

- There are so many new tools and technologies—do I need to learn them all?

- I manage donors for our nonprofit. I know I need to represent our organization in the best light when I see them face-to-face, but what do I do about that online?

- It felt great to make that customer so happy on Twitter. How do I share that with my manager? Is it worth reporting in some way?

- How do I communicate my misgivings about how unorganized we are with all this social media stuff?

When we as individuals move into social media in a business context, we find ourselves in unfamiliar territory. The mix of business and personal leaves us guessing, and despite the familiar terminology, we really don't have precedents that help us truly understand what the business implications are of friending, liking, or commenting. Dave Fleet, a PR and communications VP at Edelman, identifies the broader issue:[7]

> When we go into organizations and explain the way communications is shifting, we're often telling people that the way they've communicated their whole career, and the way they see things working, is changing. We're telling people that their comfort zone is no longer in the right place.

If it is only an issue of comfort zone, then can't we do something to make people more comfortable? It sounds like we need to send our people through some training programs so they will better understand what to do in this crazy world of social media.

Maybe.

But first you should understand more thoroughly the sources of these behavior problems in social media.

What Is Behavior Anyway?

In comparison to culture and process, our understanding of organizational behavior is simpler. When we talk about behavior in the context of social media and organizations, we are essentially talking about interpersonal behavior. Even before social media, the way the people both inside (employees) and outside (customers) the company related to one another was at the heart of the organization. Despite our focus on culture and process, every organization can be broken down into various

---

7. Fleet, Dave. "The Biggest Challenge Digital Communicators Face | Davefleet.com." Exploring the Intersection of Communications, Marketing and Social Media with PR Professional Dave Fleet. 14 Oct. 2011. Web. 01 Feb. 2011. <http://davefleet.com/2010/10/biggest-challenge-digital-communicators-face/>.

groups of individuals relating to one another: communicating, exchanging information, building relationships, having conflict, working it out, and so on. You may discover this basic yet inescapable fact if you ever have to explain to a child what you do for a living. Unless you're lucky enough to have a job with clearly identifiable behaviors that children already understand (for example, firefighter, race car driver, superhero), then we guarantee your explanations of your job will confuse the children until you finally boil it down to what most of us do: "I go to meetings." We wake up, we go to work, we interact with people (okay, and machines too), and we go home.

The rules for these types of interpersonal behavior are frequently different at work in comparison to other contexts. The way that we communicate or have conflict, for instance, is likely to be different when it is with a coworker or our boss, than it would be with a friend or family member. And, as we indicated previously, organizations with different cultures have different rules about which behaviors are appropriate and which are not. But we always have a collection of interpersonal behaviors that define what we do in the workplace.

Behavior and Social Media

Before social media, the rules were clearer. Although the area right around the proverbial line between "personal" and "professional" behavior might have sometimes been blurry, for the most part we understood the differences. We dressed differently at work than we did on the weekends, and we used different words, different tones, and interacted at a different pace. Much of that is still true, but thanks to social media, much of that is changing as well. Personal information gets shared right next to professional exchanges on Twitter and Facebook, for example. We used to be able to manage our identity in discrete packages, where work friends and personal friends would rarely interact, but that is becoming less and less feasible for many people in the age of social media. Social media was originally banned from many workplaces in an effort to enforce productivity, because engaging in such "personal" things as Facebook or reading blogs was not considered work. Those walls have come crumbling down in most places, and it's harder to tell what is "personal" behavior online versus what is professional. This confusion makes leveraging the power of social media in organizations more difficult. We have seen three ways it can interfere: identity management, relationship building, and knowledge management.

Identity Management

Managing your identity is different in the digital age. Although it varies from individual to individual, overall we are putting much more of ourselves online these days. We have always put effort into managing others' perception of who we are, but that task has been transformed in the last 10 years thanks to the Internet. To understand the magnitude of this change, first we think back to the simpler times of what we call the "analog age."

In the "analog age" (when the authors and, we assume, most readers of this book were growing up) identity was easier to manage. As you grew up, you built relationships with those around you, but different groups would end up with different pictures of who you were. Your family knew you best of all, and maybe some of your closest friends. You could let down your guard with them and show them more of your inner self. Other groups of friends might not have gotten as much access to you, though they probably knew you well. As you went to school, you might have noticed that you acted differently around the teachers. You chose a different set of characteristics when interacting with that group of people. Moving on in life, you developed relationships with coworkers, neighbors, the parents of your children's friends, the people in your book club, and so on. Each group might have a different set of (often unspoken) rules about how to behave. And each of them could have a substantially different view of who you really are.

For the most part, conflicting views of who you are would never be exposed. Only in rare and awkward moments (like when one of your father's friends ends up at the same bar where your friend is having a bachelor party) would you provide information that would contradict one group's view of you. It's not even that your father's friend would not have assumed that you might frequent a bar with your friends. But in most cases, you could control when that information was verified (or not).

In the analog age, we kept our identities compartmentalized. This was particularly true at work. To get the job the most you needed to share was a one-page resume and two or three hand-picked references. And even your references had only a limited view of your identity. It might take years at work before some of your coworkers had a more intimate view of who you are, what you care about, or what you value.

In the digital age, that whole picture is different. Interestingly, as we first started to engage in social media, many individuals worked hard to maintain a compartmentalized identity. They had their Facebook profile they shared with their college friends, and then their LinkedIn profile they shared with their work colleagues. They may belong to specific social networks or online communities where they could behave differently based on the makeup of the community. We might behave differently on the online bulletin board with our cycling friends than we do on the email listserv for the local PTA.

Thanks to Google, most of those efforts are in vain. The Internet and its seemingly endless array of dark corners provides what looks like a great opportunity for multiple identity management, but then Google swoops in with its army of virtual flashlights that illuminate everything on one big stage. When you Google yourself, you will frequently find hits from various aspects of your life, including both professional and personal. More important, so will other people, including that hiring manager.

Now, in the midst of our newly found difficulties in managing our identity, we are asked to participate in our company's social media efforts. We are told to like the Facebook page or leave a comment on the company blog or provide an answer on LinkedIn, and suddenly a whole host of people to whom we were not planning on revealing our true identity is given a road map to sources that will reveal it. Employees at all levels may want to engage in our social media efforts, but they will be unclear as to how to behave. Which account should they use when leaving a comment or liking a post? Even basic things such as which email to use are unclear. Usually no rules are in place to guide them. Engaging in social media is hard enough simply because it is new. But when you add on top of that the uncertainties of online identity management, you could be spelling disaster for your fledgling social media initiative. The how-to social media books reinforce the need for authenticity in our social media efforts, but they fail to inform us that the rules for what it means to be authentic have changed.

Relationship Building

Even if we get a handle on managing our identity, we still have to navigate new rules for building relationships online. Again, the how-to books emphasize the importance of relationships in social media. If you use your social media outposts simply for spamming potential customers with your marketing message, you will likely drive people away. But relationships, we are told, keep potential community members engaged. We agree with that statement, but that does not make it any easier to implement.

Back in the analog age, we had a clearer sense of how to engage in relationship building, and typically chose different paths depending on the nature of the relationship. We might start faster or slower depending on the social status of the other person in relation to us. We would know to talk about work things in a work-relationship context, but would introduce other topics in social relationship building. Like the identity issue, our relationships are often being mixed together in the digital age, making it harder to know how to develop relationships.

Let's say you join an online community organized around a topic relevant to you at work. You start engaging and interacting regularly with others in the community. How up front can you be with someone in this community? The topic may be relevant to work, but you logged in with your personal email account, and the tone of the conversations is informal. What if someone makes a negative comment about your company? Can you defend it? Do you have to disclose that you are employed by that company, or will that cause you to lose credibility in the community. Even worse, what if you agree with the negative comment? Can you disagree with your employer publicly?

Plagued by questions like these, the easiest response is to simply withdraw and stick to the contexts where you know the rules. But what if you are one of the more active members of the community? Assuming others have these kinds of doubts and worries, you might soon find that the people who would be likely the most active community members are withdrawing, and the communities start to wither.

Knowledge Management

They say, "It's not what you know, it's who you know," but that is more of a cute saying than an enduring truth. The fact is, it's both. It is both if you are trying to get a job (the context in which we hear that phrase most often), but it is also both when you are trying to get your job done. In your organization, the relationships you have with people in other departments or people up and down the chain of command are critical to your ability to get things done. Of course, you also need to have the knowledge—of your product, your processes, your field, your customers, and so on—or else knowing the people will only generate embarrassment for you when they realize you are all schmooze and no knowledge.

In the analog age, figuring out what you needed to know to do your job was simpler. It is always hard work, mind you, to stay on top of knowledge demands, particularly as we moved into a more information-based economy. But the areas in which you needed knowledge were more circumscribed. If you did sales, you needed to know the details about the customers. If you were the designer, you needed to know the details about the product. If you were in logistics, you needed to know the details about the factory schedules. We each had our own little domain that more or less identified the knowledge demands. The high performing individuals might have known more within the domains, but there was not a high demand to know things outside your domain.

In the digital age, this is shifting. As we pointed out in the culture section, engaging in social media has generated a push away from centralized cultures and toward cultures that embrace decentralization because that is part of social media's power. In the process section, we also talked about the need for more systems thinking, where different departments could bust through the silo walls and share more information to make social media efforts more effective. This trend toward being more open extends down to the individual behavior level in the context of knowledge. Individuals today need more knowledge outside their traditional domains if they are going to leverage the power of social media.

Social media enables micro-collaboration, both within your employee base and sometimes reaching outside it. The only way this kind of collaboration supports the overall strategy is if some of those people engaging in the collaboration know about the strategy. In the analog age, we could survive just fine, frankly, when only the top of the organizational chart knew the strategy. I know we have advocated for broader knowledge for years, but for the most part we have not achieved that, and we still managed to get our jobs done. That will be less true in the digital age. With more people empowered to get work done in social media initiatives, it is more important that strategic understanding be pushed down and out in the organization. Otherwise, as we have seen, the social media initiatives can end up spinning their wheels.

On the other side of the coin, those in more senior positions or outside the marketing and PR departments also need to extend their knowledge of what the company is doing in social media. In a networked world, we each may find ourselves as a connection point, being asked by the outside world to share information related to our initiatives. Referring that request to an individual in another department is fine, but it slows down the process, and social media is spoiled. It has known fast all its life, and when it encounters slow, it is quick to judge. We say we want nimble organizations, and to deliver on that promise, senior leaders and department-specific employees have to expand their knowledge base, because they will frequently be called on to share information outside their traditional domains.

Now What?

The collision course that we described at the beginning of this chapter seems to be playing out, unfortunately, just as it was scripted. Social media is proving to be a great challenge to our organizations, sometimes even to the ones who are attempting to fully embrace it. Many of our organizational cultures have at their foundation assumptions about risk, authority, and control that run counter to the assumptions that have driven the success of social media. Some of our most fundamental workplace processes and structures, such as departmental divisions, hierarchical reporting relationships, and basic organizational metrics, end up throwing up hurdles to the success of social media initiatives in ways we would not have predicted. And social media has brought with it new rules of engagement that are so different from our traditional workplace protocols, we often find individuals willing—but unable—to figure out how to behave effectively in this new social work world.

The question is, of course, what do we do about it? There is a temptation to fall back on what we already know (or think we know) about organizational change efforts. Aren't there books and consultants to which we can turn, to help us with these problems? If our culture is not progressive enough to deal with social media, then we should work on changing it. Let's find people for our culture transformation team and start a long-term project that will result in a new, twenty-first century culture for our organization. Or if it is a process problem, then let's start reengineering them. We can start a change management project where our managers can identify the process changes that we need to make social media more effective. And if it is only a matter of behavior, then there must be some skill training programs we can implement. We can train our people to manage their identity and build relationships online, can't we?

We don't think so.

We believe in the power and potential of culture change, process redesign, and skill training. They are all good. But we are not convinced that they will get us to the next level. Not with what we are facing today. The fact that we encounter resistance and failure at all three levels of culture, process, and behavior leads us to believe that the problems we have here will not be solved by implementing yesterday's solutions or using yesterday's tools.

As we explain clearly in the next chapter, yesterday's tools were all developed within a singular framework for understanding our organizations: Organizations are like machines. It's not a new framework. We have been looking at the universe as if it were mechanical for centuries, and not all mechanical metaphors are bad. But the social media revolution is demonstrating to us that mechanical metaphors for our organizations are, in fact, bad. They leave us with organizations that cannot take advantage of one of the most powerful and revolutionary movements to hit us in a long time.

What we need are organizations that are more human. We explain what that looks like in the next chapter.

5

Social Organizations Are More Human

What's happening to markets is also happening among employees. A meta-physical construct called "The Company" is the only thing standing between the two.

—Doc Searls et al, "ClueTrain Manifesto," Thesis 13

It is ironic that a significant advance in technology—the explosive growth of the Internet and social media—would shine the light on our need to have more human organizations, but that is precisely what is happening. As blogs and Facebook and Twitter have expanded faster than we could have imagined, more and more of our "best practices" in the organizational arena have begun to fail us. This is not just a coincidence. One of the most important reasons social media has been so successful and grown so quickly is that it has tapped into what it means to be human. It's the "social" in social media that has made the difference.

Human beings were born to be in a community. We were born to create and share elements of our experience of life through art and through storytelling. We have been coming together in communities from the beginning of our existence. We are simply not solitary beings; being connected to others is critical. It reconfirms our existence, whether we realize it or not. And look at the stories, pictures, and art that are attached to refrigerators in the family home. Children love to create and share, though typically their reach is limited to the audience walking past the refrigerator. As we saw in Chapter 2, "We Can't Go Back," social media has changed the way in which people can form communities and create content and share experiences.

More specifically, it has orchestrated a massive transfer of power to do these things, away from centralized institutions and organizations, and toward individuals. With social media, we can create and share on a much broader scale. We have the ability to connect to people and form communities over much larger physical distances and across boundaries that society puts in place (intentionally or not) to keep these connections from happening. In short, social media has given all of us the power to do what we as humans always wanted to do. Social media allows us to be more of who we are, and that's a key reason why it has grown exponentially in ways that still stagger our imagination.

The Machine World

As powerful as this trend is, it still hits roadblocks, however, when it runs into our organizations. This is somewhat confusing. After all, human beings have been forming organizations for thousands of years as well, so why would they be any less compatible with the very human work of social media? Plenty of organizations, in fact, are designed to facilitate the very human activity of creating and sharing. There is no way the human population could have expanded to nearly seven billion if it weren't for the magnificent achievements of our organizations, so one would think that the organizations we humans have created would easily embrace human-focused social media.

But something else is going on here. Human beings may have been creating organizations for thousands of years, but that does not necessarily make these organizations particularly human. Remember, we have also been creating machines for thousands of years. From the first use of tools to the proverbial invention of the wheel to the subsequent and rapid advances in technologies that gave us plows, ships, clocks, printing presses, adding machines, assembly lines, transistor radios, computers, nuclear power plants, and GPS navigators—machines have been integral to our growth as a species as well.

In fact, maybe they have been a little too integral. Since the 1600s, the western world has had a decidedly mechanistic view of the universe. Some attribute the start of this movement to Sir Isaac Newton and his contemporaries, who, in a relatively short amount of time, completely transformed science and our collective understanding of the universe. These scientists identified planetary orbits, they invented calculus, and Newton, of course, is famous for his theory of gravitation. These scientists were simultaneously philosophers (and also frequently deeply religious), and they wrote directly about how their scientific discoveries and theories were related to a deeper understanding of the entire universe. According to historian Edward Dolnick,

> When Isaac Newton learned how gravity works, for instance, he announced not merely a discovery but a "universal law" that embraced every object in creation. The same law regulated the moon in its orbit round the Earth, an arrow arcing against the sky and an apple falling from a tree, and it described their motions not only in general terms, but precisely and quantitatively. God was a mathematician, seventeenth-century scientists firmly believed. He had written His laws in a mathematical code. Their task was to find the key.[1]

When you go to work, you may not be thinking about Newton, Galileo, or Descartes. When you are trying to implement that marketing plan for the product that is set to launch next month, you may not be considering whether the universe operates like a perfectly and divinely designed clock, as Newton thought it might.

But maybe you should.

As we go about our daily, weekly, and yearly routines in our organizations, we don't particularly notice that nearly all of our organizations have been designed based on a Newtonian, mechanical view of the universe. Just look at the language we use. We *run* organizations, or we at least determine how they are *driven* (customer-driven, strategy-driven, data-driven, and so on). They are composed of parts that work together so that the whole will work better (much like a clock, actually). We work on *integrating business units*. We have a *chain of command*. We *reengineer* our *processes*. We *measure outputs*. We track *key performance indicators*. Even the terms we use for managing our people have a decidedly mechanical ring to them—*human resource* management, or the even less human term that is popular today, *human capital* management. Our organizations are meticulously divided into *divisions, units, teams,* and *product lines* because in machines, each part is distinct and knows its place. Machines have transformed our world in the last few centuries, as have the

---

1. Dolnick, Edward. The Clockwork Universe: Isaac Newton, the Royal Society, and the Birth of the Modern World. New York, NY: HarperCollins, 2011. xvii.

organizations that we have "built." It's no wonder we take this mechanical view of organizations for granted.

So here is the conflict.

Social media has taken off because it taps into what makes us human, but it has done so in a decidedly nonmechanical way. It has grown in a way where the on/off switch does not exist, or at least not in a way that is controlled by one person. It is as if all those tiny parts within our perfect clockwork universe suddenly took on lives of their own and created their own timepieces. This, ultimately, does not blend well with our organizations that were built on a mechanical model. It doesn't render them completely incompatible, of course. Plenty of organizations use social media effectively and achieve results…to a point. But it hasn't always been easy. It frequently looks messy, and as it grows we don't know how to understand it, and the tactics we employ often miss the mark.

It is the equivalent of what quantum physicists were discovering in the early twentieth century. As they began to successfully observe activity at the subatomic level, they realized that the rules of Newtonian physics did not apply. More importantly, their breakthroughs really began when they abandoned the requirement that subatomic particles must move in ways governed by the "laws" of Newtonian physics, and with this freedom they went on to develop a theory of quantum mechanics. There is mathematical precision in their theory, but in a way that allows for paradox: for light to be both a particle and a wave (depending on how it is measured) and where particles can travel from one position to another without necessarily having traveled the space in between.

Going against centuries of scientific truth is not easy, even for the scientists who led the way. Quantum physicist Neils Bohr said, "Anyone who is not shocked by quantum theory has not understood it."[2] We have collectively struggled to find language that describes the strange reality of quantum physics. One astronomer said "the universe begins to look more like a great thought than a great machine."[3] Having grown up in a world of machines, we have a hard time figuring out what a thought actually looks like.

So it is no wonder that we are collectively having a hard time figuring out how to use Twitter. The reality of social media and its explosive growth can only be partially explained in our machine-based organizations, but part of it has eluded us. As we look externally to see the success of social media and then try to fit these new tools into our existing machinery, they don't work.

---

2. Wheatley, Margaret J. Leadership and the New Science: Discovering Order in a Chaotic World. San Francisco, CA: Berrett-Koehler, 1999. 31

3. Wheatley, Margaret J. Leadership and the New Science. 32.

What we need right now is the equivalent of the quantum physicists' release of the Newtonian restrictions, so we can figure out a better way of moving forward. Or to put it in more contemporary popular culture terminology native to the movie *The Matrix*, we need that red pill that allows Neo's mind to be freed.

Unplugging from the Matrix

"But I can only show you the door. You're the one that has to walk through it."
—Morpheus, in *The Matrix*, 1999

In this book we advocate a new way of understanding organizations—one that is not based in a mechanical understanding of how things work in the world. We don't abandon mechanics altogether (neither did the quantum physicists), but we recognize that we need to step boldly out of the comfort zone of our mechanical view if we are going to create organizations that can thrive in today's more social world. We don't need our organizations to be better machines. *We need our organizations to be more human.* If we want to fully take advantage of the real power of social media, we need to make a dramatic shift away from our mechanical model and toward a more human way of running our organizations.

This book presents a guide for changing organizations to be more human. It is inspired by what we, the authors, have learned in observing and being a part of the social media revolution. The point is not to simply make your organization compatible with social media. The point is to make your organization healthier and more powerful. And social media is a part of that power.

A quick aside. We specifically did not call what we're presenting here a model. "Model" is a word that comes straight out of the mechanical paradigm, actually. It implies a singular design that could then be replicated in your particular organization, and we don't think it will play out that way. *This is not a model to be copied.* We can give you a guide, but the only way you will end up with a different organization is if you get into the middle of it all and re-create it. It's going to be your new organization, not a copy of our model. We could have called it a framework, though that has a certain mechanical ring to it as well, within the context of construction. A framework is a skeletal structure designed to support or enclose something. (In this case, that something is your organization.) Note that the framework does not give you the new organization—that is still your job. But it helps you build it—or grow it, to move out of our mechanical metaphor.

So—bear with us—let's call it a *trellis*. A trellis is a latticelike frame used to support growing vines or plants. Depending on what particular aspect of the cultivation process you focus on, the plant's growth is affected by many different factors, including the environment, the season, the soil, and how much you water it or leave it alone. It might be totally wild and beautiful, or it might be controlled and pruned—and still beautiful. Everyone has different gardening skills (or none at all), but the trellis that supports the plant helps get things going. We are giving you a trellis to support the cultivation of more powerful organizations—ones that will thrive in a social world.

A Trellis for Cultivating More Human Organizations

Our simple but powerful trellis (see Fig. 5.1) for creating a more human organization is based on four core elements of being human:

- **Open.** Human beings need to be open to our inherent connection to the rest of the system to grow personally. Individuals who close themselves off from connections end up closing themselves off from responsibility and will stall in their development.

- **Trustworthy.** Human beings also need trust to develop. Without trust in our relationships, we divert energy and attention to basic self-preservation efforts, leaving nothing left for growth and advancement.

- **Generative.** We must be generative—building, creating, and growing new things and new relationships in our lives. Limiting our focus to maintaining the status quo and just getting by is not a recipe for growth.

- **Courageous.** Nothing is more limiting to human beings than fear. Courage—figuring out how to move forward in the presence of fear—is a hallmark of the human development process.

Being open, trustworthy, generative, and courageous are critical to our growth as human beings. These are not the singular defining characteristics of human beings, of course. We could have chosen happy, sad, violent, fickle, loving, generous, or a thousand other adjectives. We chose these four intentionally because they are the critical ones we all need to master personally, interpersonally, and organizationally to reach a new level of development as humans, and therefore to grow our organizations in a way that allows them to thrive. We know that these human characteristics are not distributed evenly across the population. Plenty of human beings would fail to be characterized as either open, trustworthy, generative, or courageous, let alone all four. When we talk about being human, we are not shooting for a lowest-common denominator list of attributes that all human beings share. We are raising the bar. As we look at our organizations today and their failure to keep pace with the innovation and growth embodied by social media, we realize that we need to set our sights higher. Open, trustworthy, generative, and courageous are aspirational characteristics. They are the ones we personally shoot for.

It is now time that our organizations started doing the same.

At the same time these elements have been at the heart of the unbelievable growth of social media. Being open, trustworthy, generative, and courageous have been visible aspects of successful social media initiatives. It may not have been collectively intentional, but we noticed these elements again and again when we were investigating (and experiencing for ourselves) the success and growth of social media. Much of what has been successful in the social media world started as open source, relying on the power of a decentralized system. Trust has been at the foundation of successful social networks, and we have seen online communities nearly destroyed by violations of authenticity or truth. Successful platforms like Twitter and Facebook have been generative—growing and changing constantly in an organic way. And the spirit of courage—the willingness to experiment and learn along the way—has arguably been one of the most important factors in social media success, as many of the icons of social media (like Twitter) were originally designed for a different purpose, but found ultimate success through continuous, iterative experimentation and learning.

Now, these elements will be at the heart of the most successful organizations in today's economy.

These attributes are not frequently associated with organizations; having relied on a mechanical view of the world for too long, we've been missing these kinds of elements in our organizations. When was the last time you heard an organization described as open, trustworthy, generative, or courageous? It doesn't seem to make sense in an organizational context. We literally don't know how to understand an organization as courageous. But our lack of vocabulary should not stop us, just as it did not stop social media. This trellis helps us collectively change our conversation about what makes organizations great.

Instead of merely integrating social media into our existing organizations, we want to use this framework to help us create more powerful and effective organizations by infusing them with the four human elements that have propelled social media in the first place.

Here's how.

In today's social world, we need to learn how to create more human organizations. This is what we mean when we referenced people-centric organizations in the title of this book. And because we are seeking to change systems, we must infuse these people-centric elements into every level of the system.

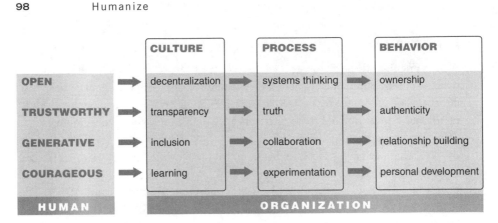

Figure 5.1 *A Trellis for humanizing organizations.*

So creating an organization that is more open requires work to

- grow a culture that is more comfortable with *decentralization,*
- design processes that embrace *systems thinking,* and
- support individuals at every level to take more *ownership* of their work.

For an organization to become truly trustworthy requires

- new levels of *transparency* in its culture,
- organizational processes that value and encourage greater levels of *truth,*
- and a much stronger individual commitment to *authenticity.*

Organizations that are truly generative

- understand the value of *inclusion* at a cultural level,
- design processes that maximize effective *collaboration,* and
- build their individuals' capacity for *building relationships,* both offline and online.

Courageous organizations

- have *learning* cultures.
- understand the value of *experimentation* and build that into their processes, and
- value—and fund—their employees' *personal development* because that kind of learning can feed back into the system and provide long-term value for the whole organization.

Human organizations are people-centric organizations. Human organizations are evolving out of our nineteenth- and twentieth-century mental models and getting ready for today's (and tomorrow's) economy. And human organizations are social organizations, that move more adeptly through social media landscapes, better able to leverage social media and integrate it into existing operations.

Unfortunately, this is probably not your organization. At least not yet, or not in every way. We see these elements in organizations today but rarely comprehensively. We do not have the perfect case study to present as a "best practice." By the time we figure that out, we are afraid the world will have changed so much that the way our model organization did the work will not be as relevant. That's why we are giving you a trellis, so you can take each one of these four human elements and dig into how you and your organization will apply it.

The Four Elements in the Real World

The revolution brought about by social media is a revolution precisely because it's shining a light on the current failures of our organizations. And because all this activity is happening online, it's publicly pointing the way to what works and what doesn't and to what society wants and what it needs from our business environment. We're seeing online what customers want from brands, what grassroots advocates want from charities and mission-driven organizations, what citizens want from their governments, what consumers want from media. Consider, for example the following high-profile examples of social media PR failures.

They each point toward elements of our trellis.

2008—The Motrin Moms Backlash

The situation: In November 2008, Motrin posted an online video ad on its website poking fun at moms who wear their babies in a sling, thus, according to Motrin, in need of some pain relief. Moms were not amused and posted a rebuttal video on YouTube[4] (followed by a whole slew more). The mom backlash spread like wildfire on Twitter over the weekend when no one at Motrin was paying attention. A Facebook group calling for people to boycott Motrin was formed.[5] The situation quickly hit the mainstream press, including *Forbes* and *The New York Times* Parenting blog, and Motrin was forced to pull the ad, shut down its Motrin.com website temporarily, and apologize—2 days (or an eternity) later.

---

4. Presnal, Katya. "YouTube - Motrin Ad Makes Moms Mad." YouTube. Nov. 2008. Web. 09 Mar. 2011. <http://www.youtube.com/watch?v=LhR-y1N6R8Q&feature=player_embedded>.

5. "Babywearing Isn't Painful. Boycott Motrin for Saying It Is. | Facebook." Facebook. Nov. 2008. Web. 09 Mar. 2011. <http://www.facebook.com/group.php?sid=36dd74fcf51f8b9efd226dce0c4d2a0e&refurl= http://www.facebook.com/s.php?init=q&q=motrin&ref=ts&sid=36dd74fcf51f8b9efd226dce0c4d2a0e &gid=46803467500>.

The resolution: Although the story eventually died down, the apology was not particularly well received as "the carefully crafted non-statement of a committee" in the words of marketer Seth Godin.[6] At the time of this writing, more than two years later, two links to blog stories about this appear in seventh and eighth position of the Google search results.

The social media lessons:

Social media is "on" 24 hours a day, 7 days a week, 365 days a year. People communicating and interacting online don't stop after five o'clock or on weekends even if your office hours say that you're closed. Motrin was left woefully unaware of the huge online firestorm that was happening over the weekend, and by the time the company found out about it, the damage to the brand (quantitative or qualitative, even temporary) had been done.

- Open organizations have processes that understand how the whole system works and use monitoring systems that operate on weekends so that they can respond more quickly.

Companies must have a social media presence to be able to respond in social spaces. Motrin was caught completely unaware, and when company officials did respond, they had to use the website. It took them two days to respond to something that could have been handled immediately.

- Open organizations support their employees in taking ownership so the people closest to the problem can solve it.

- Open organizations have people ready and willing to respond immediately and effectively.

Speed trumps polished and crafted. David Armano, senior VP at Edelman Digital, advised that Motrin should "think like a blogger, Tweeter, community & citizen journalist";[7] people (aka consumers) can create rebuttal content faster than you can get on the phone to your lawyers. Learn to bypass those approval hoops and find ways to respond quickly and honestly.

- Trustworthy organizations learn how to get the truth out as quickly as possible, knowing that silence speaks volumes.

- Open organizations are decentralized, empowering many people in the organization to speak for it without having to be approved at every step.

Companies have an online community. There are people out there *right now*, believe it or not, who care what companies do and say and who praise or criticize those things.

---

6. Godin, Seth. "We Feel Your Pain." Seth's Blog. 17 Nov. 2008. Web. 09 Mar. 2011. <http://sethgodin.typepad.com/seths_blog/2008/11/we-feel-your-pa.html>.

7. Armano, David. "Moms Give Motrin A Headache." Logic Emotion. 16 Nov. 2008. Web. 09 Mar. 2011. <http://darmano.typepad.com/logic_emotion/2008/11/moms-give-motri.html>.

- Generative organizations take relationship building seriously, even when it extends beyond the organizational chart, and embrace (reactively) or create (proactively) communities where feedback is welcome and addressed, whether positive or negative.

- Courageous organizations listen to feedback and learn from it.

Companies must involve their community in their development. Whether it's in relation to testing new products or developing marketing campaigns, the community around a company or organization should be given access to provide feedback. In the case of Motrin, testing the video first on a small group of moms would have helped them realize that the idea would never fly.

- Generative organizations collaborate with their audiences and their community and include them in testing of ideas.

- Courageous organizations build experimentation and learning into everything they do.

2009—United Breaks Guitars

The situation: Musician Dave Carroll of the band Sons of Maxwell became furious and frustrated after spending nine months trying to get compensation from United Airlines for destroying his $3,500 custom-built Taylor acoustic guitar. He wrote and filmed a video of a song titled "United Breaks Guitars" and posted it on YouTube. The video received 150,000 views on the first day; today, the video has more than 10 million views. A follow-up song, in which, according to Dave Carroll's website,[8] "Dave takes a closer look at his dealings with [hapless United employee] Ms. Irlweg and the flawed policies that she was forced to uphold," has more than one million views.

The resolution: United eventually apologized and said it would use the video as a learning tool. United issued this statement:

> This has struck a chord with us. We are in conversations with one another to make what happened right, and while we mutually agree that this should have been fixed much sooner, Dave Carroll's excellent video provides United with a unique learning opportunity that we would like to use for training purposes to ensure all customers receive better service from us.[9]

8. Carroll, Dave. "United Breaks Guitars Trilogy | Dave Carroll Music." Dave Carroll Music - Perfect Blue and United Breaks Guitars. 2009. Web. 09 Mar. 2011. <http://www.davecarrollmusic.com/ubg/>.

9. CBC News. "Broken Guitar Song Gets Airline's Attention - Arts & Entertainment - CBC News." CBC.ca - Canadian News Sports Entertainment Kids Docs Radio TV. 8 July 2009. Web. 09 Mar. 2011. <http://www.cbc.ca/news/arts/music/story/2009/07/08/united-breaks-guitars.html>.

The social media lessons:

Social media can spread stories virally. People now have avenues for expressing frustration and criticism that can potentially reach millions of other consumers.

- Open organizations encourage employees to respond and deal with complaints before they get to PR crisis stage.

People don't need record labels to share their creativity. The things shared through social media are those that captivate and motivate others. Creativity flourishes through social media in ways that marketing or advertising falls flat; and people don't need to go through traditional channels—like getting a recording contract before publishing a song.

- Courageous organizations experiment with different ways of conversing with their audiences in different social spaces and adapt their messages to the culture of the particular online space they are interacting with people in.

- Generative organizations understand how to encourage creativity and personality in the interactions that they have with their audience.

Complainants want to be heard, they want a response, and they want reasonable resolution. Dave Carroll never would have written, videotaped, and posted his song had the matter not dragged out over months and months. He was frustrated because he felt he was treated unfairly and repeatedly dismissed in an unreasonable way.

- Trustworthy organizations are reasonable and not unnecessarily rigid when it comes to policies and procedures.

- Open organizations listen to feedback and treat people in their community (both staff and consumers) with respect.

Sometimes company policies suck. The (presumed) reason the situation dragged on so long? Because there was no flexibility in the policy Ms. Irlweg followed when she denied Dave Carroll compensation again and again.

- Trustworthy organizations start from a position of trusting their customers and stakeholders. They assume people have legitimate concerns worth treating fairly, until proven otherwise.

- Courageous organizations are willing to admit they are wrong and act to change things that are not working.

- Open organizations empower staff to use their own good judgment to make decisions.

2010—The Gap Logo Reversal

The situation: In October 2010, the clothing chain Gap was forced to abandon its logo redesign one week after consumers revolted with thousands of comments on the Gap Facebook page, a "Make your own Gap logo" spoof website, and a protest Twitter account.

The resolution: Marka Hansen, president of the North American division of Gap, announced a reversal through the comments of Gap's Facebook page.[10] She said,

> We've learned a lot in this process. And we are clear that we did not go about this in the right way. We recognize that we missed the opportunity to engage with the online community. This wasn't the right project at the right time for crowd sourcing. There may be a time to evolve our logo, but if and when that time comes, we'll handle it in a different way.

Since then, Gap dumped its longtime marketing agency responsible for the debacle for the slightly more social media savvy Ogilvy. According to *AdAge*, [11]

> Gap's behavior has taken a turn-for-the-transparent. Asked what's behind the new approach, [spokesperson] Ms. Callagy acknowledged it was a conscious move on behalf of the company, and said: "There's a level of transparency that's expected now from consumers, who want to have a dialogue and not just be spoken to."

The social media lessons:

Consumers "want to have a dialogue and not just be spoken to." Enough said!

- Generative organizations are inclusive, listening to their community and building relationships.

- Trustworthy organizations are reasonably transparent about reasons for major business decisions.

- Courageous organizations are not afraid to ask their communities for their opinions.

10. Halliday, Josh. "Gap Scraps Logo Redesign after Protests on Facebook and Twitter | Media | The Guardian." Latest News, Comment and Reviews from the Guardian | Guardian.co.uk. 12 Oct. 2010. Web. 09 Mar. 2011. <http://www.guardian.co.uk/media/2010/oct/12/gap-logo-redesign>.

11. Parekh, Rupal. "Gap Names Global CMO, Taps Ogilvy as New Agency in Series of Major Changes | Agency News - Advertising Age." Ad & Marketing Industry News - Advertising Age. 02 Feb. 2011. Web. 09 Mar. 2011. <http://adage.com/article/agency-news/gap-names-global-cmo-taps-ogilvy-advertising-agency/148605/>.

Consumers want to be involved in major company decisions. A logo redesign might seem to be something purely in the realm of marketing experts, but consumers care. They care very vocally.

- Courageous organizations "fail fast and smart" (more on that later) and experiment iteratively and inclusively with their audiences.

- Open organizations embrace systems thinking, meaning that their core values are known to all in their community.

2010—The BP Oil Spill

The situation: As if the worst oil spill in U.S. history along the Gulf Coast in April 2010 was not bad enough, BP added insult to injury by failing to share information with those affected and with the public at large. It ignored the social media sites where people were clamoring for the truth about what was happening. For example, BP neglected to send out any tweets about the disaster until April 27, a week after the spill happened—an eternity in social media, by which time it was universally derided as uncaring. Josh Simpson, a comedian, created a parody Twitter account, @BPGlobalPR, and his dry tweets were at first almost indistinguishable from the official account; it grew to 180,000 followers (compared to 18,000 for the official account today).[12] A parody video on YouTube (BP Spills Coffee—"a very small spill on a very large table") has 11.5 million views to date. A Google search for "BP Twitter" still has the parody Twitter account as the top search result, and, as of this writing, every link except one on the first page of results is about that parody account.

The resolution: The situation is ongoing. BP allegedly continues to spend millions of dollars on Google Adwords to get its official sites back up to the top in search results.[13] The company has been managing its social media sites slightly more proactively. The BP_America Twitter account and Facebook accounts are active, although not apparently responsive to any comments—a quick glance at a Twitter search for @BP_America (messages directed at BP) is enough to show it has a very, very long way to go. A Boycott BP Facebook group is currently very active, with 823,000 followers.

---

12. Mascarenhas, Alan. "BP's Global PR vs. BPGlobalPR - Newsweek." Newsweek - National News, World News, Business, Health, Technology, Entertainment, and More - Newsweek. 4 June 2010. Web. 09 Mar. 2011. <http://www.newsweek.com/2010/06/04/bp-s-global-pr-vs-bpglobalpr.html>.

13. Scott, Cameron. "BP Buys 'oil Spill' Ad Words: The Thin Green Line." San Francisco Bay Area — News, Sports, Business, Entertainment, Classifieds: SFGate. 7 June 2010. Web. 09 Mar. 2011. <http://www.sfgate.com/cgi-bin/blogs/green/detail?entry_id=65205>.

The social media lessons:

Companies must ensure their social media presence is well defined and populated before someone else defines it for them.

- Open organizations are clear about what they stand for and what they are about.

- Generative organizations build relationships with people in their communities and are willing to share themselves.

Companies must be transparent and give people the facts. The public just wanted honest answers about what was happening.

- Trustworthy organizations share information freely.

Companies must be honest and admit when they don't have all the answers. BP was accused of lying about the true extent of the damage. BP and the other players in the crisis (including Halliburton, TransOcean, and Deepwater Horizon Oil) were seen as pointing fingers at each other rather than coming together as quickly as possible to find a solution. The social media backlash was severe in the face of obvious spin.

- Trustworthy organizations tell the truth.

Companies must collaborate with people who want to help.

- Generative organizations encourage collaboration with all people in their communities.

- Generative organizations are inclusive and able to listen to differing viewpoints.

2011—Etsy's Offensive Art Versus Censorship Debate

The situation: Etsy, the online website for people to sell homemade and vintage wares, was hit with a customer revolt after it ignored requests for a seller to be banned from the site. He was selling offensive and defamatory cards, including cards offering congratulations on being raped, for having AIDS or cancer, or for having a child with Down syndrome. Etsy ignored requests to shut down the seller, until a Change.org petition garnered 16,000 signatures.

The resolution: Etsy finally compromised by removing the offending cards (though not the seller) and changing its terms of use policy to include prohibition of items that promote misogyny or homophobia and disparage people with disabilities. [14]

---

14. Jeffries, Adrianne. "Etsy Bans 'Congrats, You Got Raped' Cards and Other Mean Things | The New York Observer." Observer.com | The New York Observer. 14 Jan. 2011. Web. 09 Mar. 2011. <http://www.observer.com/2011/media/etsy-bans-congrats-you-got-raped-cards-and-other-mean-things>.

The social media lessons:

Social responsibility matters. Although this particular situation led to a debate about free speech with valid arguments on both sides, the key point is that people in the Etsy community were vocal about asking the company to remove content they felt was inappropriate.

- Open organizations are decentralized, with power residing in all parts of the system.

Members of a community have other networks they can call upon for help when needed and access to online services that can amplify their reach. When Etsy at first ignored calls for the seller to be removed, the complainants reached out to other networks, including Change.org, an online campaign-building service.

- Generative organizations are networked and connected to others inside and outside their industries.

Members of a community are joint owners of its marketplace. In Etsy's case, the company's rigidity in first refusing to respond to its community of sellers reflected badly on it. It would have hurt the sellers themselves if the situation had resulted in the loss of paying customers.

- Open organizations are made up of individuals who have ownership of their role in the organization and their personal responsibility for its success.
- Trustworthy organizations listen to their community and share reasons for their decisions.
- Trustworthy organizations don't ignore conflict.

These examples are all related to PR crises; though there are many, many more smaller instances of similar situations. These examples succinctly illustrate how the four human elements of our trellis for humanizing organizations appear everywhere in terms of social media lessons learned. We dig deeper into our four elements and get a lot more practical and concrete about what this means for you and your business in the next four chapters, but let's pause here for a moment and get on the same page about exactly how we define our four human elements.

Open

The twenty-first century meaning of "open" in a business and technological context has its roots in the open source movement—pioneered by Linux—with "software whose source code is published and made available to the public, enabling anyone to copy, modify, and redistribute the source code without paying royalties or fees."[15] The concept has many applications in all kinds of industries beyond software companies, but today it's most commonly referred to as simply the idea that anyone can work on developing a particular system because we all have access to the information we need to do that. The same concept applies to being human. As we develop as human beings, we must be open to the rest of the world, rather than closed off from it—open to new relationships, connected to different parts of the systems we operate in and communities we live in, even open to new ideas or new situations.

In investigating the lessons of social media, we saw the desire—or demand—for openness as one of the first elements causing friction between people and the companies they interact with. Ideas like

- People want responses from organizations regardless of the traditional constraints of office hours.

- Employees at any level should be able to respond on behalf of an organization.

- Employees at any level should be able to act on behalf of an organization and take responsibility for ownership of a problem until it's resolved.

- Organizations are too slow because they are hampered by approval processes and by having only certain "spokespeople" empowered to respond.

- There's now a demand for direct response to online feedback, whether positive or negative.

In light of these types of issues, all of which are related to the openness (or lack thereof) of organizations, we're seeing that openness means different things at each of the three levels of challenges we discussed in Chapter 3, "We're Not Moving Forward." Being open is not the same thing at an organizational culture level as it is at an internal process level, and it's not the same thing at an internal process level as it is at the individual behavior level.

From the point of view of organizational culture, openness means decentralization: The various parts of the system can act on behalf of the whole. To embrace a culture of decentralization in our organizations, we need to become much clearer on our core values. We need to be able to share that throughout the entire organization in such a way that everyone is aware of why this particular organization or business exists. How do we do that? We need to learn how to share control among the many,

---

15. "Open Source." Wikipedia, the Free Encyclopedia. 09 Mar. 2011. Web. 09 Mar. 2011.
    <http://en.wikipedia.org/wiki/Open_source>.

not the few. How do we change our traditional hierarchies and flatten the organizational chart while still steering the ship? How do we establish a culture of listening, where our employees can feed back what they hear in conversations online into the system? How do we encourage evangelists for our businesses, who know what we're trying to achieve and are willing to help us to achieve it?

At the level of internal process, openness appears in systems thinking, the idea that each individual part of a system must be aware of its relationship to the whole system. Specifically in terms of problem solving or growth and development, all parts are interconnected and working toward a common goal (namely the health of the system), as opposed to working independently in ways that could cause future problems or hinder growth and development. Systems thinking has been in the business literature for 20 years, but we still have rigid silos, approval loops that no longer make sense, miscommunication, top down strategy, and other processes and systems that sap our organizations' potential. Social media shows us how to engage all parts of the system in new ways that enable faster and more targeted action. (In the next chapter we examine how to achieve openness and systems thinking as it relates to processes like strategic planning, staff meetings, cross-functional collaboration, performance reviews, and more).

At the level of individual behavior, openness is found in what we're calling "ownership." Although social media asks us to dismiss traditional notions of control, individuals at all levels of the system need to build their capacity for true ownership—clarity on what is theirs to do (and theirs to *not* do) in a networked and decentralized system. Empowering any employee to speak for an organization does not mean anyone can be out there saying anything. True openness at both the culture and systems level helps individuals figure out exactly what their role is in the system, how they can play that role internally and externally in building relationships with their audiences and stakeholders, and how their actions affect the current and future health of the whole organization.

We explore openness in Chapter 6, "How to Be Open."

Trustworthy

Human beings value trust. It is at the heart of all relationships that we would describe as deep. The power of trust lies in its ability to help us reduce complexity and save us energy and attention. When we trust someone, we are willing to risk more because we trust he will not take advantage of us, and that means we don't have to devote our attention and energy to protecting ourselves from the infinite ways he may betray us. With all that off the table, we can focus on deepening the relationship and getting things done. Low-trust relationships stay at the surface and never really get to anything where the stakes are high. There is nothing inherently wrong with that, but you can see that the potential for growth, or achieving great things, is limited.

Trust has also been a visible factor in the growth of social media. We all have had those moments where we are unsure if we should approve a "friend" request (is he really my friend?) or connection on LinkedIn. Sure we know who the person is, but we don't know him well. Will it be safe for me to share the information that I share with my friends with this person? In short, can I trust him? Social networks by default are about sharing personal information, and that involves risk. So without trust, the social networks won't thrive. And in social media failures, we begin to see how the trust factor can be at the center of tension among stakeholders in an organizational context. People expect organizations to tell the truth and be more transparent. (Silence is certainly no longer golden.) Rigid policies (somewhat the opposite of trust) are not tolerated as much as they used to be. It is no longer enough for organizations to make their decisions—stakeholders, both internal and external, want to know why the decisions were made to determine trustworthiness.

So for people-centric organizations, trust plays out in different ways at the levels of culture, process, and individual behavior. It is never truly as simple as an individual customer trusting the organization or not trusting it. The characteristic of trustworthiness is developed when an organization can truly embrace the ideas of transparency, truth, and authenticity.

Transparency comes into play when we look at organizational cultures, and, frankly, this one is going to be hard to grow. Too many organizational cultures view transparency as a dangerous threat, and these organizations will find it hard to be more human. As you work on re-creating your organization to be more compatible with social media, you need to examine how your culture can embrace transparency more than it does now. What information is shared, with whom do you share it, and when does it get shared? The answers to these questions, in general, are changing. It does not require complete or radical transparency, necessarily (the particulars will always vary depending on the organization), but until now the culture's view on transparency has likely not been challenged, and more often than not the default has been to retreat to the apparent safety of opacity. It is true that erring on the side of being opaque can be safe. The problem is, it is difficult to trust an organization that is opaque.

When we move further down into the area of organizational process, we confront the issue of truth. When we try to figure out how to make our processes more human, we invariably come back to the issue of truth. This is not an oversimplified understanding of whether we lie in our processes. It's about how we structure our communication, and how we manage conflict. It's about how we support our ongoing interactions so that more truth is spoken both within the organization and out to external stakeholders. Social media has already been pushing us in these areas: when customers demand to be part of the process, departments need to share more information with each other, or the reasons for decisions need to be visible to stakeholders. The current, more mechanical processes we have in our organizations don't support the increase in truth that is demanded by social media. The result is a reduction in overall trust with the organization.

At the level of individual behavior in organizations, trustworthiness shows up in the notion of authenticity. The word is almost a cliché in social media circles, but here's the rub—an organization talking about authenticity is not the same as actually being authentic. To be authentic in the digital age is not the same as it used to be, and if anything the stakes have been raised. People expect more of it, and social media thrives on it, so we need to figure out how we can support our people in actually being more authentic. You would think authenticity is something we all know how to do. But just ask the CEO of the corporation as she tries to write a blog post in an authentic voice, or how honest an employee can be about his or her political beliefs on a personal blog, or whether a marketing manager can actually use the standard marketing copy when she is tweeting. The rules have changed, and if we don't figure them out, we run the risk of damaging the trust our companies have developed with customers, employees, or other stakeholders.

Chapter 7, "How to Be Trustworthy," explores how organizations can be more trust-worthy in full detail.

Generative

Being generative is a characteristic that has been particularly fascinating to watch in the development of social media tools. For example, the huge online ecosystem of Twitter-related applications, which are built to integrate with Twitter's platform but owned by many hundreds of startup companies, have added to the value of Twitter. Over time, Twitter (the company) has acquired and incorporated a few of these into its core functionality and has grown and developed its core system through these additions. But the company has left the huge majority of other applications to hap-pily (for the most part) coexist with Twitter and play their part in the future health of the online ecosystem in which these tools exist. So like our openness element, being generative has its roots in software development, but it's also a deeply human quality that we need to foster in our organizations.

To be generative means to create new things. This is true for human beings at the most basic, biological level, of course, but it is also an important part of a fulfilling life. The alternative is to be stagnant. This is why people continuously try to progress in their careers, seek out new challenges, build new relationships, and deepen existing ones. It is a fundamental, human desire to create and experience new things. Without it, we do not grow. Organizations face the same dilemma, and we are not only talking about growth of the bottom line. The quality of an organization's existence depends on its ability to be generative. The world around us has been changing constantly, so if we are not keeping pace, we will start to atrophy. As W. Edwards Deming famously quipped, "It is not necessary to change. Survival is optional."

And social media has been raising the bar when it comes to being generative at an organizational level. Our ability to be generative used to be focused internally—do we have the internal resources to keep up with change? Social media revealed that being generative crosses traditional boundaries. Consumers expect a dialogue now, not just to be the targets of advertising. Organizations do not have the luxury of staying separate from the community. You need to have been a part of that community *before* you can leverage it in crises or opportunities. It is a given today that communities will have opposing views and perspectives, so organizations can no longer sit back and blame others when things go wrong. Generative organizations are inclusive, they collaborate effectively, and they focus on relationship building. These, in fact, correspond to our three levels of culture, process, and behavior.

Generative organizations have cultures that value inclusion. Inclusion means more than just allowing all parts of a system to know what's going on in the rest of the system; it means having a culture where diversity of ideas and identity is nurtured and cultivated. How can ideas from lower-level (or younger) staff be heard and rise through the system? How do we create a culture and system that pushes innovation forward? How could crowdsourcing, being able to dip into the talent pool both internal and external to our business, help with finding new voices and new ideas? How do we create a culture that embraces diversity, not just via lip service, but in a strategic way that encourages development and pushes our business or our industry forward? To include others is a lot easier said than done, and generative organizations cultivate cultures that figure out how to do it.

At the level of internal process, being generative requires collaboration. Social organizations are being forced to change internal processes, because building (and managing) social communities emerging around the organization demands collaboration across departments and hierarchies. New interdepartmental teams are emerging simply to be able to deal with multifaceted social communications, and these new ways of collaborating need to spread through the entire organization.

And as for individuals' role in being generative, the key is in relationship building. Social media is teaching us how to build relationships online, but for many people, this is continues to be a huge challenge. It's time-consuming, we're not sure how to set boundaries between our professional and personal personas, some of us may find the social tools hard to figure out, and we're confused by adding online relationships to the face-to-face interactions we are already managing with our customers and stakeholders. Social media is teaching us that building relationships means sharing some of our true selves. It means more than transactions. It requires more personality, more creativity, more personal risk. And frankly, even before social media, relationship building was not particularly valued in organizations, so the core skills of managing conflict, communicating effectively, and negotiating boundaries are typically under developed.

Chapter 8, "How to Be Generative," delves into how organizations must create new value.

Courageous

We've all, by now, heard the Google mantra "fail fast, fail smart" about continuous experimentation and learning from the results of that experimentation, both successful and unsuccessful. Today we see this idea in every software beta test (both "open-beta" and "closed-beta"), when technology companies test their products on a core group of interested users and integrate their feedback before launching more publicly and widely. The speed of entrepreneurial activity and startup culture, too, in Silicon Valley and pockets of tech innovation all across the world continues to accelerate and reflects the "fail fast, fail smart" philosophy. But despite the positive press about this philosophy, it has not been widely adopted. In traditional businesses and organizations, failing fast is not only still counter to "how we do things," it is also risky, scary, and difficult to implement. No one but Google is Google, right? So what we need is the courage to pursue this philosophy even if we are not Google. It is not about being Google. It is about expunging fear from our organizations.

Franklin Roosevelt felt the same way about human beings with his famous "the only thing we have to fear is fear itself" quote. Fear is a natural human emotion, so we should never have the goal of eliminating fear. But human beings who evolve and develop always learn how to move forward despite the presence of fear. Each stage of human development requires moving through and past greater levels of fear. We all know people who refuse to accept that challenge and retreat to a more comfortable (but less powerful) existence in which the fear is not confronted.

Once again, the same is true in our organizations. In our previous social media examples, you can see how fear in the organization prevented people from doing what they needed to do to succeed. We are afraid to ask our community for their opinions. (What if that means we need to change?) We are afraid to admit we are wrong or change what is not working. (Will I get blamed for the mistake?) We are afraid to build learning and experimentation into everything we do in our organizations. (What if it reveals we made bad choices?) Thousands of books on management are available, and they are all frequently filled with excellent advice that simply dances around the underlying problem: fear. That is why people-centric organizations are courageous. They develop learning cultures. They figure out how to bake experimentation into all their processes, and they are not afraid when their employees develop personally.

A culture of learning is much easier said than done. "Learning organizations" have been touted for decades, but we are not sure most people really understand what that means or requires of the organization. It requires that people have time to learn and time to talk about what they are doing (rather than running 100 miles an hour to keep doing what they are doing). It means that failure is not only "an option," it is normal. It means that answers are not valued as much as questions. It requires us to be willing to abandon long-held beliefs when the evidence is clear. These cultural elements are diametrically opposed to the cultures of many organizations today, which is precisely our point. We need more courage, and learning cultures are a big part of it.

When you translate learning cultures down to the process level, the key word is experimentation. Most existing processes and systems are designed to avoid mistakes, which has an obvious logic. But one of the unintended consequences of a focus on avoiding mistakes is a fear of experimentation. People don't try new things because being wrong would bring on some kind of punishment. People don't suggest new ideas because they have learned the hard way that they have to get approval far up the chain of command to try something new, and the hoops they have to jump through are just not worth it. We strive for consistency and efficiency (which is fine), but in the process we have totally removed experimentation. People-centric organizations learn how to balance efficiency and experimentation. They make sure that their processes all have room for experiments so their people can learn how to do it (rather than only being told how to do it).

And finally, fear at the level of individual behavior is addressed primarily through personal development. As competency increases, fear decreases, so people-centric organizations are focused on developing individuals at all levels. If you have been involved in social media, then you know it is all about stepping out and making a difference. It's much more than broadcasting marketing messages; it is about building relationships with people around common interests and goals. When you do that, you invariably learn new things, and the more you learn (related to a particular community), the more active you will be. It is risky, of course, because there are times when you might reveal your ignorance, but that is the only way to learn and develop. Social organizations foster that quality in their staff and value people who want to add value to the organization, who want to be more than just relevant to their communities, and who develop in ways that their organizations might not have imagined.

We look at examples of courage in organizations in Chapter 9, "How to Be Courageous."

Making It Happen

At this point, we hope you have generally been nodding in agreement with our premise: The future will belong to more human organizations that understand how to embrace and leverage being open, trustworthy, generative, and courageous. To be honest, however, we also hope that you have been jotting down questions along the way, like "Okay but how do you make this happen?" or "But I am not the CEO, so what role do I play in trying to change our culture?" Those are the kinds of questions we explore in the next four chapters. Chapters 6 through 9 takes on each of our four elements, one at a time. As we explore each human element we examine specifically how organizations can become more human at the three different levels of culture, process, and individual behavior.

And each of the four chapters get specific about how you can make this happen, recognizing that the "you" who is reading these words right now will range from CEO to mailroom clerk. We don't want a book that only results in nodding heads as it is read on the train. We will not even be satisfied with a book that is powerful enough to change a few conversations in our machine-based organizations that are on the brink of failure. We want people to use this book to help them make change today.

In that regard, we created worksheets that are accompany each of the four chapters on being open, trustworthy, generative, and courageous. We present the basic ideas behind the worksheets along with some of the questions here in the book. The worksheets are also online at www.humanizebook.com, so you can download them and work through them in your organization.

Each worksheet provides guidance on what questions you need to ask when assessing how well your culture handles things such as learning, inclusion, or transparency. It goes on to help you identify specific next steps you can take to start changing the culture in that direction. Both the assessment and the action planning steps will be different, depending on where you are in the system. Those at the top of the organizational chart (executive) need to direct their attention and their actions to different areas, as compared with others without that authority. The worksheets take that into account and provide guidance for different levels in your organization.

Whatever you do, do something. Read each of the next four chapters and download the worksheets so that you and your colleagues can start building more human organizations right away.

Ready? Let's roll up our sleeves and get to work.

6

How To Be Open

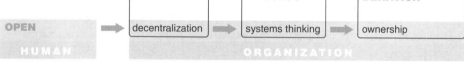

OPEN	CULTURE	PROCESS	BEHAVIOR
	decentralization	systems thinking	ownership
HUMAN	ORGANIZATION		

"The social model is more human, less burdened by departmental silos, fluid with its communications (both internal and external) and with a much flatter operational structure. ... In a bizarre twist of irony given that modern technology is responsible for making the model possible, it is very much a return to basics. It is how business was done hundreds of years ago: face to face, one handshake at a time. The difference is that now, scale is no longer a hurdle. Companies can, if they want, build loyalty 140 characters at a time, shake hands from hundreds of miles away, and have "'face to face'" interactions with tens of thousands of customers per day."

—Olivier Blanchard, *Social Media ROI*

Openness is the foundation of human organizations, as it has been the foundation of social media's success in the last ten years. The social media revolution distributed power away from the center and toward the periphery. Suddenly the masses could do their own publishing, create their own entertainment, and write and distribute their own product reviews. They could build and nurture communities where it used to take a centralized organization with pooled resources to get that done. They could make news without the help of a PR agency. They could create industry discussion forums, job boards, and resource libraries without the help of a professional association. Only a few years ago, centralized power meant a lot more than it does today, and where power was centralized, the need for openness was diminished.

Or at least the ability to *demand* openness was diminished. We took for granted that the power of the individual (or dispersed groups of individuals) was relatively low compared to the power of groups where control and authority were centralized. So as we created institutions and centralized groups with power, we accepted the fact that systems would be closed, information would be controlled, and responsibility would be concentrated among the individuals who held certain positions in the hierarchy. Those strategies seemed to work. It was the price we were willing to pay to get the increased potential that came with our organized groups.

We're lucky that social media opened our eyes to the potential of openness because the characteristics of an open human existence—individual empowerment combined with a connection to the broader system—are in desperate need of attention these days. As human beings, we thrive when we are able to step into our power as individuals while simultaneously engaging effectively with our community, our network, our family, and the system at large. It is a bit of a paradox to combine the power of the individual with the power of the system, but we see it in the individuals we admire and look up to as leaders in our communities. On one hand, they are comfortable with themselves and show us that they are powerful, without having too strong an ego, and on the other hand, they are also comfortable being a small part of the bigger picture. They celebrate others and deflect attention to the system. They are open. Human beings can certainly survive in a closed existence. They can focus on individual survival and pull back from the community. They can focus only on their own career goals, their own power, and their own success. Or they can subsume themselves to the system, constantly reacting to the needs of others. You can survive in these ways, and you can even amass substantial power and riches doing so. But that is not how we thrive as a society.

Today, the same is true for organizations. **To humanize our organizations, we need to make them more open.** We need to embrace that same paradox organizationally: the power of the individual combined with the power of the whole system. Frankly, this is not a skill that is particularly well developed in today's organizations. We tend to reject the paradox as impossible, and instead, we make choices. We give more power to the top of the organizational chart. We don't let certain individuals take ownership of what they are doing because the inconsistency and unpredictability of individual ownership causes us to lose our efficiency. We value control and see it is a limited resource, so much of our collective organizational lives are spent in that fight for control in one form or another. The results, as we show in Chapter 3, "We're Not Moving Forward," and Chapter 4, "Challenges to Socializing Business," are less than impressive.

So it is time to make a change. It is time to stop paying lip service to openness and figure out how to make it happen. We need to divert our attention away from vapid corporate values statements and toward efforts that make real change in our organizations. We need to make changes that help us practice openness at all levels of our organizations. This is part of what made social media so successful, and in this chapter we explore each level of our trellis for humanizing organizations as it relates to becoming open. We talk about how to build open cultures that embrace decentralization, how to create open processes based on systems thinking, and how to support open individual behavior where people take ownership of what they do.

Open Culture: Decentralization

The Matrix is a system, Neo. That system is our enemy. But when you're inside, you look around, what do you see? Businessmen, teachers, lawyers, carpenters. The very minds of the people we are trying to save. But until we do, these people are still a part of that system and that makes them our enemy. You have to understand, most of these people are not ready to be unplugged. And many of them are so inured, so hopelessly dependent on the system, that they will fight to protect it.

—Morpheus, in *The Matrix*, 1999

In Chapter 4, we discussed the challenges social media poses to organizational cultures. Specifically, we identified the issues of risk, authority, and control. More often than not, an organization's culture is relatively risk averse on the one hand, and values command and control on the other. Social media repeatedly clashes with cultures like this because social media's success has been partially dependent on our collective ability to take risks, try new things, let users control the development of what happens (rather than the central publisher), and actively move across established boundaries when it comes to participation.

In short, our cultures are centralized. All organizations (like all systems) have power at both the center and on the periphery, but today's organizational cultures tend to value the power at the center more. Part of this comes from our centuries-old machine metaphor for understanding organizations. In machines, there is a central power source, or engine. That engine produces the core motion that enables all the disparate parts to be in motion and carry out their various functions. If something stops working or needs repair at the periphery, the impact is typically contained within that locality. If the core were to break down, though, the whole system is in jeopardy. Thus we value the center more, and that's where we put our energy and resources generally.

Interestingly, another source of our fondness of centralization comes from one of the underlying values in the culture of the United States—individualism. One might think that a spirit of individualism would lead us to favor a more decentralized approach. That certainly happened politically during the birth of our nation, as reflected in the delicate balance between state and federal powers in the way the U.S. government works. But when it comes to organizations, we have to remember that nearly every organization started the same way: Someone founded it.

Part of our spirit of individualism is the freedom for each individual to pursue their dreams, often in the form of starting and running a business. Not every individual wants to take advantage of this opportunity, of course, but many do, and they are the ones who have created and are creating the organizations in which the rest of us are now working or will work in the future. And here is a simple truth about organizations: They start small, and when they are small, their culture is defined by the founder and/or the founding family.

Sometimes the founder's culture is rejected early on, in which case the founder typically leaves the company and those who remain build a new culture. But either way, the culture starts by being defined by the values, approaches, and principles of a small number of individuals. During those beginning times, there is little doubt about who is in charge and few people question that person's authority when it comes to creating a culture. They might suggest some shifts, but if that is not the direction the founder wants to go, then the others typically accept the decision.

This is the birth of our centralized cultures. Granted, some individuals possess a set of values that demand a decentralized culture in their organization, and those organizations certainly exist. But their decentralized nature is still determined, at least initially, by the founder. Right out of the gate in our organizations, we assume that the people who start them are in control, and as such they get to set the culture. So it should be no surprise to us that even as those organizations grow beyond the founders or the founding families, even to the point where they hire consultants to help create a more attractive work culture, the core value of centralized control is rarely challenged. It is simply a given that the people who are at the top get to have most of the control, partially because that is always true at the beginning of an organization's life. Even as we introduce new staff people, create new departments, or institutionalize external stakeholders such as stockholders, it is all done within a context of at least some measure of centralized control.

It doesn't have to be this way, and if we want to grow organizations that can thrive in a social world, we need to create more open cultures that are not as dependent on centralized control. Open cultures embrace decentralization, just like social media does. Open cultures actively shift the balance of power, away from the center, where it has existed historically, and toward the periphery. However, it is not a complete decentralization. This is not some kind of communist revolution for organizations where "the people" take over (which never actually happened in communism, for that matter). There is still room for a center in an open culture, and there are always differing levels of control. But the balance has shifted, and as a result, organizations can tap into power and effectiveness that has previously been left untapped.

To do this, you need to understand what your culture is and how you need to change it. Remember what we said about culture in Chapter 4: It is inherently stable. The stability of cultures is reassuring, even when we don't like them. So as you move to change the culture, be ready to help people through a transition that may not always be pleasing to them. Also recognize that culture is both deep and broad. Your change efforts must address all three levels of walk, talk, and thought if you are going to successfully shift to a more decentralized culture.

Walking the Walk: Who Steps Up?

To embrace a more open culture, you have to change the way "centralization is done" in your organization. We recognize that is an odd phrase, but in fact every organization "does" centralization in particular ways. It frequently revolves around the idea of "who." Who gets to decide? Who solves the problem? Who represents the organization? Who is invited to the meeting? Who gets to speak at the meeting? As we mentioned in Chapter 4, command and control cultures are determined by how they establish their boundaries, both internally and externally. The more centralized cultures tend to have more opaque boundaries. They don't let information or people move across the boundaries freely. This is true both horizontally, across departments, and vertically, across levels in the hierarchy. There are three primary types of "who" issues: who *decides*, who *speaks*, and *who acts*.

As you start to change the "walk" of your culture, pay attention to these issues of "who" in your search for ways to open up some of your boundaries.

Who Decides

Who decides is the one piece of our culture walk that is most frequently associated with centralization and decentralization. In centralized cultures, decision making rests at the top. Decisions about allocating resources and hiring people tend to be placed higher up on the organizational chart. In some large bureaucracies, you will find "lower level" employees who complain they have no autonomy and are simply required to follow instructions and established processes.

The more decentralized you get, the more decision making authority you find floating around among the cubicles. As you examine your culture, take a look at what decisions people can make on their own, versus which ones require approval. You don't have to inventory every single decision. Just identify some categories that make sense in your context. Who can make a hiring decision, for example, and who must submit a candidate for approval? Who can purchase equipment for a project? Who gets to decide how they spend their time?

That last question has been covered extensively in the business press thanks to the much-publicized policy at Google called "20% time." The policy enables engineers to spend one day a week on any project they want, even if it is outside their job description. Google's incredibly successful Gmail product was originally developed during an employee's 20% time. (Remember Google was originally just about search, not mail software.) Google is not the only company to embrace this idea, and it is a good example of a culture of decentralization. It doesn't give complete free reign to every employee (extreme decentralization), but it carves out a piece where the employee has control about the decision of where to pay attention, at least for that one chunk of his or her weekly paid work time. For example, on the Google blog, one employee wrote about how he used Google 20% time to create a new keyboard shortcut for Google Reader. No one had to assign that task to him; it was his decision to devote attention to that project. But when he did come up with the idea, he still had to get it approved and implemented through established channels in the company.

The concept here is about creating containers. By offering 20% time, Google gives its employees a limited container within which they have leeway, flexibility, and freedom. This is the hallmark of a decentralized culture. You are not completely inverting your organizational pyramid structure. You are simply figuring out how to give the maximum freedom to specific pockets within the system, while still being able to maintain the integrity of the enterprise. Centralized cultures, on the other hand, put in controls to prevent the chaos they assume would ensue were the controls not in place. They limit who can decide, and they demand records of time spent that map back to job descriptions and task lists (typically with a punishment for noncompliance). Decentralized cultures place limits, too, but they do it at the lowest level possible. They look for ways to create pockets of chaos because they know that's where the power of a decentralized system is unleashed. But they have to be real pockets of chaos. You actually have to let people make the decisions in those contained realms and then be clear about what happens after. Let people spend time on projects they deem important (some of the time). Increase the budget that department has to bring in outside consultants or buy equipment. The challenge is in making the pockets of chaos as big as possible, while still having controls on what emerges out of the chaos. Implementing new practices like these helps create a more decentralized culture.

Those types of actions are very visible, which is important when addressing the "who decides" part of your culture. You must remember, though, that there is an equally important—but much less visible—piece of your culture when it comes to decisions. All organizations have a formal hierarchy that obviously impact decision making, but all organizations also have what Art Kleiner calls a core group. [1] The core group is a collection of individuals or stakeholder groups whose influence and status in the organization are great enough to exert some kind of gravitational pull on the organization's decision making. In short, these are the people you think about before you make an important decision, wondering how they might react or what they might think of what you're doing. Kleiner argues that given the complexity and strategic contradictions most of us face in organizations, we need a simple guide for making decisions, and the core group gives us just that.

In that sense, we actually need some people to matter more than others. If everyone has the same weight, then we have no guidance in our decision making, but if we can pick out a few key individuals or groups, then in a pinch we can at least guess about the guidance. Guessing is a key point because we may not always know what the core group thinks, but we still make decisions on the direction we *think* they are headed.

In a centralized culture, the core group typically mirrors the top of the organizational chart. In fact, in a highly centralized culture, nearly everyone outside key leadership positions is excluded from the core group. In a less centralized culture, the core group is constructed differently. It is not simply an expanded version of a centralized core group. That defeats the purpose of the group. Having 139 people in your core group is impossible because it leaves you with the complexity and contradiction that you were trying to avoid in the first place. But core groups can be more fluid and situational. In decentralized cultures, multiple core groups with varying membership emerge depending on the nature of the situation.

Let's say you're in the IT department and you have a fairly standard organizational structure. Eight people are in your team, one of whom is the team leader, and she reports to a director, who reports to a vice president, who reports to the CEO. In many organizations, your core group may be your team leader, the director, the VP, and the CEO. Those are the people who control your job, so you think about them when you are making a decision. But in a decentralized culture, you would be open to relying on other people, not because of position or control they might have, but based on their ability to help you get the job done. You know that Colette in marketing has been doing social media since the early days and has knowledge about many of the technical details you are working on. She may end up being someone you rely on in decision making, even though she's not in your set of boxes on the organizational chart.

For this to happen, though, you need to know Colette, so some process changes might need to be implemented for that to happen. (We talk about that later.) But more important, the people in authority positions need to demonstrate that they, too, look outside the lines and boxes when it comes to seeking advice and learning. The vice president of operations (who oversees IT) needs to (a) know and (b) have

---

1. Source is Art Kleiner, *Who Really Matters: The Core Group Theory of Power, Privilege, and Success,* (Currency/Doubleday, 2003).

the guts to acknowledge publicly the expertise of someone like Colette in marketing. Another set of challenges arises for middle managers who may end up coordinating work that cuts across department lines. These are the things you need to change about who makes decisions if you want to create a decentralized culture.

Who Speaks

The second element of walking the walk of a decentralized culture is who speaks, or who gets a voice in the organization. This can be external, like who gets to represent the organization publicly, or internal, as in who has permission to speak in meetings. This actually follows a similar pattern to our discussion about decision making. In centralized cultures, fewer people are allowed to speak. The authority to "represent" the company is given sparingly, and until the right people can figure out what needs to be said, silence is the norm. In decentralized cultures, on the other hand, a larger and more distributed group can do things like speak up in meetings, write blog posts, and engage on social media sites. There are still centralized communication points in decentralized structures (the official spokesperson is still the official spokesperson), but it is accepted as fact that in addition to the official spokesperson, employees at all levels will still be listening, speaking, and engaging—and in doing so, they represent the company, even if not officially.

In short, in decentralized cultures, people speak up. People in one department speak to people in another department. Lower level employees speak up in meetings, even with higher-level employees present. The right people get together for a meeting, even if they are not the department heads or weren't preauthorized to meet. Of course, it is not enough just to demand that a culture be open and decentralized like this.

We can see it now: A progressive executive reads the newest book about how social media is changing business and then calls an all-staff meeting. She shares some new information with the whole staff, maybe even information that used to be housed only within one of the silos. She speaks authentically and powerfully about the potential impact of this information and acknowledges that the challenges they are facing need everyone's help if they are going to make it through. Knowing that a decentralized culture will likely allow her to take advantage of more of her resources to address this challenge, she boldly asks for direct feedback, imploring her staff to share their concerns, ask the tough questions, and provide some out-of-the-box ideas. She looks eagerly to her assembled staff to unleash their decentralized power. And what happens? Nothing. Silence. Crickets even.

An open, decentralized culture is not something created on demand. It is not an idea that a few people come across and then implement in their organization. Yes, walking the walk of a decentralized culture includes more people speaking up—even in a meeting where the boss passionately asks for participation. But it doesn't happen simply because the boss wants it to happen in a given moment. (That is still centralized.) It happens when people at all levels of the system value the power of a decentralized voice. It happens when everyone, over time, is rewarded for speaking up. Think about W. L. Gore's flat structure discussed in Chapter 3, where the people who call meetings that other people want to attend are the ones called "leaders." That kind of structure empowers people to speak up and call meetings, regardless of traditional lines of authority. If you want to create a decentralized culture, then you must figure out where the opportunities are to expand the voice of your people.

Social media, of course, is one obvious place to do this. Who in your company is allowed to have a blog? Who in your company is given permission to write posts on the company's official blog? How many people in your company have active Twitter accounts? Are they identified when they tweet, or is there a single, generic, mono-lithic @blandpartyline Twitter account? In the early days of social media, giving employees this kind of voice felt too dangerous. And obviously, there is still room for clear and effective social media policies. Every individual should not be the offi-cial company spokesperson. But allowing more people to speak, knowing that they will be speaking in their own unique and uncontrolled authentic voice while also being recognizably part of your company, helps build a decentralized culture. We like to cite NTEN, the Nonprofit Technology Network, as a great example of this. NTEN is a membership organization whose mission is to help nonprofits effect social change through technology, and it works to achieve that partly by leading by example. On Twitter, each of NTEN's staff members have their own NTEN-related Twitter handles (@ntenhross, @annanten, @sarah_at_nten, and so on) as well as their official Twitter account @NTENorg. Their audience and their community know and trust each of their individual voices.

Even in larger organizations where multiple people tweet from one Twitter account, they might sign the end of their tweets with their initials so that their followers know who wrote it. Even with hundreds of thousands of followers, each follower is an individual, and they want to know who wrote what they are reading.

And to reinforce an organization's commitment to giving employees a voice, it is also critical that the people in authority positions demonstrate visibly that the employees' voice really matters. Giving employees the space to participate in social media is a great start, but the impact will be much greater if the higher ups actually show that they are reading what's being posted and acknowledge how it is support-ing business goals. Too often employees feel their voices are unheard. So if you're in a position of authority, make sure you connect (out loud and visibly) what your employees are talking about to what actually gets done in the organization. Even if you already knew that it was a good idea to reach out to that government agency in preparation for the product launch, make sure that the department head who sug-gested it in last month's all staff meeting is publicly acknowledged for suggesting something that is being implemented. While open, decentralized cultures are marked by everyone having a voice, do note that the people at the center/top must be very intentional about what they say to make it happen.

If you can provide venues where you can give your people a voice, and show them that it makes a difference, then the one time you really need their participation in that all-staff meeting, you'll be more likely to get it.

Who Acts

The third area of walking the walk in a decentralized culture is who gets to actually take action. Who gets to solve the problem, make the sale, address the complaint, or design the product? Of course, there are always people who have it in their job description to do each of those things. Obviously they take action in appropriate ways. But what we are discovering in this social world is that limiting action to the people who have been assigned authority for that action is a recipe for disaster. That is part of our crumbling, Newtonian view of organizations, where we can successfully separate thought and action, and the HR specialist can design the perfect organization, predicting how the future will play out so the customer service representative is in precisely the right place at the right time to meet the needs of the customer, or the design department can be fed the perfect information at the perfect time to come up with the perfect product.

Centralized cultures are comfortable when people are doing the jobs they are supposed to do. But life does not always work that way, and decentralized cultures can better adapt to the more organic way in which life unfolds. Yes, we still have job descriptions, and people perform those jobs. But that is rarely enough to thrive. So we have to find ways to enable more people in the system to actually step up and take action when it's needed, even if it is not in their job description. In fact, one way of measuring how centralized your culture is in this regard would be to count the number of times during a given time period that you hear people say, "It's not my job." There are many different versions of that statement. (X department handles that, let me check with my supervisor, I'm not at liberty to say, we are not authorized to do that, and so on.) At any given moment it is uttered, it might be the appropriate response. But keep an eye on the overall count because the higher it gets, the more centralized your culture.

How can you enable more people to solve more problems? What has to happen to allow Ms. Irlweg at United to actually solve Dave Carroll's problem of the broken guitar? How can you have more people listening to social media so important issues are addressed immediately, rather than waiting for some designated spokesperson to respond? Decentralized cultures are filled with people who are ready and willing to solve problems. That is not because those particular individuals are rare breeds who are self-starters or top-notch talent. They are ready and willing to solve problems because they are given tools and access, and are rewarded for doing so. One plumbing company in the Washington, DC, area trains its field technicians in the contents of its high-end fixtures catalogue, recognizing that the best time to make a sale on many of those products is when the technicians are in the homeowner's residence, probably working on a completely different issue. Referring the customer to a call center or a website could mean a lost sale, but instead, this company—that makes several thousand service calls per year—has an "army of salespeople" ready to respond to the customers on their terms.

The focus here is on giving people closest to the problem the resources to solve the problem. When an airline desk employee marches 50 feet down to the other end of the counter, simply to print out a document to verify your seat was, in fact, cancelled, she is not working to solve the problem. She is working to get you out of the line. When you then complain that it is not fair to ask you to pay $500 for a seat on the *exact same flight* for which you had already paid $500 for a ticket (before your seat was mistakenly canceled), and she suggests you call the 800 number, then she is definitely not working to solve the problem. At that point, the airline has most likely lost a customer for life. Not that this has happened to either of the authors. Ahem.

Talking the Talk: Less Is More

As the previous section illustrates, it is not easy to move from a centralized culture to a decentralized one, and that is the challenge most organizations face as they try to be more effective in a social world. Identifying and making changes to the "way centralization is done," however, is only one piece of the puzzle. You also need to pay careful attention to the "talk" side of culture. How will your organization change its words so that it can facilitate the action identified in the previous section? What do you tell your people to generate a decentralized culture?

This is actually quite a challenge. Of course you cannot create a new culture simply through words. Too many organizational leaders make up their minds about what culture they want and feel that they can somehow declare it into being. These are the organizations with the pretty posters on the wall with inspirational sayings. Culture can't be created by the marketing department.

But what you say is important. If you don't say anything, or if the messages are mixed or unclear, then your people will simply invent what they think the culture is supposed to be. So we need to choose our words (public statements, policies, company marketing messages, and so on) carefully.

Ev Williams, CEO of Twitter, presented the company's guiding principles in his keynote at the 2010 South by Southwest Interactive conference.[2] (The keynote itself, an interview run by Harvard Business Review blogger Umair Haque, was panned by the audience for not living up to the hype, but let's focus on the substance of it). Williams talked at length about his company principles, paraphrased here from the talk:

- Be a force for good.

- Pay attention.

- Be open—assume there are more smart people outside the company than inside.

- Experimentation creates value.

- Partner only when everybody wins.

- Amplify weak signals. (Give the most disadvantaged a voice.)

The lesson here is that if you can narrow down your guiding principles (or your core values, or your mission) to something that fits on one page or less, don't just share them internally—share them everywhere. Share them publicly. Hold yourselves accountable to them.

But when it comes to moving toward a decentralized culture as part of a more open organization, especially for one that has been around a while, we are faced with an additional challenge. When you create a decentralized culture, you are ultimately putting forth the argument that the people in the authority positions are intentionally not clinging to power and control. That is the nature of decentralization.

So how do you order people to accept the fact that you are not in control? It's a paradox. The more you try to make it clear that you are not in charge, the more you look like you are in charge. The more you insist that others need to do the talking and take the action, the more you end up talking and taking action yourself. So the mantra when trying to shift to a decentralized culture is "less is more."

Decentralization is typically achieved by using the fewest number of words possible. If you have to produce a 300-page manual to instruct everyone about how decentralization will happen, you are missing the point. The classic example of the extreme opposite approach comes from Nordstrom, the successful department

---

2. Haque, Umair. "Twitter, SXSW, and Building a 21st Century Business – Umair Haque - Harvard Business Review." Business Management Ideas - Harvard Business Review Blogs. 17 Mar. 2010. Web. 10 Mar. 2011. <http://blogs.hbr.org/haque/2010/03/twitter_sxsw_and_building_a_21.html>.

store. For many years, they distributed to new employees a single 5 x 8-inch card as its new employee manual that read:

Welcome to Nordstrom

We're glad to have you with our Company. Our number one goal is to provide outstanding customer service. Set both your personal and professional goals high. We have great confidence in your ability to achieve them.

Nordstrom Rules: Rule #1: Use best judgment in all situations. There will be no additional rules.

Please feel free to ask your department manager, store manager, or division general manager any question at any time.[3]

Apparently these days Nordstrom does also hand out a more detailed manual along with this card, which doubtless has some important legal information in it. But the power of the clear (and brief) statement is still real.

Certainly Nordstrom's policy manual is on the more extreme end of the decentralized scale, where all employees use their best judgment. But no matter where you are on that scale, it is important to follow Nordstrom's lead in its clarity and careful word choice. One reason to avoid a 300-page policy manual is that it will likely be too controlling and centralized. When you spell everything out in immense detail, then it is the center (who wrote the manual) telling everyone else what to do.

But the other reason you need a brief manual is that you need people to be able to memorize it, or at least the key components of it. If you are going to have a decentralized culture, then the center needs to have the ability to articulate its guidance in small, memorable chunks. Using few words is required because in a decentralized culture, the periphery is expected to use their own judgment and solve their own problems, but in a way that is consistent with principles that come from the center. If people can remember the principles, then the system can achieve some cohesion and consistency, without robbing the periphery of its autonomy.

That is one reason why lengthy strategic plans fail, and many companies are adopting clearer statements of strategic principles or strategic directions that can fit on one sheet of paper. Different units may end up creating more detailed work plans to guide things on a local basis, but the center's role is to create a set of clear principles that are easy enough for everyone to internalize and apply to every situation.

We have even seen this same drive for clarity and brevity in the new area of social media policies. We see a lot of organizations working through the process of setting

3. "Nordstrom." Wikipedia, the Free Encyclopedia. 6 Mar. 2011. Web. 09 Mar. 2011.
    <http://en.wikipedia.org/wiki/Nordstrom>.

social media policies to feel more comfortable with allowing employees to begin responding to customers on social media sites. In the policies we have seen, we have noticed some themes. The best policies tend to

- Be built on trust, or the belief that staff want to do the right thing.

- Reflect the organization's core values, its mission or vision, which dictate the reasons why it is important to be participating in social media activities.

- Be in plain language, so everyone understands them.

- Be site-agnostic, because social media tools change faster than policies can keep up.

- Be focused on individual behavior.

- Supplement existing conduct policies, not try to replace them or include everything.

- Contain more DO's than DON'Ts, because too many prohibitions on social media activity are impossible to monitor and enforce. The friendlier the policy, the more likely it will be followed.

- Be widely shareable, either internally only or internally and externally.

All these principles for a good social media policy point to the overarching idea that they should be simple, easy to understand, easy to abide by. There must be clear direction for why it's good for business for the organization to participate in social media. There must be some key behavioral guidelines that basically say, "We expect you to act in a professional and responsible manner online just like offline."

Less is more is no easy task. We doubt Nordstrom developed its one-sentence policy manual in five minutes. It required deep strategic clarity and a well-thought-out operational plan to make it happen. But creating decentralized cultures requires both that effort and that discipline.

Thought: Cultural Assumptions

The foundation that supports both the "walk" and "talk" of culture change is a set of assumptions about the way things are that is widely shared among people in a system. There is no formula for modifying these assumptions, and it is not always easy to even articulate your starting point, let alone where you are headed. But if you want a decentralized culture, you need to examine and probably shift some of the underlying cultural assumptions. We cannot tell you what your existing cultural assumptions are, of course, and we cannot hand to you on a silver platter what your cultural assumptions should be. (That would not be very decentralized of us, now would it?) But we start you off on the path to discovering your specific cultural assumptions by providing you with a set of themes that we feel capture the essence of the decentralized culture found in open organizations.

We Are Not Alone

Decentralized cultures operate on the assumption that the solutions to problems are probably distributed across multiple people or departments. We assume that some-one else, somewhere, has part of the answer to my problem, just as we assume that some of my knowledge, expertise, or experience will be needed to solve other peo-ple's problems that we have not even considered. This runs counter to traditional organizational cultural assumptions. Traditionally, we assume that we have hired properly based on expertise and problem solving ability, so each individual in the system should be doing her job and answering questions on her own. It is assumed to be inefficient to push your way into solving other people's problems.

In fact, the days when problems stayed local and clearly defined are pretty much behind us. In today's fast-paced and social world, if we are not working with others, communicating across department lines, and connecting to customers and other stakeholders—then our inefficiency makes us come up short more quickly. We're lost, but we're making good time. Look how technology is no longer the sole realm of the IT department. Notice how younger employees often need to do "reverse mentoring" with senior management to get them up to speed on social technolo-gies. Work to articulate cultural assumptions that emphasize our connectedness, our dependence on each other, and the power of distributed networks.

Protect and Serve

It is important to understand that a decentralized system is not the same as a sys-tem without a center. It merely reflects a distribution of power away from the center and toward the periphery. The center is still there, and the center always has a vital role to play in any system. The "protect and serve" theme is about that role. In decentralized cultures, those in the center—those with positions of authority and those who control resources—understand that it is their role to basically get out of the way of the rest of the system so they can get the job done. It is the center's role to protect and serve the periphery. This is not a new concept; other texts on man-agement and supervision say that a supervisor's primary role is to run interference for his or her employees and protect them against the quicksand of the bureau-cracy. Employees are not there to make the manager's job easier. It is the other way around. The center still has a tough job. It is never easy making choices about resources. The trick is to make those tough choices with the system's health in mind and recognize that the power to achieve great things lies more in the work of the distributed periphery than in the inner workings of the center.

Proceed Until Apprehended

In decentralized cultures, the default is action, rather than approval. As people move through their day, creating value and solving problems, the underlying assumption is that they can go ahead and do what they think they should do, not needing to get approval first, but knowing that someone will stop them if they go too far. This means, by the way, that the responsibility for appropriate "apprehension" can be anywhere in the system. If you are a lower level employee in a decentralized culture, you may step in and question a colleague who you think has gone too far, rather than simply sending an email to your boss suggesting that he contact your colleague's boss, and so on. This cultural assumption says that it is okay to push the limits, and it is also okay (not a punishment) to be stopped.

Leadership Is a System Capacity

Leadership, paraphrasing Peter Senge, is defined as the system's capacity to shape its future. This is a critical assumption for a decentralized culture because it realizes that our traditional notions of leadership that focus on individuals in positions of authority are not enough to propel the system to the next level. Leaders are everywhere, and leadership is not some personal characteristic or quality that we assume exists in people who get attention in organizations. Leadership development takes on a whole new meaning, moving away from preparing people to get promoted into management toward making sure the system has the capacity in every corner of the system to adequately respond and move forward in ways that generate results.

Clarity Over Control

The days where a command and control culture consistently translates to organizational success are behind us. In the first chapter of her book, *Open Leadership*, Charlene Li declares that giving up control is inevitable.[4] Her basic definition of open leadership is about giving up control while inspiring commitment in others[5] (which we talk about later). But we hate to break it to you: Giving up control is the easy part. The point is not to abandon control and then just see how everything plays out. Thriving in a system that is not dominated by control requires more work, not less, and one of the key areas of work is developing and maintaining clarity. A decentralized culture works best when the different parts have a clear and shared understanding of key organizing principles. It is not a set of marching orders, but a clear direction. If the center focuses its work on the "macro-managing"

---

4. Li, Charlene. Open Leadership: How Social Technology Can Transform the Way You Lead. San Francisco: Jossey-Bass, 2010. 3.

5. Li, Charlene. Open Leadership. 14.

job of generating clear strategic principles, for example, then the periphery can better translate that guidance into everyday action without needing "micro-management" from the center. That kind of clarity is not easy, and decentralized cultures make it a priority, devoting the time and resources necessary to achieve clarity.

Open Process: Systems Thinking

Today, the org chart is hyperlinked, not hierarchical. Respect for hands-on knowledge wins over respect for abstract authority.

— The "ClueTrain Manifesto," Thesis 50[6]

As we try to make our organizations more open, we will probably encounter significant obstacles at the process level. Our processes have been at the very heart of the machine-based approach to organizations that has dominated the last century. Through our mechanically inclined process improvement, we transformed the productivity of our people. In today's social world, however, we are hitting the limits of these productivity gains. Social media has shown us a new level of both realized and potential productivity based on a more organic and human approach to getting the work done.

Systems thinking has been at the heart of these new achievements. We explain the basics of systems thinking in more detail later in this chapter, but the fundamental premise behind it is that systems are not only complicated and complex, they are also dynamic and changing. Only when we can see the broader system dynamics (including as they change over time), will we be able to apply the right types of leverage to move the system in the right direction.

The mechanical worldview understands systems, of course, but it never fully grasped their dynamic nature. Machines have much more rigid boundaries than natural systems, so when we work on machines, we can focus on shorter time frames and a more limited number of variables. They are still complex systems, but they possess what Peter Senge calls "detail complexity," rather than "dynamic complexity."[7] It is hard work to manage all the details correctly to keep the mechanical system running, but at least that fix you applied to that one part of the system will *always* be the fix that you apply to that one part of the system in the future. The solution to clogged fuel injectors (a common cause of engine hesitation at low RPMs, by the way) is to clean them. When it happens again in 60,000 miles, the solution will still be to clean the fuel injectors. That is mastering detail complexity.

---

6. Levine, Rick, Christopher Locke, Doc Searls, and David Weinberger. "The Cluetrain Manifesto - 95 Theses." The Cluetrain Manifesto. 1999. Web. 9 Mar. 2011. <http://cluetrain.com/book/95-theses.html>.

7. Senge, Peter M. The Fifth Discipline: the Art and Practice of the Learning Organization. New York: Doubleday/Currency, 1994. 71.

Natural systems don't work like that. As you fix one part of the system, the solution you implement might end up having an impact on other parts of the system that you will not be able to observe for some time. That can end up changing the system so much that either new problems emerge or the original problem can flare up again, but now resistant to the original solution. For example, the introduction of nonnative wild pigs to some channel islands in California enabled the protected Golden Eagle species to build up their populations there. This seems like a great success for environmental advocates. As the Eagle population grew, however, an endangered native fox on the island almost became extinct.[8] The increased number of eagles reduced the number of foxes, but more important enabled an increase in the number of spotted skunks (that used to be killed by the foxes). It turns out the skunks and the foxes competed for the some of the same food sources, and as the balance shifted, the foxes were unable to thrive in the new system. Managing dynamic complexity requires a more constant adapting to changing systems, rather than only a static understanding of complicated relationships or structures.

Human organizations have dynamic complexity, which is why we need them to be open. We need them to be appropriately connected to the broader system, and at the process level, this means a proper application of systems thinking. In Chapter 4, we defined organizational processes as the collections of rules, instructions, and shared understanding of how we do the work. We see processes operating on three basic levels: structural, internal, and external. In this section we define systems thinking more clearly and then explore how it can be used to change our approach to processes at the structural, internal, and external levels.

What Is Systems Thinking?

The concept of systems thinking was not created by Peter Senge, but he was instrumental in accelerating its popularity and application to the business world through his widely popular 1990 book, *The Fifth Discipline*. Systems thinking is the fifth of his five disciplines of learning organizations, all of which are explored in the book, but he starts with systems thinking because it is a prerequisite for mastering the other disciplines. The simplest definition of systems thinking, according to Senge, is

> Systems thinking is a discipline for seeing wholes. It is a framework for seeing interrelationships rather than things, for seeing patterns of change rather than static "snapshots."[9]

In too many organizations, we lack the discipline to see wholes. We have become very skilled at examining things (rather than relationships), and we value those who can quickly make sense of static snapshots, but frankly we tend to reject those who

---

8. http://www.pnas.org/content/99/2/554.full.pdf

9. Senge, Peter M. The Fifth Discipline. 68.

try to point out broader patterns of change. Senge provides a great example of the lack of systems thinking in action in his depiction of a computer simulation called "the beer game," where retailers, distributors, and manufacturers each make things worse in managing supply and demand because they fail to take the whole system into account in their decision making. It's the classic blind man/elephant analogy. Each knows his own part of the system but doesn't see the other parts and draws different conclusions about what is going on and what should be done.

The challenge, then, is to understand the dynamic complexity of systems (rather than detail complexity), as mentioned previously. One of the keys is to start thinking about circles and loops, rather than just straight lines. Our culture values a very linear understanding of cause and effect. We study cause and effect through experimentation. We start a process, add variables, and measure change. That is how we understand how things work. Senge points out that dynamic systems don't operate in a linear fashion that way. Although the United States-Soviet arms race might have made sense from a one-sided, linear perspective (the Soviets added to their arsenal, which was a threat to the United States, so we should add to our arsenal), when you understand that each response triggers an even greater response on the other side, you quickly see that there is no end to the escalation.

Senge points out three basic patterns that we need to have in mind when looking at systems: reinforcing loops, balancing loops, and delays.

Reinforcing loops are system dynamics that end up reinforcing the effect of a certain action or set of actions, causing growth or acceleration. If you have a great product, and sales increase, you now have more customers out there to spread positive word of mouth. This triggers more sales, which gives you more customers, and so on. It is a snowball effect. Of course, the reinforcing loop can be negative as well. Social media certainly makes loops like that quite visible.

Balancing loops are system processes triggered to bring the system back to a preestablished norm. When it gets cold, you put on a sweater to get your body temperature back to where you want it to be. When your company's cash gets low, you borrow more to bring it back to the appropriate cash balance. Like reinforcing loops, balancing loops can be positive, negative, or neutral, but they can become dangerous when they remain undetected as you try to change things. The more you change, the more the balancing loops push the system back to the way it was. It can be quite frustrating.

Delays refer simply to the delay between action and consequence in systems. If the consequences were instantaneous, it would be easy to figure out when a reinforcing loop causes things to accelerate more than we want them to, or when a balancing loop prevents us from implementing change. But consequences are not instantaneous, and we are not patient with delays. We turn the hot water on for a shower, and when it comes out cold, we turn the hot water on even more. By the time the water feels right, we get in, only to discover it is getting hotter than we can stand. So we turn it down a bit, but it is still too hot, so we turn it much more...you get the picture. We do that in business all the time, particularly related to manufacturing and supply chains. Understanding delays and reading the impact on the system is an important part of systems thinking.

When you put these three elements together, you are better able to keep the whole picture in mind when analyzing what is happening in your work environment. Senge goes on to describe some typical system dynamics, namely a limits to growth scenario and a shift the burden scenario. In limits to growth, companies do something that works, and things start growing, but they don't realize that the ramping up of the successful activities generates unnoticed balancing loops, and the results start to falter. As a result, they push harder on the initial successful work, but that only increases the balancing loop, and the results are never achieved. In the shift the burden scenario, people either don't see or don't want to confront the bigger problem, so they focus on creating elegant solutions to the more limited symptoms. The symptoms go away, but of course the bigger problem remains unsolved, new symptoms crop up somewhere else in the system, and in the end everyone is unhappy.

Arguably every organization would benefit from systems thinking. That is certainly Senge's point in stressing the importance of learning organizations. But we think it is particularly relevant when seeking to create more open organizations, specifically in the context of organizational process. In each of the three areas of process—structural, internal, and external—we demonstrate the value of systems thinking in making the organization more open.

Structural: Silos That Work

Organizational silos have long been identified as a problem in management circles. They prevent information from being shared, they reinforce unnecessary competition among departments, and they keep people from seeing the big picture. They are the structures that breed the ugly, political turf battles that we constantly disparage (yet somehow always find ourselves fighting). Open organizations, of course, do not tolerate this kind of wasted energy. The solution, however, is not necessarily to flatten the organization completely and put everyone into the same department. From a process perspective, open organizations still need groups of people who possess particular expertise or who work more closely with each other on particular areas of the business. The trick is to apply systems thinking to the structural solutions to prevent these organizational boundaries from creating problems larger than the solutions they provide.

One answer is to make sure all the silos are "reading from the same sheet of music" or all can "see the big picture." We tend to boil it down to an issue of focus (as evidenced by all the visual metaphors we use to make our points). If you can keep your head up and "see the forest from the trees," then you will recognize the need for your department to cooperate with other departments to meet the larger organizational objectives. As much as we say that, however, we rarely see it working. Most organizations have big-picture strategic plans, or at least some kind of unifying mission or vision statement, but we've had those for decades, yet the problem of silos persists.

Management consultant Patrick Lencioni offers a slightly different wrinkle to this idea, which reveals how systems thinking can transform the problem of silos. Lencioni argues that organizations can break down the silos and the turf battles if they can provide a single, unifying "rallying cry" for all the different departments.[10] He calls it a "thematic goal," and it is something that all departments focus on for a limited amount of time. Maybe it is to successfully implement a merger, or to reposition your company for a more health-conscious market, but whatever the thematic goal is, it is fairly time limited.

It may not sound different than asking all departments to contribute to a strategic plan, but the way these thematic goals are time limited is the key. Thematic goals obviously have a set of more specific objectives tied to them, but those objectives (creating a unified marketing message for the merged organizations, for example) are always different than the standard set of operating objectives you already have (like managing profitability by product or managing employee turnover), which remain more consistent over time.

When organizations simply pursue their standard goals and objectives over time, they work into ruts of reinforcing and balancing loops. Because the standard objectives always get more specific and different in each department, you end up reinforcing the silo behavior. Solving problems in one department often ends up causing problems in other departments (Senge's shifting the burden scenario), but as long as we focus on our traditional objectives, we do not see it.

By introducing a new, time-bound, and cross-functional focus, you can shake the system out of its patterns. You change the way people do things in ways that reveal the limiting patterns that were previously invisible. It does not matter whether you call it a rallying cry, thematic goal, or something entirely different. What matters is that you assume your units and divisions need to be periodically distracted from their traditional, year-in-year-out goals and objectives. It is not that you become completely unfocused, jumping from one random objective to the next. The "distraction" is actually a critical part of the system's health, and it always remains connected to the core strategy or direction of the organization. The distraction acknowledges that over time, the system changes, so if you only focus on your original objectives, you will end up off course. Manage your structure intentionally to

10. Lencioni, Patrick. Silos, Politics, and Turf Wars: A Leadership Fable about Destroying the Barriers That Turn Colleagues into Competitors. San Francisco, CA: Jossey-Bass, 2006. 17–208.

help everyone see the system dynamics. This is how you manage the structural end of process in an open organization.

Internal: Perpetual Motion

Applying systems thinking to internal processes to create a more open organization can also shake things up, but mostly in the form of transforming linear or disjointed processes into circular, flowing, and dynamic ones. It requires reexamining your internal processes to make sure they account for the dynamic complexity of your organization, not just the detail complexity.

One of the most obvious places to make this shift is in your organization's strategic planning process. In Chapter 3, we pulled back the curtain to expose some of the fundamental flaws behind strategic planning, demonstrating its developmental roots in the machine-based view of organizations. Its formalized processes force us to predict the future and somehow suspend time while we do our strategic thinking. After we have the plan in place, we then start the clock again and implement the plan for the next five years. We don't think this process ever was effective, let alone in today's more social world, and proponents of systems thinking would agree.

Today, we need strategy processes that work with the principles of open organizations and are rooted in systems thinking. This requires strategy processes that are not so tied to our calendars. Strategic challenges and opportunities do not pay attention to your strategic planning schedule (for example, the 3-to-5 year plan based on when Board meetings are scheduled and your fiscal year ends). The timing of that moment when you need to respond, or the insight that is required to make the appropriate pro-active step, is not predictable. So instead of designing a detailed strategic planning process based on your annual calendar, figure out ways to create opportunities for ongoing and coordinated strategic conversations. Yes, this can include specific meetings of specific people that can be put on a shared calendar. Some of the conversations can be scheduled, particularly when you want to convene a large or diverse group of people (which you should) as part of the process. You can't always spontaneously convene representatives from your North American, European, and Asian divisions every time specific strategic inflection points arise, so it is okay to schedule some strategic retreats periodically.

But it also should include ongoing strategic conversations at different levels in the organization, based on presenting information rather than on organizational calendars. Leaders of specific departments need to be able to find time on their calendars with relatively short notice to schedule a half-day meeting to address a particular challenge, which includes time to do some homework and gather some data on the topics. Social media can also play a part here. People in your organization need to monitor, listen to, and participate in the social media conversations in your industry to feed insight from those conversations into broader strategic conversations. Feeding the insight into strategy conversations, however, can be a challenge, because the people we have listening and engaging in social media are not, quite frankly, the ones we invite to the strategic planning sessions. To make a strategy process continuous, you will need to shift who is involved, who gets to speak, and who is required to listen—all in service of connecting the emergent needs and issues of customers and stakeholder to the people who are making the strategic decisions.

This decentralized approach to strategic conversations makes more sense in an open organization, whose culture is already bound to be more decentralized, but it also meshes with systems thinking. One of Mintzberg's main problems with strategic planning is the way it separates thought from action. This is parallel to system thinking's recognition of the delay between action and consequence. If you create a three-year strategic plan (over a weekend!) and then start to implement it, your initial actions (over time) will impact the system in ways that render your original thinking about strategy during that weekend somewhat obsolete. You may plan periodic strategic reviews of the plan, but they start by retrospectively looking at the plan, rather than a more holistic view of the system dynamics. An ongoing process of strategic conversations works better with an understanding of systems and the natural delay between action and consequence.

Another process shift you can make to address the dynamic complexity of systems (that is perhaps not as obvious as strategic planning) is in the way you manage data. With computers and the Internet came the age of information, which brought along with it ongoing and extensive challenges in managing data. There is no single answer to this problem, but it is critical for open organizations to examine this issue closely, particularly if your company's business model is not specifically based on data exchange. Where data exchange is central (like banking, for instance), companies are more likely to investigate the systems thinking implications of data sharing and management. The rest of us certainly rely on data exchanges (just look at your inbox), but we often do not think through the implications for how we manage our data.

Just look at computer hard drives. If we take a 30,000-foot view of your organization, it will appear to be a large collection of data, information, analyses, and insight. You've got hundreds or thousands of employees all working together in their little buildings that we can see from our vantage point in the sky. Groups of people work together and get things done. As we move closer, however, we begin to see that although those hundred people all work in the same office and can maybe even see each other if they peer over the tops of their cubicles, the information they are working with is nearly all located safely within the individual hard drives of each employee. True, you probably set up shared file servers a long time ago, which are used with varying degrees of completion and success. But even so, we end up emailing documents to each other, adding our initials to the end of the document name so we know whose changes were put in last. We save drafts of things on our hard drives because we are not ready to share them with the rest of the team. Or worse, we don't want those people over in X department to get their hands on it because they just don't get it!

These practices are the remnants of our old, control-based system. We like our hard drives and our email inboxes because it gives us the illusion that we can be in control of what we are working on. We do obviously exert some control on our work (we talk more about that when we discuss the topic of ownership), but our practice of "securing" our data within our individual email boxes and hard drives creates more harm than good. The result is our data are not shared together centrally where different parts of the system have access to what they need, when they need it. Instead, data are isolated from each other. In essence, we have created a "knowledge archipelago"—a string of tiny islands, all very close to each other but also all with their own unique boundaries. From 30,000 feet up, it might look like a solid land mass, but when you get closer you see that you can't get from one end of the island chain to the other as easily as you thought.

By keeping the data separate, you effectively render the system blind to the dynamic complexity. You extend the delays between action and consequence because people don't have access to the information. You can't see the loops that are balancing out your efforts. Open organizations make sharing data a priority, where documents can be edited in real time, and data can be entered from different parts of the system. It feels messier and out of control, but it also unleashes the power of a decentralized system.

External: Open Community

Part of your organizational processes always extend beyond your organizational boundaries. Everyone has customers, stakeholders, suppliers, members, constituents, and so on, but not everyone can honestly say they have a community. That is something an open organization might be pursuing. Traditional organizations usually have a clearly defined (and defended) boundary separating the organization from the outside. We welcome customers to enter our stores, give us money, visit our websites, watch our ads, and use our products, but we have security at our corporate offices and in our product development centers. Of course we are trying to keep our competitors out, but until recently it would have been ludicrous to suggest letting the public inside our organizational walls. It simply is not done.

In today's social world, that is changing. You should be familiar with the experience of Dell Computers. In the mid-2000s, Dell was taking considerable criticism for its poor customer service, and much of the bad press they received was coming not from the mainstream press but from the newly active blogging community. Dell did eventually respond using social media tools (including a blog in 2006), and it also launched IdeaStorm, which is a site where customers can make suggestions and post comments that simply tell Dell what to do. Dell is not the only company to create such a site—Starbucks' MyStarbucksIdea site is the exact same concept. Customers can log in, make suggestions, and engage in discussions about the ideas and rank some ideas as better than others through voting. It is an online way to leverage the wisdom of the crowds (à la Jim Surowiecki) and get the customers more engaged with the company.

Of course, it is not enough to just create the site. You actually have to listen to what the customers are saying (and voting on) and, more important, you have to respond. You actually have to make changes (at least some of the time) based on what they are saying. In Dell's case, this meant it started building computers that had the open-source operating system, Linux. Customers asked for it, and even though the people at Dell certainly had concerns (how to provide support, for example) and it never turned into a big part of their business, its decision to produce these machines showed that Dell was listening and willing to respond.

This is a good example of systems thinking in action. Dell had a good thing going (more or less) in building Windows computers for its customers. When the suggestion to make Linux machines came along, it would be rational to reject it. When you look at Dell's manufacturing, supply chain, and technical support systems, the added costs to do it differently might not be justified by the limited financial return in sales. But that looks only at one aspect of the system. If you broaden your view, you see a customer base that is actively engaged in this new thing called social media, and they are already unhappy. If you ignore the Linux requests, you run the risk of contributing to a negative reinforcing loop. Dell customers who are already frustrated by Dell's poor responsiveness find a new reason to blog about it and spread negative opinion about the company, which can impact sales negatively. By letting the customer into the decision making process and acknowledging the broader system impact they can have, the company ends up making smarter decisions.

Opening up your organizational world to the broader community does not mean, however, that you abdicate all decision making power. In Starbucks' case, it received plenty of suggestions that it intentionally chose to ignore. Actually, ignore is the wrong word. It listened carefully to the suggestions, but after an appropriate systems analysis it determined that the request could not be met. One such suggestion was to create a system in the store where regular customers (who already have their exclusive black Starbucks card) could actually program their regular drink order into the card. That way, they could swipe the card as they get in line, and the order is automatically put into the queue, rather than having to wait behind all the Starbucks newbies who have to call their order several times before they get it right. The idea gained a lot of support from customers and was welcomed by Starbucks initially, but eventually it was shot down because of the cost and process changes that would need to happen in each store. Basically each store would have to be completely rewired. Broader systems thinking addressed the secondary effects of a change (that would not have showed up for some time) before the decision was made. As an open organization, Starbucks created a community where it could have this extended conversation with people outside the official chain of command in the organization. Both Dell and Starbucks have strengthened their brand reputations through establishing goodwill relationships with their customers (and the public at large) through these collaborative spaces.

Open Behavior: Ownership

Why, Mr. Anderson? Why do you do it? Why get up? Why keep fighting?
Do you believe you're fighting for something? For more than your survival?
Can you tell me what it is? Do you even know? Is it freedom? Or truth?
Perhaps peace? Yes? No? Could it be for love?
—Agent Smith, in *The Matrix Revolutions*, 2003

As we said in Chapter 4, nothing really changes in our organizations unless behavior changes, and when it comes to creating an open organization, the lens through which we need to view individual behavior is ownership. Like a lot of words we use in this book, the way we understand ownership can be different from others in the management literature. In this case, it is substantially different. So before we talk about what ownership is (to us), let us be clear about what ownership is not.

Ownership is not some magical quality or spirit that causes individuals to go above and beyond the call of duty. There is no chorus of angels singing as that fry cook suddenly takes on a spirit of "ownership" and starts picking up trash in the parking lot on his way into the burger joint. Ownership is not an attitude that can be developed by convincing employees that they should feel like they have some kind of financial stake in the company (even though they do not). In addition, ownership is not merely the same thing as initiative—as if only those who take initiative, are proactive, or get things done can really can take "ownership" over their job.

If we are exaggerating our characterization of the state of the current management literature, it is only slightly. A lot of people in the management community are making a fervent call for more ownership among employees, and the basic frame of reference is the actual financial owners of companies. Although they do not often say it explicitly, it is implied that the people who actually own the company are perhaps the only ones who are willing to do anything to see it succeed. They would wash dishes, work nights and weekends, mortgage their house, ignore their friends…the list goes on. True owners do what it takes. So when we look at our employees—the ones who only work 8:30 to 5:00, or ignore opportunities to serve the customer because it is not in their job description, or conveniently only have sick days on Fridays, we get frustrated and wish they would act like "owners."

This view is flawed. It is true that owners, particularly entrepreneurs, often put in enormous amounts of time and energy to see their business succeed. We get it. Entrepreneurs invest a piece of themselves in the business, so they want to see it succeed. But the idea of having everyone act like an entrepreneur makes no sense and should not be a goal. Part of what drives an entrepreneur is that literal owner-ship. The entrepreneur has a personal stake in it. Trying to fabricate that feeling, that personal stake, will not work. And even if you could, you would then have an organization filled to the brim with owners, and that creates a host of new prob-lems. If you don't believe us, try coordinating a group of independent consultants on a long-term project...but perhaps that is another book.

Yes, ownership is an important concept here, but the goal should not be to get peo-ple to literally act like owners. The goal should be to get people to take ownership of their job so that things get done. There is a big difference. In open organizations, you strive for a decentralized culture and processes that embrace systems thinking. The last thing you want is for all your people to think they own the whole organiza-tion—that sounds more like centralization and myopia. Literal owners are in con-trol, and as we emphasized, the cultural assumption in open organizations is one of clarity over control. So ownership in the context of open organizations has a simple definition that is not about control.

Ownership means you don't have an excuse for not taking action. For an open organization to work, the entire system needs to be primed for action. Anything less, and the system will not perform to its full capacity. In too many organizations, capacity is wasted because the individuals are not given what they need to truly take ownership. Think of the "hapless Ms. Irlweg" in the United Breaks Guitars saga. She is faced with a customer who has one of those obvious cases that should be rectified but clearly falls outside the written policies. She is forced to simply fol-low the letter of the policy.

What she cannot do is really take ownership of the relationship she has with that angry customer. In an open organization, Ms. Irlweg would have the tools at hand to take ownership of that relationship. She would be aware of United's strategic principles as they relate to customer service. She would know enough about not only her job, but the job of the baggage handlers and the customer service reps that Mr. Carroll had already engaged. She would have a better sense of who Mr. Carroll was and where he was coming from—and probably the fact that he was a musician who posted videos to YouTube as a matter of course. She would be able to manage the interaction with the angry Mr. Carroll with integrity and respect. If she had all that going for her, then she would have been able to take appropriate action to resolve the issue. Ownership leads to appropriate action. Consequently, when ownership is not present, the result is inaction.

But the question remains, how do we ensure ownership is present in our organizations? The United example points to several different factors, but they can all be put in two categories: knowledge and skills. What did Ms. Irlweg need to know that would have enabled her to take appropriate action in that case? What skills would have helped her move forward rather than choosing the more passive (and destructive) path of just saying no? These are the questions you need to answer in your organization. For all your employees, from the CEO to the mail room clerk, what areas of knowledge need to be developed, and what areas of interpersonal skills need to be honed for more ownership to be present, where more people take appropriate action, rather than backing off?

Knowledge: Integrating Multiple Perspectives

Systems thinking comes in handy as you look at the knowledge challenge. It is a given that more knowledge is better. So you will not get far by simply imploring your people to expand what they know about the company, the customers, the suppliers, and so on. Yes, that is a good idea, but they really already know that. Ms. Irlweg thought she knew what she needed to know to do her job. It is not just about more knowledge, it is about knowing the right things about the system that can enable more action throughout the system.

One place to start is with your new employee orientation process. Every company is different, of course, but we are guessing that most follow a similar pattern, depending on the size of the company and the location of the employee in the hierarchy. The new employee is inundated with manuals, documents, and reports, and then is typically introduced to the various people around the organization who are supposed to provide the new employee with information related to their piece of the organization. You meet the leaders of other departments who orient you as to what their department does and how it interacts with your little world. You get maybe an hour with each person, and in larger organizations, you end up meeting with more people from each department. It is a huge volume of information, and most employees have difficulty assimilating it all. (This is largely due to a poor understanding of how adults learn, but that's a topic for another day.)

But even if they can assimilate all the information, we have to recognize that what the employees just got is the official employee orientation. This is important and necessary, but it is not sufficient. They also need the unofficial orientation. This is the orientation where people tell you the truth. Like the fact that Juan in product development is the only one in the department who responds to email within a month. Or the fact that marketing really calls the shots. Or that it's not the head of that department you go to when you need an answer, it is a couple of layers down.

Or even that your own supervisor has no intention of managing and is really just trying to make a lateral move to a better paying technical position two departments over. This is the kind of information that helps you understand who the real core group is in your organization. It helps you understand how things get done and where the capacity exists in the system, and where it does not.

This kind of unofficial orientation is critical for enabling action because it reflects a more comprehensive view of the system. Even though it is not scheduled, all employees always receive this orientation. The problem is, they only get it partially, or from a limited perspective. You tend to get the "truth" from people in slightly hushed conversations from coworkers who want to spare you the pain or frustration that they have experienced. As a result, the orientation you get is biased. Some of the information is valuable, insider information that you can use later to help you get things done, but some of it is biased information that blames other parts of the system for the current problems, often unfairly. The facilities department? Oh they just get taken to lunch by vendors but don't do any real work. The people on the line? The union ensures they can't work too hard, so don't rely on them. The management team? A bunch of people who couldn't cut it down here in the real world, so they stuck them in management.

Open organizations know that the information in the system contains bias, and they figure out ways for individuals to cut through it. They don't dismiss it. It would be a mistake to tell your people to ignore that biased information and insist that the party line is the only truth. But they make sure that the individuals in the system have access to enough information and insight from various perspectives to balance their perspective. They encourage open conversations about these issues so more people end up knowing more about the system. The truth is complex and dynamic, and open organizations have individuals who can handle that.

The American Institute of Architects, for example, have put their 2010–2015 strategic plan online on their website, with an accompanying toolkit that allows any of their components to map their programmatic activities to the mission, vision, and strategic goals of the national organization's plan.[11] The purpose is not to ensure that the hundreds of state and local chapters all do exactly as the national organization commands. The goal is to facilitate better conversations at the local level by injecting a clearer understanding of what is already happening at the national level. Better yet, they are using online technology to allow the results of those local conversations to be shared throughout the system. Instead of being worried about "exposing" contradiction among the component parts, they willingly shine light on the contradictions because they are part of the messy but important truth of what the local components want, need, and are currently doing.

---

11. "The American Institute of Architects - 2010–2015 Strategic Plan Toolkit, Strategic Plan." The American Institute of Architects - AIA Homepage. Web. 12 June 2011. <http://www.aia.org/about/initiatives/strategicplan/AIAB082451.

It's not only internal differences that can generate bias. Part of your orientation also has to include external perspectives. To have real ownership over a relationship with a customer or client, you must have a good understanding of what their experience is, but most organizations seem to be afraid of this. Organizations typically design their processes with internal needs in mind, more so than the needs of the customer (despite their marketing slogans about the customer coming first).

In the movie, *The Doctor*, William Hurt portrays an accomplished surgeon diagnosed with throat cancer. He is suddenly forced into a world he knows in great detail (hospitals and health care), but from the wildly different perspective of a patient. In the process, he realizes that the actions he takes as a doctor end up impacting patients in ways he could never see. As a result, at the end of the film, he has all the staff in the hospital actually go through and receive all the treatments that they prescribe to patients (including the rather uncomfortable ones) so that the staff truly knows what the patient is going through. This kind of knowledge promotes the type of ownership we are talking about here. It is knowledge that spurs appropriate action, as the doctor thinks twice about the procedure based on the impact it has on the patient, in combination with the medical diagnostic impact. It does not mean they will only prescribe comfortable procedures, but it does mean the doctors and staff can better address patients' fears and concerns. The whole interaction becomes more human. To get to the point where you can be this human, you need to do the types of things that enable your people to know much more than they do now about how the entire system works.

Another way to expand the knowledge needed for employees to effectively take ownership is to more fully and carefully disseminate information on organizational strategy. In the previous section about open process, we discussed a more decentralized, systems-thinking approach to strategy making that focuses on more ongoing strategic conversations. But even if you accomplish that, the results of those strategic conversations need to be shared. Strategy has to be much more broadly distributed to facilitate ownership. This is part of the logic behind Lencioni's idea of a "thematic goal" that we discussed in the context of reducing silo-based politics. The strategic clarity enables people to appropriately move across silo boundaries. That is ownership without needing total control.

Note, however, that to truly follow Lencioni's suggestion, you need to have one, singular thematic goal. This is a lot easier said than done. When it comes to disseminating strategy, organizations tend to either shoot too high or too low. One approach is to boil the strategy down to one or two sentences. We have all been a part of those painful word-smithing sessions where senior managers spend the better part of a day during an offsite retreat debating whether the strategy statement should say "customer-focused" or "customer-centric." Although the debate and discussions are well intentioned (it is good to understand clearly what strategically drives success), the resulting "strategy" that is disseminated ends up more like a fluffy marketing brochure. These in-the-clouds statements of strategy (our goal is to be the preeminent, customer-centric market leader, driven by innovation, quality, and a culture of respect) might have a motivational quality, but they don't help people make decisions. They don't help people take appropriate action. They are hard to translate at the level of implementation.

The common alternative, of course, is to offer all employees a copy of the inch-thick strategic planning binder that includes lengthy bulleted lists identifying specifically what each department is expected to achieve by the end of each quarter. These are designed to be more applicable at the level of implementation, and they are, but when they become that specific, they end up taking the decision making part out of the equation. This comes from the outdated mechanical model, where we assume we can design the perfect plan and then expect our constituent parts to each do their part. We know reality to be different because things rarely go according to plan, so we need our people to be able to take ownership. The 39 bullet points in the plan work against this.

What is missing from too many organizations is what we call middle-level thinking (in general, but also particularly in the area of strategy). Instead of relying on only the high-level platitudes and the in-the-weeds tasks on the to-do list, we need strategic clarity at the middle level. This is essentially what Lencioni is shooting for with his "thematic goals." They are time-limited and different from ongoing operational targets, which brings them down from the platitude level, but they also cut across all departments and are not unique to any one group, which brings them up out of the weeds. When you can provide middle-level strategic guides, you end up giving your employees enough guidance to make good decisions, without taking the decision making authority away from them. This is the essence of ownership.

Southwest Airlines seems to have been successful in communicating some middle-level strategic clarity to its employees. Southwest understands that its business is driven by customers who enjoy the flying process. Southwest actually realizes that it is better off not competing with the other airlines, but competing with passengers' automobiles. It wants to make flying cheaper, faster, and easier than driving. With that in mind, employees all know that turnaround times make the difference, so Southwest is famous for having its captains out side-by-side with the cleaning crew preparing the cabin for the next flight. That is ownership—not because the captain thinks she owns the airline but because the strategic clarity makes it easier for her to take appropriate action.

Zappos has gained notoriety for its strategic emphasis on customer service that enables call center employees to take ownership of their relationships with customers. There is no limit to the amount of time they can spend on a call with a customer. In 2009, Zappos posted to its company blog a video from Jennifer S., an employee who spent four hours on a single call from a customer with peripheral neuropathy, a condition where the individual cannot feel her own feet. Jennifer said she talked to the woman about the problems she had, like losing shoes without realizing it, or finding shoes that would fit around the bandages she had to wear. She said she also talked about dogs, and early life stories, and the ins and outs of the disease. "That's what I love about Zappos," she said. "There aren't any scripts and you can really connect to the customer."[12] That is ownership. That is more human.

Skills: Tools for Action

You don't hear a lot about "ownership skills" in the management literature because ownership is considered more of an internal attitude than a skill. We disagree. Ownership is about generating appropriate action, and you can develop this in your organization through skill building just as much as you can develop the dissemination of knowledge. The focus is on developing skills that prevent inaction and that help us move past the excuses we tend to generate as to why we cannot move forward. Many different skills can help with this, but three worth singling out are skills that we see are well developed in organizations with high levels of ownership: managing conflict, communicating across media, and managing your ego.

Managing Conflict

The dysfunction that most organizations have around conflict actually goes way beyond ownership. Conflict is frequently misunderstood and labeled as destructive and something to be avoided. That is not without reason, of course. We have all lived through some dreadfully negative conflicts in our work lives. These are the ones where relationships are permanently damaged, people quit or are let go, projects fail, money is lost, and time is wasted. But the problem is not the conflict itself. The problem is how we handle the conflict, particularly in the early stages. Too many of us lack the most basic conflict resolution skills, so when the conflict first emerges, we ignore it. It feels too risky because we are unsure how to handle it and fear the conflict will escalate. Of course by ignoring it, we usually guarantee it will escalate and become more difficult to manage in the future.

This is particularly damaging to our capacity for ownership in organizations. Ownership is all about taking appropriate action, and when we are afraid to deal with conflict in the system, we almost always choose inaction. We convince ourselves that avoiding it in the immediate term is a wise plan. It gives us time to get the facts straight, or get advice from a colleague about how to approach the conflict,

---

12. C., Jason. "Zappos CLT Longest Call Record, with Jennifer S." Blogs | Zappos.com. 23 Feb. 2009. Web. 11 Mar. 2011. <http://blogs.zappos.com/blogs/inside-zappos/2009/02/23/zappos-clt-longest-call-record-with-jennifer-s>.

or to clarify our thinking, or maybe to gather more allies on our side. There are certainly instances where taking your time, rather than reacting impulsively, is a good idea, but in most cases we are fooling ourselves. In most cases, we need to know how to move toward the conflict, address the issues calmly and clearly, and stay with it until both parties are in agreement about what to do next. A number of concrete skills in interest-based negotiation, communicating in challenging situations, and emotional intelligence can help people in your organization manage conflict more effectively.

When they do, you will see more ownership. What happens in your organization when an employee from one department walks into another department to give them feedback that the way they respond to customer complaints is ineffective? Better yet, what would happen if someone from another department walked into your department to say that your people are not managing the customer needs effectively? Here is our best guess as to your response: You would listen, express concern at the problem, maybe ask a weak question or two, and quickly end the conversation with a vague but pleasant promise to address the situation.

That is not ownership.

But that is what we see over and over again. We are afraid to confront the conflict. Even worse, after that person leaves your office, you would probably have a conversation with her supervisor about the inappropriateness of crossing departmental lines like that. This would get back to the person who brought over the feedback and ensure that she never did that again. So the next time she sees your people screwing up with the customers again, she will simply look the other way.

That is not ownership.

Do you see the problem? What if you had moved toward the conflict and really embraced it? What if you got excited to hear this feedback, and you quickly called together key people in your customer support team to have a meeting about it? What if you welcomed her feedback and asked her clarifying questions so you could learn more? You might discover in the process some performance issues on your team, so you would then address that conflict with the team members—not to "hold their feet to the fire" with accountability, but to problem solve with them about how to improve performance. (How sad is it, by the way, that we have workplaces where the idea of holding someone's feet to the fire is viewed as a good thing; this is an indicator that things have gone wrong.) You might end up with some new lines of communication being opened on a regular basis because your team did not realize that they have an impact on this other department. You can change your processes in ways that enables better customer service.

That is ownership. And managing conflict gets you there.

Communicating Across Media

Another skill that can build ownership capacity is the ability to communicate effectively in several different media. Training in communication skills is ubiquitous, but these programs rarely address the issue of communicating effectively in different media. Speaking in a meeting is different from writing a letter, and both are different from composing an email. Then we add social media to the mix and it gets very confusing. But the fact remains, the business world now involves all these kinds of communication. To say that you don't "do" Facebook is quickly becoming a career limiting move.

If you want ownership in your organization, then it serves you to build the capacity of your people to communicate across different types of media. The companies that were early adopters in social media faced this issue. As staff start blogging, or tweeting, or posting to Facebook, they probably have to learn what tone is appropriate, what kinds of information to share in what contexts, and how to speak in an authentic voice. Even the effective use of email, which is not a new communications technology by any means, is a skill that many employees need to develop.

With email, it is not even an issue of basic etiquette. True, plenty of people still don't have a clue how to use the bcc: field, and we still hear many stories of "reply all" disasters and the ridiculous overuse of the cc: field (particularly when there is conflict, actually), and general email overload has been written about for years now. But all of that is not nearly as damaging as our collective inability to understand how the use of email can actually sap our organizations of ownership.

George Bernard Shaw has been quoted as saying, "The single biggest problem with communication is the illusion that it has taken place." This is precisely the problem with email. In a busy world, we use email to shoot out a response or a question to someone because it gives us the illusion that we actually did work on that topic. We have an extensive to do list, and we manage it by plowing through our inbox and sending out the appropriate responses and questions. In some cases, our email responses are just what was needed. But in too many cases, our response only further delays the actual resolution of the issue or solving of the problem. In short, email gives us the perfect excuse for inaction. We get the illusion of having done work (yeah, I'm on that, I emailed him yesterday), but the problem is no closer to being solved.

That is not ownership.

To get real ownership, we need to develop our skill in discerning the difference between an issue that can be handled in an email exchange and one that cannot, and we need the discipline to take action when it's needed. Understanding how to behave in the Twitter or Facebook contexts enables the same kind of appropriate action. You don't post things just because the marketing department said we need to be on social media. You engage appropriately with members of the community. The more skilled you are at doing that, the more you can take appropriate action.

That is ownership, and skills in communicating across multiple media can get you there.

Managing Your Ego

This is really a subset of emotional intelligence, but the skill of keeping your ego in check is critical in today's social world. It's not that egos are evil. We all have them, and they certainly serve a function. But they can trip us up when it comes to the issue of ownership. Ownership is about taking action, and one thing that frequently stops appropriate action is the fear of being blamed, and that is about ego.

Psychology is not frequently welcomed as a tool in the workplace. It is considered "touchy-feely" and not appropriate for professional conversations. This is a shame, because we are all human beings, and humans have emotions, egos, and all that go with them. So part of our human condition is that we want to be loved. We want to be approved. We want to know that others are glad we are there and a part of their lives. We are social animals, so it is in our nature to care about this stuff.

Let us get back to the issue of being blamed. Because we have the human need to be loved and approved, we have a natural fear of being blamed. Our ego tells us this is a problem. If we screwed up, the other will blame us and not want to be in the relationship any more. We have to avoid that, so we of course try to keep from screwing up. Unfortunately, the easiest way to prevent screw ups is to avoid actually doing anything. If you do nothing, you can't screw up, and you can't get blamed. As such, this ego-based fear of being blamed can be a major driver of inaction. That is not ownership.

This means we are afraid to make a concession for an angry customer—what if the higher-ups don't agree with the call I am making? We are afraid to collaborate across departmental lines—what if they don't come through and I am left holding the bag? We are afraid to stand behind our employee who is experimenting with a new process—what if it doesn't work out and you get called on the carpet at the senior management meeting? Well, what if those things happen? Will you actually die or get fired? Probably not. This is where managing your ego comes into play. The ego sounds the warning alarm anytime the *potential* for blame exists, but we have to learn how to distinguish between low risk and high risk situations because the ego won't. Blame, in fact, is tolerable, and if you are smart, you can transform a blame conversation into one where everyone learns how to do it better next time because that will help enable appropriate action in the future.

That is ownership, and managing your ego can get you there.

Open For Business

We said at the beginning of the chapter that openness is the foundation of human organizations. It was really the first area where we saw the applicability of social media principles to management and leadership (as has been documented already by others; see Charlene Li's *Open Leadership,* cited in the "Must Read" section). But it is very important to understand that what we are talking about in this chapter—and in this book—goes way beyond social media. Being open is not only about having your employees participate in social media. It is also about a more fundamental decentralization of your culture, about embracing processes that better understand system dynamics, and giving your employees the knowledge and skills they need to take more ownership over their jobs. Feel free to employ social media in that campaign, but don't limit yourself to that kind of openness.

Being open is about humanizing your business. It is using decentralization, systems thinking, and ownership to generate sustainable business results—the kind of results that the machine-based organizations of our past have not been able to achieve. Then make openness your launching pad for humanizing in other ways, for example by creating an organization that is built on the principle of trust, which we cover in the next chapter.

Must Read

As you dig into making your company more open, with a decentralized culture, processes infused with systems thinking, and people who understand and take ownership, we recommend you take the time to read these three books in their entirety, in addition to this one. Li's *Open Leadership* is a good start on the culture/decentralization topic. Her book is written primarily for senior management, and it has a strongly defended position about letting go of control. Senge's *Fifth Discipline* is the Bible of systems thinking, so it should guide your work on creating more open processes (and has the added benefit of covering other aspects that can help you build a true learning organization). And Pfeffer and Sutton's *Knowing-Doing Gap* is the best book we know to get you thinking about why people don't do what we all know they should do—turning knowledge into action is at the heart of ownership.

> Li, Charlene. *Open Leadership: How Social Technology Can Transform the Way You Lead.* San Francisco: Jossey-Bass, 2010.

> Pfeffer, Jeffrey and Robert I. Sutton. *The Knowing-Doing Gap: How Smart Companies Turn Knowledge into Action.* Cambridge: Harvard Business School Press, 2000.

> Senge, Peter M. *The Fifth Discipline: The Art and Practice of the Learning Organization.* New York: Doubleday/Currency, 1994.

Get Started Today: Worksheet

Enough reading. Let's get started!

Download and print the worksheet accompanying this chapter at www.human-izebook.com.

In the end, we are activists. We love to think and write about these issues, and we have been for years. But we have never been content to let the words be the end of it. We want action. We want change. We want better organizations. We have always recognized that ideas by themselves are not going to change things. Our mantra: If you do what you've always done, you will get what you always got. So as we conceived of this book, we knew from the beginning that we would be designing a set of action-oriented worksheets that would help translate the ideas into immediate action.

There is one worksheet for each of the four main human elements we cover in the book: Open, Trustworthy, Generative, and Courageous. The worksheets are all structured in the same way. The first section helps you assess how open, trustworthy, generative, or courageous your organization is, and includes a quiz and some open-ended questions. In the second section we guide you through conversations with others in your organization about that topic. And the last section gets you going on an action plan.

The quiz for the Open worksheet is 30 questions where you give your organization a rating on a scale of one to ten about how open your organization is, covering all three levels of culture, process, and behavior. Do people closest to the problem have the authority to solve it? Are people all clear on policies and values in the organization? Can anyone call a meeting or participate in social media? At the process level, do external stakeholders have an impact on the work? Do departments actually work together? Is everyone involved at strategy at some level? In terms of behavior, can your people handle conflict? Is the orientation process up front and honest? Do people have what they need to do their job?

You will then add up the scores to get a sense of how open your organization is going into this process, though obviously the score is only a rough measure. The more important purpose of the quiz is to get you thinking about these topics and taking a closer look at what's going on in your organization because the next step is to have some conversations with others about these topics.

Because the change we are talking about here cuts across culture, process, and behavior, the change involved is, in the end, going to be substantial. Becoming a more open organization, or becoming more human as an organization on any of these dimensions, is not going to be a matter of a few tweaks. This means you won't be able to dictate the change through a memo or hire a few new people to make it happen. It needs to come from within, and that requires ongoing conversations. Obviously the conversations will vary somewhat depending on who is involved. If the senior management team convenes to talk about how to be more open as an organization, for instance, they will likely be talking about different topics than a group of middle managers might. They simply experience the issues differently. So in each of our worksheets, we provide some guidance about how to approach these conversations, depending on where you are in the organizational hierarchy. We provide this advice for the Open conversations:

Executives. This is a good opportunity to explore how open you are as a senior team. Without anyone else in the room, you might get some more openness in the conversation, so muster up some courage and focus on you (not the "others" who are "out there" and are the source of the problem). You'll need to be clear on the ground rules, particularly confidentiality. You'll need to come to agreement about what sort of "reporting out" to people outside the room there will be.

But it's also critical that people at other levels see you having conversations about openness, so you can't keep it all behind closed doors. Talk about these issues with middle managers and line staff. Don't dominate the conversation, and don't worry if your people aren't 100% open with you in the room. (You knew that would be the case, right?) Have the conversations anyway, and try to balance your questions and curiosity with your own open expression of your opinions. (Too many questions and not enough statements and your people will feel like they are being interrogated or tested; too many statements and not enough questions and it will feel like a mandatory lecture.)

Middle Managers. The challenge at this level is having too many different people and groups to talk to about being decentralized, embracing systems thinking, and supporting ownership. One approach would be to have conversations with people at the "exchange" points between and among departments. Middle levels can often be bottlenecks that prevent decentralization and that would be a good topic for a group of middle managers. But you may also want to engage groups of direct reports and really focus on the issue of ownership and facilitating right action. Or you could work with senior folks on clarifying the business case for being more open. Don't get paralyzed by your options. Pick some conversations to start and see where it leads you. Remember that you don't have to solve all these problems yourself. You need to connect the right people together and let them help solve the problem.

Front Line Employees. As a front-line employee, you may feel you don't have much (if any) say in taking action to make your organization more open. But you wouldn't have read this book if you didn't think you could do something. What areas do you have responsibility for that you can examine? Who at higher levels might support you in this endeavor? What kind of data can you present (say, for example, social media conversations) to make your case for more openness? As a front-line employee, we are assuming you are the closest to your organization's customers. Gather data from them, as well as from what similar organizations are doing, to help you make small breakthroughs. You don't have to convene formal meetings and conferences on this topic—just keep gathering data and sharing it with people that can use it with an eye on how to change behavior and processes in ways that matter.

As we said, the ultimate point here is to take action, so as you have your conversations and take your notes, make sure you start moving to the point where you can do something about it. The third section of the worksheet is a simple framework for action planning. We urge you to look at things that are already working well so you can do more of that, as well as making both small and large changes to introduce new openness to the organization.

Ultimately, the changes we advise throughout this book are necessary, they are possible, and they start with you. Don't wait for permission or the perfect timing. Are *you* ready? Go.

How to Be Trustworthy

	CULTURE	PROCESS	BEHAVIOR
TRUSTWORTHY ➡	transparency ➡	truth ➡	authenticity
HUMAN	**ORGANIZATION**		

"Technique and technology are important, but adding trust is the issue of the decade."

—Tom Peters, in Stephen M.R. Covey, *The Speed of Trust*

We have to be careful with the idea of trust because as an idea, it has achieved a status dangerously close to notions like motherhood and apple pie. When ideas become that universally (and sentimentally) favored, we tend to overlook them in the end and take them for granted. Trust is, of course, universal. All human beings have an experience of what trust is, and it usually connects closely to things we all value deeply. It is a central element of the parent-child bond, so we are destined to link trust with very deep feelings. Beyond our parents, though, we all also have extensive experience in our relationships with both trust and distrust. The good relationships are the ones based in trust, and the ones we are bitter about almost always have some kind of betrayal of trust in them. In every context, from family to workplace, trust is cited as a good, important thing.

Trust is often treated as a touchy-feely aspect of the workplace that would be nice to have in the abstract. Once every couple of years when you gather for a senior management retreat or staff team-building exercise, trust gets about an hour of air time as people solemnly promise to build trust in the organization because it is so important. Or worse, you'll actually be forced to fall backward into the arms of your teammates in the classic "trust fall" exercise. Then you go back to your offices and your emails and your deadlines and your existing culture, and it all goes back to the way it was. We tend to treat trust as some kind of emotional issue that requires our resolve, and that is a misunderstanding.

Emotions and resolve are part of it, but so are reason, analysis, negotiation, productivity, leadership, and time management. Trust is a much more fundamental part of organizations than we tend to admit. The reason is that trust (and distrust, for that matter) is used by everyone to meet a critical need in the business world: It reduces complexity. The act of trusting someone or a group of people is powerful because it removes certain outcomes from your internal contingency planning. When you trust someone, you don't have to spend time figuring out how to protect yourself against the potential opportunities the other person has to take advantage of you. That is the essence of trust: I trust you will not take advantage of me.

That simplifies things. When there is trust, a significant number of potential bad outcomes are basically taken off the table, and that simplifies how we work through our environment. There is a risk, of course, associated with this simplicity. There is no trust without risk. But the act of simplifying can be powerful. It allows you to get things done with increased speed and at lower costs.

Stephen M. R. Covey calls it the "trust dividend," and it allowed Warren Buffett of Berkshire Hathaway and Wal-Mart to conclude a $23 billion acquisition deal of Wal-Mart's transportation division in about one month, initially over a handshake.[1] It allows managers to focus on strategic challenges rather than checking up on employees. It allows organizational silos to share information with each other. It allows senior executives to directly confront each other when they disagree about important issues. Trust is a critical driver of organizational performance.

Trust has also been central to the growth of social media. At one level, it is a natural extension of social media being so open and decentralized. Social media represents a major shift in power and control, away from the center and toward the periphery. In many cases in social media, this shift seems almost accidental. We simply created the technology that allowed the decentralized masses to have more control than they used to, and they took advantage of it. There didn't seem to be some kind of epiphany where the central authorities suddenly decided to trust the masses.

---

1. Covey, Stephen M. R., and Rebecca R. Merrill. The Speed of Trust: the One Thing That Changes Everything. New York: Free, 2006. 15.

But after it happened, we realized that we had to trust them, at least more than we used to. We worried a lot that people would post inaccurate information or make inflammatory statements when we opened our websites to user control, but we discovered that those instances were greatly outnumbered by positive contributions; and when they did happen, the community tended to rise up to manage it. When we started trusting people to get things done, a whole lot more started getting done (look at Wikipedia). Where we used to look only to authoritative subjects for trusted information, we can now use social media to filter what we find valuable based on trusted relationships. We follow the links that come from people who we trust or at least whose judgment we trust. Think about how trust issues can quickly take down successful social media initiatives, like when followers discover that a thought leader is not actually writing his own tweets or when a blog is being ghost-written.

Companies that use social media effectively understand the importance of trust. Their social participation is often geared in a simple but powerful way to provide some evidence that they are doing what they said they were going to do.

General Motors' former Director of Global Social Media, Christopher Barger, pointed out in a 2010 interview with ZDnet that social media was a critical component of building trust for GM in the marketplace:[2]

> Being in social media and taking part in online communities is helping us win back some consumer trust a lot sooner than we might have without it. … The more people see us proactively using these networks and communities to take care of our customers, the more people will realize that we do care and do try to make things right when we get it wrong.

Just because trust has driven social media, however, does not make it a new concept in the business world. Edelman has been doing global research for years on how much people trust various institutions like businesses, nongovernmental organizations, the government, and the media. In 2011 when Edelman surveyed U.S. adults (see http://www.edelman.com/trust/2011/), less than half (46%) gave high marks on trust to business, which was a significant decline from 2010. (Though if it makes you feel any better, Media only hit 27%.) When Edelman's survey asked what matters when it comes to corporate reputation, 65% of respondents ranked "Company I can trust" eight or nine on a nine-point scale of importance. "Transparent and honest business practices" received an identical score, and the only answer with a higher score was about high quality products.

---

2. Leggio, Jennifer. "GM's Christopher Barger: 'We're Headed toward a Social Media Version of the Dotcom Bubble Burst' | ZDNet." Technology News, Analysis, Comments and Product Reviews for IT Professionals | ZDNet. 15 Dec. 2010. Web. 25 Apr. 2011. http://www.zdnet.com/blog/feeds/gms-christopher-barger-were-headed-toward-a-social-media-version-of-the-dotcom-bubble-burst/3369.

So, yes, trust matters in business, but people-centric organizations do not need survey results to convince them of that fact. People-centric organizations are trustworthy at their core. Trust is not something they turn to when economic times make it hard, in order to position themselves better against competitors. For people-centric organizations, trust becomes a platform from which they operate continuously by embracing the ideas of transparency, truth, and authenticity. Trust is not some highbrow ideal. It is real, concrete, and a regular part of business, from the executive suite to the front line. Like the other three elements of human organizations, being trustworthy plays out on all three levels of culture, process, and behavior.

Trustworthy Culture: Transparency

"I honestly believe that if Redfin were stripped absolutely bare for all the world to see, naked and humiliated in the sunlight, more people would do business with us."

—Glenn Kelman, CEO, Redfin, in "The See-Through CEO" by Clive Thompson, *Wired* Magazine 15.04

We all aspire to be trustworthy, and if we care even a little about our organizations, we would hold them to the same standard. We want organizations we can trust. A necessary component of trust is transparency. Whether it is an individual or an organization, when too much is kept behind a curtain of secrecy, then trust becomes difficult. Unable to see intentions or actions clearly, we naturally become suspicious of motives, and instead of trusting, we demand proof. Alternatively, when faced with transparency it is easier to trust, and we can give the other the benefit of the doubt.

Given the universal appeal of trust, then, it would make sense that we would embrace transparency in our organizations. The more that is visible, the easier it will be for employees, customers, members, and other stakeholders to trust us. To some extent, organizations do embrace transparency. Few want to be known as the organization that hides information and keeps everything secret. That's what evil governments do. That's what the bad corporations do before they are exposed and then convicted for their wrongdoings. No, we are not like those bad people. We embrace transparency and are happy to reveal appropriate information to show that our corporation (or government, nonprofit, family business, and so on) is one of the good ones. At least that's what we tell ourselves.

Then along comes social media and its demand for actual transparency. Suddenly we change our tune. What if one of our employees posts something we don't like? What if a commenter asks for information we are not willing to share? Is it really a good idea to let all this information out there? Maybe our employees should get permission from a central authority before posting online? While we say that we like trust and its cousin, transparency, when push comes to shove, it makes us nervous, and we often default to our more familiar and comfortable value: control.

This is something that people-centric organizations need to figure out. They will push past the high-level agreement about the value of trust and transparency and actually get clear on what transparency really means, at a practical level, where the proverbial rubber meets the road. This is hard work. Human organizations always leverage the power of trust, and this requires more transparency than we have been used to. Trustworthy organizations embrace transparency. They get the information that matters to the people and groups to whom it matters, and, importantly, they know why it matters.

That is the essence of transparency: sharing information. Organizations that want to create a culture of transparency must figure out how to do the work of sharing information more effectively. This is not a binary issue: sharing information or not sharing. It is subtle and complex and requires hard work. As in all organizational cultures, it shows up at the three levels of walk, talk, and thought.

Walking the Walk: Strategic Transparency

Being transparent is easier said than done. The simple answer is "share more." And that is part of it. Transparent cultures absolutely do share more than traditional organizational cultures that control information and release things on a "need to know" basis. The problem, however, is that most of us, frankly, have spent much of our work lives in traditional cultures. Even though we may have personal beliefs about the value of transparency and sharing information, when the moment hits where we have the opportunity to be transparent, we too often hold back. We check with someone else first, provide only part of the information, or explain that we are not allowed to share that kind of information.

So, starting an initiative to change culture with an announcement about the value of transparency and the directive to employees to "share more" is not going to get you very far. It's not an on/off switch where you go from being not transparent to being completely transparent. We don't expect Coca-Cola to share the formula for its soft drink in a spirit of transparency. There are still things that are kept secret, and that is okay. But that is why the blanket directive of sharing more information is not helpful. Most understand that proprietary formulas behind a company's competitive advantage are not to be shared, but what's appropriate to share may not be as clear. Can we share salary information internally? If a customer asks why a major program has been changed, are we allowed to tell her the strategic thinking behind our move? People need a clearer understanding of what transparency really means. The meaning will vary across different stakeholder groups in the system—customers need a different kind of transparency than investors do. But for any group, transparency has three elements to it:

- What do we share?

- With whom do we share it?

- Why does sharing it matter?

Clear answers on these three questions move the conversation from simple transparency to a more important idea: strategic transparency. We don't share more information because transparency is generically good. We share more information because we understand how the information will be leveraged by others in the system to generate a result that is good (or at least better) for everyone involved. We know what we're sharing, with whom, and why.

Take the issue of compensation data. A few years ago, coauthor Jamie Notter suggested on his blog that organizations might want to be totally transparent with their salary data (internally at least). The reaction in the comments was negative—that this was perhaps a good idea in theory but wouldn't work in practice, or that it would create hard feelings and destructive competition among employees. Jamie wrote several posts on the topic, and each one garnered roughly the same types of comments each time, describing the idea as "insanely bad" and concluding that salary information was the exclusive purview of an employee, his family, and the boss—and that's it. Even Don Tapscott's book *The Naked Corporation*, which explores transparency in great detail, dismisses salary information up front as something that should be kept secret.

The successful grocery chain Whole Foods, however, would disagree. Since the 1990s, any Whole Foods employee can look up the salary information of any other employee, and teams within the same store can see how their bonuses were calculated.[3] More than just compensation data is available. Information on daily store sales, team sales, and profits for each store are all available to any employee. Part of the reason for doing this was philosophical. This was part of an overall philosophy at Whole Foods of a high-trust organization driven as much by a mission of creating a better world ("Whole Foods, Whole People, Whole Planet") as it is by the goal of building a successful and profitable company. But the other part is profits. When team members are able to see the performance of other teams, they are better able to make shifts in their own work that will generate better results. When individuals see who in the company is making what kind of money, they can make choices about their personal development and career path, which leads to more effective employees. Whole Foods shares this specific information because they see how it can be leveraged by groups within the company to generate better results. That is strategic transparency.

---

3. Hamel, Gary. The Future of Management. Boston, MA: Harvard Business School, 2007. 75.

We are not arguing that sharing salary data internally is a "best practice." (And you know how we feel about those.) But we do argue that if you choose not to share it, you should truly understand why you have made that choice. And the answer "because things might go bad if we share it" is not adequate. A culture of transparency—of strategic transparency—holds itself to a higher standard around sharing and not sharing information. Although not everything needs to be shared, a trustworthy organization puts some effort into figuring out how to share the right information with the right people to get results. Just like open source software companies have realized that sharing the source code with a community of passionate users generates a better product, organizations need to intentionally pull back the curtain in areas so employees, customers, or other stakeholders can get information they need to generate better results for the system.

In another example, the Private Client Group of Prudential securities implemented what they call a "transparency architecture" designed to create more openness among all stakeholders, both internal and external. They share financial, strategic, and operational information with all their financial advisors, which enables them to better handle situations as they arise. For Prudential, this resulted in increased employee retention. After implementing the transparency architecture, the annual attrition rate dropped from the historical annual rate of 23% down to 11%. Local branches, which used to complain that the headquarters just "doesn't get it" (like nearly every other large, distributed organization), changed to become much more engaged with the company.[4]

The nature of that transparency architecture varies by organization, but that is where you need to focus to walk the walk of a transparent culture. Make a list of the things that are currently controlled and kept behind barriers and think through whether the release of that information could be leveraged to produce better results. Obviously you have to weigh both the pros and cons of being more transparent, and certainly you have to stay aware of privacy concerns and legal restrictions on what can be shared and what cannot.

But given how closed our organizations have been historically, there are likely to be a number of opportunities to increase transparency in ways that can improve results. When your senior management team engages in annual strategy conversations, what gets shared with the whole organization? Obviously the results get shared—a carefully edited strategy document that reflects the end point of those conversations. But what if there were some critical conversations—where the team had to work through extensive conflict about the strategic value of two different departments, for example? Many organizations would be afraid to share that kind

---

4. Tapscott, Don, and David Ticoll. The Naked Corporation: How the Age of Transparency Will Revolutionize Business. New York: Free, 2003. 104.

of information—it would be considered part of the "confidential" senior management conversations.

This makes perfect sense, but it is a potentially huge missed opportunity. They would be missing the more subtle but important element of what the other senior executives thought about the strategic value of each department. That is valuable feedback, and there are scarcely any opportunities for the employees (outside the most senior levels) to get access to that information. It might help them to realize they need to share more information about what they do to correct the executive's view. It might represent insight they did not yet have about their department's work, and they could use that insight to actually change what they are doing to be more effective. Most organizational cultures shy away from sharing that subtle feedback. It is either too difficult (not enough time) or too sensitive (someone might take offense).

But trustworthy organizations learn to enable that kind of strategic transparency so they get information into the hands of the people who will use it to create better performance. It should be clear, also, how strategic transparency is valuable in open organizations that have decentralized cultures, because it is focused on increasing the capacity for more effective action at all levels of the system.

Sharing the nuances of a strategic conversation at the executive level is just one example of an opportunity to be more transparent. In your organization you need to do some kind of inventory of these opportunities and then piece them together into an overall transparency architecture that doesn't reveal everything to everybody, but intentionally provides more extensive access throughout the system to the information, thinking, analysis, data, and insight that can produce better results.

Of course, the architecture also needs to be supported and reinforced by the behavior of individuals throughout the system. When asked for information, people need to share it. When given information, people need to use it to solve problems and increase performance of the system. A culture of transparency grows out of your employees' discipline to share more and do more with what they get. We talk more about that later in the two sections on process (telling more truth) and behavior (more authenticity), but you also need to reinforce the behaviors around sharing and problem solving to support a culture of transparency.

Talking the Talk: The Power of Consistency

In Chapter 6, "How to Be Open," we emphasized the maxim of "less is more" when it came to talking the talk of a decentralized culture. The more you try to convince people your culture is decentralized, the more it sounds like the center is calling the shots. With a culture of transparency, though, almost the opposite is true. Talking the talk is critical in a transparent culture because the end goal here—being a trustworthy organization—is driven by consistency. It is a basic tenet of trust. When your actions are consistent with your words, you are more trustworthy. Inconsistency breeds suspicion.

So if the goal is to establish a culture of transparency, the actions of your transparent culture (your transparency architecture) must be matched with consistent statements and messages about transparency.

In organizational terms, this means if you want a culture of transparency, you not only must be transparent, you have to tell everyone that you are transparent as well. Through that consistency you will become more trustworthy as an organization. So how do you do it? The first step is to work on making your values more visible.

You may already have some kind of company values statement. They are popular. Googling "company values statement" gives you 84 million hits to scan through if you want to see examples. Having a published values statement does not make your organization transparent by default, but trying to convince someone that you have a transparent culture without telling people what your values are is going to be a tough sell. Certainly if you are actively building a transparent culture, then you want to have language up for all to see about your commitment to transparency and sharing information. But beyond that, it is helpful to simply take a clearer stand on who you are as an organization and who you are not. The words "transparent" and "clear" are synonyms for a reason. The clearer you are about your organizational identity, the more consistent your claims of transparency will be.

There's one problem, though. When you look at company websites to determine their values, they often sound identical. Consider this excerpt from a company values statement:

> As a company, and as individuals, we value integrity, honesty, openness, personal excellence, constructive self-criticism, continual self-improvement, and mutual respect.[5]

It is a fine values statement, reflecting values that pretty much anyone would admire. But that, actually, is part of the problem. If your values statement stops at merely staking a claim to universally admired values, it isn't really serving the function of clarifying as it should. The preceding statement above belongs to Microsoft. Does that really help us understand the organization better?

Maybe a little, but it would require much more explanation than that. If the goal is consistency, the high level platitudes don't cut it because they give us nothing to measure against. As a customer or a business partner of Microsoft, how can I test

---

5. "About Microsoft: Your Potential. Our Passion." Web. 25 Apr. 2011.
   <http://www.microsoft.com/about/en/us/default.aspx>.

my experience with them against the value of integrity or personal excellence? Unless I happen to have a really bad experience with someone there, they are sure to pass the test, because a platitude is hard to prove wrong. Being clear about your values, particularly if you are trying to be transparent, means taking a bit more risk and sharing in more detail what you are really all about.

Whole Foods, mentioned earlier as an example of a company walking the walk of transparency, is also very clear and vocal about its values. The values statement on the Whole Foods website (www.wholefoodsmarket.com/values/corevalues.php) is more than 1,000 words and is divided into seven sections, including "Supporting Team Member Happiness and Excellence," and "Creating Ongoing Win-win Partnerships with Suppliers," not to mention the not-so-warm-and-fuzzy "Creating Wealth Through Profits and Growth." Each section spells out in detail what it means, and the first two talk about transparency specifically. In supporting team members, they talk about how they provide open and timely information (including the annual compensation report) because they feel that knowledge is power and that team members need information relevant to their jobs. In their supplier section they talk about "farm to fork" transparency regarding production, planning, ingredients, and safety to ensure they bring safe and high quality products to market. These types of statements are clear and connect what they believe and value (transparency and openness) with what they actually do, and that makes it real.

Whole Foods also connects its organizational values and identity very directly with its transparency architecture, and that is the next step in talking the talk of a transparent culture. Just like you are taking a stand on who you are as an organization, you have to make it clear that transparency is part of your culture. You have to tell everyone that you will do the work of transparency, and you have to tell them before they need to know it. Your policies should spell it out clearly. Your new employee orientation should talk about it, and your managers should mention it frequently in their interactions with their direct reports. It's not enough to say it in the policies and the annual report and then hope everyone reads it. You need to weave it into the stories that get told around the boardroom table. You need to revisit it as you engage in a post-mortem analysis of a project.

The reason is simple: To create consistency across words and actions, the more words there are, the more easily the consistency is acknowledged. Look for ways to point out to employees and stakeholders how you have set up your transparency architecture. Even if you think they know it, find a way to tell them again.

Transparency is by its very nature a risky venture, and that is true for all levels in the organization. There is often hesitation. So the more you communicate it, the more comfortable people will be to be a part of it. Employees coming in to your organization or new business partners you are engaging as part of the business will likely come from environments not rooted in transparency, so the work of overcommunicating the cultural norms is important to help these new employees and partners to engage in different behavior.

Thought: Assumptions Behind a Culture of Transparency

Transparency, as you might have guessed, is not a culture that you can fake. You can't purchase it from a branding agency. Although you always have to identify and change underlying assumptions when working on culture change, it is particularly important to get it right when you are trying to elevate the importance of transparency. If you aren't authentically behind them, it will obviously become visible quickly. Because this is so important with transparency, we also cover in this section the additional challenge of identifying existing cultural assumptions that are actually destructive and lurking in the background. They are not the assumptions and values you see referenced in your official values statement—you may not even be fully aware of how prevalent they are, but they can make culture change difficult.

We will start with the assumptions that truly support transparency.

Knowledge Is Power

A transparent culture goes hand in hand with a decentralized culture because it recognizes the distributed power in the system that is unleashed when knowledge is shared. The purpose of transparency is to allow the right people to get access to the right information, and when they do they can accomplish more. So an underlying assumption of a transparent culture is that knowledge is power and power is multiplied when it is distributed. Previous organizational models tended to value the consolidation of both knowledge and power. You kept knowledge in the center because that's where it could be controlled and manipulated. In transparency, you are actively looking for ways to share that knowledge outside the center. You want information to be liberated. You want people on the outside to get access to information on the inside. (And "inside" could mean within the organization or within a specific team or department.)

No Risk, No Reward

There is no trust without risk, so there is no culture of transparency without risk as well. Transparency means exposing the truth and showing more than we are used to showing, and that is always risky. It feels risky to the people at the top of the organizational chart because they feel like they are pulling the curtain back on their part of the office. It also feels risky to middle managers and line employees because (a) the rules seem to have changed and (b) with transparency comes responsibility. So it is important to support a culture of transparency with the underlying assumption that risk is a good thing. Risk is needed to reap the reward of a trustworthy organization. It is the risk of transparency that allows you to take advantage of the speed of trust.

Responsibility Matters

You really shouldn't aim for a culture of transparency if you are ashamed of what exists behind your curtain. Implied in transparency as a goal is the understanding that you generally have your ducks in a row and do not have anything to hide. So really, before you think about transparency, make sure you have your house in order. That means that one of the cultural assumptions underlying transparency is that responsibility matters. It is not good enough simply to have a company that makes a profit and does not visibly violate the law. You have to have an organization rooted in responsibility and built on clear values.

One reason Whole Foods is comfortable being transparent about individual compensation is that it started with a clear set of intentions and values about how it pays people. Its policy is to ensure that the ratio between the highest paid person in the company and the lowest paid person in the company is no more than 19:1 (in the average Fortune 500 company the ratio is more than 400:1).[6] Think about your organization and how strongly you stand behind responsibility. If there is too much leeway—the feeling that you can get away with things because no one will know— you should work on that before you start building the transparency architecture.

We Can Work It Out

Transparency is not the easy path. With transparency comes difference, conflict, and contradiction. This, however, is a good thing because there is no growth without conflict. Transparency shines a brighter light on the whole system, which means differences that were before obscured are now made clear. So underlying a culture of transparency is the basic idea that when differences or conflict emerge, we will be able to work through them. If you are petrified of conflict, you won't like transparency. If difference is not welcomed, transparency is going to be abrasive. People in the organization need to work on their approach to difference and conflict before they will be willing to embrace a culture of transparency.

The Dark Side

When you are working on organizational culture, it is critical to acknowledge that along with all the aspirational work where you try to create the ideal culture, you also need to confront the less idealistic side of things. These are the assumptions

6. Hamel, The Future of Management. 75.

and philosophies that are rarely acknowledged in cultures but exist nonetheless, and actually get in the way of achieving our ideal culture. They are not purely negative—like an assumption that people are inherently evil. They are merely contradictory to our aspirations. For example, as we explore both decentralized and transparent cultures, it is important for each of us (and our organizations as a whole) to be clear about where we stand about human self-interest. Will people go after their self-interest over everything else? Will they take advantage of us if we expose ourselves through transparency, for example? Some cultures will say yes. It does not show up on their corporate values statement, of course, but it is real, and when you look closely, you can see it in policies and practices. We are mentioning this "dark side" of cultural assumptions here, but it is something worth exploring in all four of the elements of human organizations.

We say that knowledge is power, but do we have unspoken assumptions about the trustworthiness of lower level employees? Would we really trust them with any power? Are they the ones who are likely to abuse power if it were given to them? Do they have the common sense to use knowledge appropriately? You don't have to give them control over the whole operation, but you should take a hard look at the assumptions you have about their capacity for responsibility and effectiveness.

We say "No risk, no reward," but are we really confident that risk is a good thing? Do we have assumptions that tell us to follow the safe route and grow incrementally rather than deal with the ups and downs of more risky ventures? Going after the speed of trust by accepting risk makes logical sense, but we have to make sure that we don't have deeper preferences for safety that get in the way of pursuing our ideal.

For every underlying cultural assumption that we talk about in this book, be prepared to also explore and challenge contradictory assumptions and commitments that get in the way of the direction you have chosen.

Trustworthy Process: Truth

"Organizations need candor the way the heart needs oxygen."
—Warren Bennis, *Transparency: How Leaders Create a Culture of Candor*

Pulling back the curtain to provide organizational transparency will end up backfiring if people don't tell the truth. As we start to talk about ongoing processes that support a culture of transparency, we need to dig a little deeper into the idea of truth in our organizations. At the process level, we need to create more opportunities for people to speak the truth in our organizations. How do we design structures that allow truth to be spoken, particularly across levels in the hierarchy? How do we change the rules of engagement internally so the whole truth gets spoken as we deal with organizational issues, particularly conflict? How do we facilitate honesty in our ongoing dialogue with entities outside our organizational boundaries? Trustworthy organizations answer these questions and design processes that support more truth.

Unfortunately, truth is like trust—it's a mom and apple pie feel-good idea that everyone can support as a concept, even if they are not so good at it in practice. No one is going to stand up and say "our organization does not value the truth," at least not publicly. But that doesn't mean that most organizations have truth wired into their DNA. This universal commitment to truth (as a concept) does not actually serve us, because in making it a universal commitment, we also tend to oversimplify it.

We love truth because we define it simply as "not lying." In the United States this has been reinforced by our national myth of George Washington as a boy confessing "I cannot tell a lie" as he admitted to chopping down his father's cherry tree. While we can all admire young George's courage in owning his misdeed, when we frame the truth as simply not telling a lie, we are setting the bar way too low. It's easy to not lie—you simply tell about half the truth. For example, you could express some sort of vague concern with the direction of the project without telling your colleague that the idea is bad and is going to be a waste of time and effort. You could agree with your boss that the governmental regulatory efforts are going to impact your new initiative, but don't mention that you think taking resources away from other areas to focus on government relations is a huge mistake. You could have that conversation with your direct report about her performance issues but don't be too direct about it (or the consequences of not improving) because you don't want to be too harsh. These half way conversations are dysfunctional—they misguide people, avoid important issues, and tolerate poor performance—but none of them is a lie. This allows us to maintain our commitment to the oversimplified idea of truth without confronting the dysfunction in our internal conversations.

We also love truth because we like narrowing things down to just the "facts." There is nothing wrong with facts, and they are definitely a part of truth, but so are the complex and subjective views of different parts of the system. You are not going to resolve the dysfunction between two departments in your organization, for example, simply by narrowing things down to just the facts. It's always more complicated than that and you need a mix of convergent (fact-finding) and divergent (open-ended) conversations to really solve the problem. By sticking to our oversimplified insistence on deciding based on facts (the truth), we consistently mishandle the complex problems that need to be solved.

We also love truth because we love personal integrity. Like facts, there is absolutely nothing wrong with integrity, but our focus on personal integrity when we talk about truth unwittingly allows us to avoid the conversations we really need to have about truth. Truth becomes almost exclusively a matter of integrity. When people in our organization don't tell the truth, or even only tell half-truths, we attribute it to a lack of integrity. Those people lack the strength or the resolve to do what is right. Although this is certainly the case some of the time, this view completely undervalues the power of culture and process in organizations. Culture trumps integrity almost every time, and so does process. People who possess integrity often find themselves behaving in ways that are not entirely consistent with their own values when the existing culture or processes don't support it.

We have to embrace the complexity of truth if we're going to use it in our organizations. And to use truth, we need to infuse it into our organizational processes in structural, internal, and external contexts.

Structural: Beyond Blowing Whistles

Truth became a hot topic in the business world after the meltdowns at companies like WorldCom and Enron in the early 2000s. We marveled at the extensive lying and fraud and celebrated the whistle-blowers that exposed the wrong-doings. One public consequence was the Sarbanes-Oxley Act of 2002, which established new rules for how companies handle their accounting practices and disclosure and includes protection for whistle blowers. While not applicable to privately held companies, Sarbanes-Oxley has had an impact on nonprofit organizations, which must now at least disclose on their tax returns whether they have a formal whistle blower policy. So believe it or not, the federal government wants more truth spoken in our organizations.

Certainly that is one way to get truth out of your organization: Mandate it and build it into the structure. Strict policies and controls on disclosure will force some truth and is an important part of preventing fraud or other ethical violations. You can also build it into specific positions within your hierarchy, such as a neutral ombudsman, with whom people could raise issues that they might be afraid to raise within the established chain of command. This structural solution can allow more people to speak the truth, raise issues, and start important conversations within an organization that can contribute to making the organization more trustworthy.

But these kinds of structural solutions are fairly low impact when it comes to supporting truth in an organization. If all you have is a way for people to expose fraud, then, yes, you are supporting some truth telling, but that typically is created to deal with exceptions, rather than everyday situations. What about all those situations that are not the worst-case scenario, where core values are not being violated or federal laws are not being broken? To grow a truly trustworthy organization, you are going to need more truth spoken than you currently have, and there are ways to do that on the structure side. But it might require a challenge to something that most people seem to consider untouchable in organizations: reporting relationships.

Although there are some examples of radically flat organizations, most have at least some hierarchy and with that comes reporting relationships. Within a chain of command, people report up the chain, and that reporting relationship is used to manage performance. Logic dictates that these reporting relationships exist within departments, where the "superiors" will have the substantive expertise necessary to evaluate the performance of the direct reports. Viewed in the abstract, there is nothing particularly wrong with reporting relationships, and they serve some obviously important functions.

But it may not be obvious that the way organizations typically manage reporting relationships can negatively impact the truth, particularly when it comes to managing performance issues. The problem here is actually illuminated by systems thinking, which we discussed in Chapter 6. Our departments are all interrelated parts within a system, so as we go to solve performance problems, it is highly unlikely that all the reinforcing loops or balancing loops that we need to address exist only in one department. If someone falls down in terms of performance, it has an impact outside just his department. If your department is the one impacted, you would likely go to the person's supervisor to raise the issue. It is normal to stay within the chain of command, and it could be viewed as inappropriate to go directly to the person in question. Again, at one level this makes sense. That employee and his supervisor can work out the details of the performance issue, which could very well involve details of that department's work with which you are not familiar. At another level, however, the way we structure these conversations discourages truth in important ways.

First, it creates an unhealthy dynamic in organizations called triangulation. When you have a problem with Person A, instead of going directly to that person, you go to Person B and complain about it. Complaining might make you feel better, but the problem is nowhere near being solved, and in your conversation with this third party, you've probably expanded upon the story of the problem without involving the other, more direct party. This blurs the truth, and it helps you to feel like you've done something about the situation, when in fact you've likely only made it worse. Of course Person A has likely been doing the same thing and is expanding his internal story about the problem without working out the real issues between the two of you. As people consistently triangulate and avoid the direct conversations about the organizational problems, the more the truth gets muddied with assumptions, stories, exaggerations, and unexpressed allegations. The result is typically heightened drama, low morale, and in worst-case scenarios, high turnover.

Ironically, our strict reporting relationships actually encourage triangulation. Let's say that Person A is in the marketing department and is not performing up to expectations. You are not in the marketing department, but Person A's work issues are definitely impacting you and your work. Instead of going to Person A, you go to his supervisor (Person B) to raise the issue, who then is responsible for meeting with Person A to solve the problem. While this makes sense and might be standard protocol, this kind of constant triangulation can be damaging to the system. It is a perpetual organizational game of "operator," where the problem is whispered to one person who whispers it to another who might understand it in a completely different way. Each single instance seems fairly minor, but the constant pattern is what is most damaging. This reinforces the idea that departments don't talk to each other, and it can often fuel bad blood between departments. ("I told Person B in that stupid marketing department about that problem with Person A, but of course nothing changes!")

Part of the solution here is simply redefining the roles and responsibilities of supervisors when it comes to performance issues and problem solving. Supervisory responsibility has traditionally been framed as an issue of control and ownership (and not ownership as in "enabling right action" as we discussed in Chapter 6, but ownership as in control, "it's mine, stay away"). Drawing that firm boundary around managing the performance of "your" people creates the pattern of triangulation. One way to change this pattern would be to shift the emphasis from control to facilitating. As the supervisor, Person B's role is actually to facilitate problem solving and performance improvement of "her" employee (Person A), which would involve bringing you and Person A together as part of the process. This would facilitate more direct feedback; you would actually have to talk directly with Person A about the issue. In fact, if other departments were impacted by this issue they might be a part of the conversation as well. Instead of "running interference" for your employees, as a supervisor you are constantly facilitating the right conversations across different departments to ensure problems are solved and "your" people are doing what they need to do for the system to thrive. That is how you can make subtle adjustments to structural elements of your organization that have a high impact on how truth is supported.

Internal: Conflict Is a Good Thing

Our best opportunity for bringing more truth into our organizations is in the realm of internal process. Internal processes are at the heart of how we do our work together, including how we communicate with one another while working. Obviously this is where the truth will come out (or not). When we do our performance review process, is the truth spoken? When we have meetings (particularly senior management meetings), do the issues get fully explored or do we hold back and settle into our comfortable pattern of speaking half-truths? If you want to create a trustworthy organization, you need to redesign your internal processes in ways that facilitate more truth telling among your employees.

To do this, however, you will invariably confront a topic that is not popular in organizations: conflict. Most organizations are conflict avoiders. There are certainly exceptions, but if you look at the fat middle of the bell curve when it comes to organizations in terms of how they approach conflict, you find many organizations avoiding conflict at every turn. It's not that everyone hates conflict. Some do, of course. These are the types who would rather get a root canal than confront someone with whom they have a disagreement. And many people in any organization simply dislike conflict. They don't like the negative energy, or the emotional charge, or would just rather people get along. But there are perhaps an equal number of people in any organization who tend to like conflict. They may not like the really angry or destructive conflict, but they would rather confront issues as opposed to ignoring them and letting them fester. The sooner you confront the conflict, the sooner it's over. And yes there are people in every system who show up to work, and if there isn't any conflict, they'll create some. These are the types who love conflict. They love the energy, and they feed off it.

Despite this broad range of feelings about conflict, however, the tendency organizationwide almost always skews toward avoidance. Certainly those who hate conflict will avoid it, but even those who like it often want it to be resolved quickly. This actually can be a form of avoidance, because they end up avoiding the deeper, stickier issues in favor of an early (but incomplete) resolution. The result is an organization that has built a series of processes that make it acceptable (even encouraged) to avoid conflict in the early stages, assuming it will either work itself out or can be worked out later if it turns out to be an ongoing problem.

This is a recipe for dysfunction. Conflicts are easiest to resolve when they are young, before they have been blown out of proportion, involve other departments, or have generated ongoing resentment. But this requires addressing the conflict and confronting it directly, early on. In other words, it requires speaking the whole truth. That first moment when you feel like your colleague is trying to take the meeting in a direction that doesn't make sense to you, or that first email where it feels like the tone is more confrontational than cooperative, or that first instance where it seems like the performance of Person A is impacting the results of your team—that is when you need to be able to put the whole truth out there and address the conflict.

Unfortunately, our processes are not designed to support that behavior. We have already pointed out the structural problems with performance management, but it also shows up on the procedural end in our performance reviews. Our review processes seem to be designed more by lawyers trying to document separations rather than leaders who care about improving performance in systems. Samuel Culbert, a business professor at UCLA, doesn't pull any punches in his assessment of performance reviews:

> To my way of thinking, a one-side-accountable, boss-administered review is little more than a dysfunctional pretense. It's a negative to

corporate performance, an obstacle to straight-talk relationships, and a prime cause of low morale at work. Even the mere *knowledge* that such an event will take place damages daily communications and teamwork.[8]

We design the process (in theory) to allow a supervisor and a direct report to work together on ways to improve the direct report's performance. Fine in theory, but everyone knows that you need to have "good" performance reviews if you want a raise, a promotion, or, at the very least, to keep your job. That goal of having a good review ends up clashing with the goal of improving performance because it pushes the direct report to (a) not be too up front about performance problems and (b) not push back too hard against the (always subjective) views of the superior (for fear of being dinged on the "can't take criticism" box). It actually discourages the airing and confronting of conflicts. We force our conversations about these potentially contentious issues into a tiny window based on a random organizational calendar, rather than encouraging supervisors and employees to address performance issues when they happen. From a systems thinking perspective, it is a perfect "shift the burden" dynamic, where instead of creating a system where problems are solved as they happen, we all can defer them to the later and more "appropriate" setting of the performance review, which fools us into thinking we are handling a problem, when in fact it is simply getting worse.

An even more basic context where our processes are designed to actually weaken our ability to deal with conflict is the staff meeting. Actually, regardless of the conflict issue, most of us need to reinvent our staff meetings. Like strategic planning, they are a process that we universally hate, but also universally practice. Staff meeting processes obviously vary widely, but they typically share the same flaw: They lack clarity of purpose. We all know that meetings are required so we can share information among team members. We all know that to make a group decision (or get buy-in for a decision), we need to have a meeting. We need meetings to plan activities, learn about our operating environment by hearing perspectives of others, break down silos, coordinate with other departments, and demonstrate and share our expertise with our colleagues. Many staff meetings mix all those purposes together, resulting in a three-hour mess that is boring, repetitive, and even confusing.

So why does every staff meeting have to do *all* of that? Project teams, for example, need to share information with each other so each team members can be aware of what the others have accomplished. That particular need could be met with a series of regular but extremely brief meetings, where team members report on their progress with little or no discussion. Or, better yet, create some online processes

---

8. Culbert, Samuel A. "Get Rid of the Performance Review! - WSJ.com." Business News & Financial News - The Wall Street Journal - Wsj.com. 20 Oct. 2008. Web. 25 Apr. 2011. <http://online.wsj.com/article/SB122426318874844933.html>.

where basic information can be shared and reviewed prior to meeting in person. You might even be able to skip the meeting altogether. The trick here is to clarify the purpose of the meeting and design the process to serve that purpose. (Form follows function.)

But here's the problem. The way we typically design meetings (where the purpose is vague or has too many pieces to it) actually discourages us from dealing with conflict. When conflict arises, it is typically viewed as a potential time suck, and we have all become weary of those three-hour meetings. Not wanting the meeting to be prolonged, we almost always avoid the conflict and defer the tougher conversations. And by "defer" we mean "ignore forever" because the next time we convene for a meeting we will once again have to endure the unstructured around the world game before we could get back to the tough issues. It may not have been intended, but the result is clear: Now conflict is routinely avoided and people get in the habit of not speaking the full truth in staff meetings.

The alternative is to structure meetings with more intention. As we mentioned above, basic information sharing can be done in a series of very brief meetings, or even by email or online. For the meetings where you need an active discussion, it is not hard to design the process so the discussion items are identified and prioritized before the discussion begins. That way, when you actually get into a particular discussion and conflict emerges you are more likely to stick with it because this portion of the meeting was actually designed to give time to solving the tactical problem at hand. Should the conflict turn out to be deeper than you thought (maybe hitting on some more challenging strategic issues), you can always schedule a later meeting to deal with that issue alone.

In fact, you should be scheduling more meetings like that, particularly when the issues become strategic rather than tactical. Strategic conflicts are incredibly important, but they tend to get brushed under the rug like all the rest, even at the level of the senior management team. The reason is basically the same: We're tired of these long meetings. So when big strategic issues emerge, schedule a separate meeting for them that blocks at least two hours, and assign people to do homework, reporting to the group before the meeting. In that meeting, you can spend a lot of time on conflict because it is through that conflict that the strategic insight emerges.

When meetings are designed with this kind of clear intention and an understanding of what processes support open exploration of conflict, then the result will be an increase in candor. It's not that you or your colleagues lacked integrity, but our traditional meeting process designs unwittingly discourage people from speaking the truth. If you want to create a trustworthy organization then you will need to make these kinds of adjustments in your processes to ensure that conflict is addressed openly.

External: Cultivating Truth in the Ecosystem

We (the authors) favor natural metaphors over the mechanical ones that have dominated the thinking about organizations over the last century. One of our favorites is that of an ecosystem. Machines are self-contained, orderly, with clear lines of cause and effect. Ecosystems have fuzzy boundaries, have dynamics operating at the big picture and the little picture simultaneously, and require more continuous and generative efforts to achieve change. Seriously, which one sounds more like your organization? When it comes to supporting more truth in processes that extend outside your organizational boundaries, a more natural metaphor will help.

If you view your operating environment as an ecosystem, then truth is the pollen.

In any ecosystem, the more pollen you have blowing in the breeze, traveling with birds and insects, and mingling among the plants and trees, then the more vibrant your system will be. You'll see more growth, more expansion, more health, and more stability in the system. Truth has that same effect in organizations. Within the operating environment, the more truth that is spoken, the healthier the organization tends to be. It is not a single, hand-crafted truth that is carefully delivered from place to place (sorry, PR and marketing departments). It is a collection of thousands and thousands of tiny statements, flowing freely within the system, sparking new ideas, conclusions, or actions in ways that are not controlled by the central authority.

So from an organizational process point of view, the challenge is to create processes that support the free flow of truth throughout the system, particularly outside organizational boundaries. There are two sides to this: Speaking your truth and allowing others to speak theirs.

Speak Your Truth

To speak the truth and have it extend outside your organization, you might need a spokesperson. But when we think of spokespeople, we tend to think of the marketing and public relations functions, and because we are talking about truth here, we feel the need to be candid: Marketing and PR do not have a reputation for being comfortable with truth. These are the official "mouthpieces" for organizations, and they have a tough job. They push out information to consumers or stakeholders that is almost always designed to convince the information recipient to believe or do something that is more likely to help the company than the people themselves. They don't do truth. They do spin.

Spin, however, is out. Spin still happens, of course, but in the digital age its value has been diminished. With the explosion of information brought to us by the Internet, the true nature of spin is more frequently exposed than it was in the past. While we might have been skeptical before, we still could not as frequently prove wrong a claim made by a spokesperson. Today, however, we can tap into social networks and always find more information than the spokesperson is delivering—frequently more current information as well. You can shout at consumers until you are blue in the face that customer service is your highest priority—and you the executive may even truly believe it—but all your carefully chosen words are going to pale in comparison to that one YouTube video of your cable TV technician who fell asleep while on hold with your own company's technical support line. "Message control" is a thing of the past, so organizational processes designed to disseminate truth out into the ecosystem need to change.

Although companies still need marketing and PR functions, the act of cultivating truth in your ecosystem invariably goes beyond these efforts. More and more companies have official blogs, including blogs written by CEOs and senior managers. Whether it is written by the CEO or a line staffer, blogs enable an organization to speak more truth. They can share information with external stakeholders that in most cases would not be included by official spokespeople. No, they should not reveal trade secrets or expose confidential information (plenty of CEO blogs are reviewed by legal counsel), but that still leaves a lot of valuable information to be shared that will help an organization build trust within its own community by not withholding the truth.

Use of other social media outlets can expand the sharing of truth exponentially. With the capability for large numbers of employees to be on Twitter or Facebook, suddenly everyone can become a spokesperson. This, of course, might make some companies nervous—what if they say the wrong thing or make a mistake? This worry has been a part of social media from its inception, actually. Trustworthy organizations—ones that design processes to support more truth—understand the risk of having so many spokespeople, but they manage that risk because the reward is significant. They invest time in training employees on how to use social media and give them the freedom to experiment and try it out before they start posting official messages for the organization. They handle mistakes when they happen—not trying to cover them up, but acknowledging them as a part of being human. The result is many voices in the marketplace speaking the truth about an organization—the pollen blowing in the breeze. It provides multiple points of connection for matching up both the words and the actions of a company. The more consistent this is, the more easily trust is developed among employees, customers, and other stakeholder groups.

In some cases, embracing this approach may require a shift in policy as well. In the days of traditional marketing and PR, the channels for broadcasting information were limited, and controlling the message was easier. In that context, the default policy in organizations was confidentiality. In any given meeting or information exchange, there was a general expectation that the information should be kept confidential, unless one of the parties made it clear that it could be released. In other words, if nothing was made explicit, we assumed it should be confidential. The opposite is true these days.

Now there is a generalized assumption that private conversations or exchange of information may be shared more broadly, even universally, unless you make it clear that it is to be kept confidential. This still allows for confidentiality, but from an internal policy perspective there needs to be clarity on the expectations. This openness built into the process allows greater truth to be shared.

Let Others Speak Their Truth

Of course, if you're worried about what kind of truth your employees are going to share about your organization, you may be even more concerned about what people outside your organization's boundaries will say in response. This is a critical piece for trustworthy organizations: They let others speak their truth. If you write a blog, then you welcome comments. If you engage with customers on Twitter, then you expect to encounter frustrated people. Part of being trustworthy is accepting the whole truth, even when it is at times frustrating, confusing, or even contradictory.

We mentioned NTEN, the Nonprofit Technology Network, in Chapter 6. They are our shining example of an open, transparent organization, and they have achieved this in part by writing their commitment to truth into their Community Values statement on their website:

- We are accountable to you and to your needs and strive to engage, listen, and be responsive to you, our members, in all that we do.

- We strive to be authentic and honest in all of our communications so our community knows that we say what we mean forthrightly, and mean what we say.

Truth is dynamic, not static. It's not just a simple fact that can be repeated. It is generated through conversations and relationships. So as much as you build processes for ensuring that your organization speaks the whole truth through its many spokespeople, there also need to be processes that actually seek out and understand the truth of others in the system. The organizations that are still missing the boat on how to use social media as part of marketing and PR are the ones that viewed social media as a new set of broadcast mechanisms. They got on Twitter and scheduled their marketing messages to go out once every 15 minutes. What they were missing was the listening. For the truth to emerge through a conversation, you actually have to listen to what others are saying. Then the truth that you are speaking is actually more relevant to the people you are trying to reach. You can talk about what is interesting to them and what matters to them.

Trustworthy Behavior: Authenticity

Neo, sooner or later you're going to realize, just as I did, that there's a difference between knowing the path and walking the path.
                                    —Morpheus to Neo, *The Matrix*, 1999

Along with trust and truth, authenticity is yet another concept that everyone likes to support, at least in theory. In general, people strive to be authentic, and we associate authenticity with the people in our lives who we respect, admire, and emulate. But like trust and truth, authenticity is a concept that is more complicated and challenging in practice than it is in theory.

The simple definition of authenticity is being yourself—living your life in a way that is consistent with who you really are. At one level this sounds pretty easy, but you have to remember that we are social creatures, and part of having a society is having socially constructed roles that we play. In the process of playing these roles, we often find ourselves behaving in ways that are not quite aligned with our deeper sense of our true identity. We call this being inauthentic. Most of the time we stray from authenticity in minor ways, which allows us to still maintain a fairly healthy and complete sense of self. But there are moments when the lack of authenticity becomes too much to bear, and the disconnect and conflict show up in the form of leaving jobs, ending marriages, and other behavior that typically requires some kind of upheaval or major shift to reestablish a baseline of authenticity.

And the closer we look at authenticity, as you might expect, the more complex it becomes. In Chapter 4's discussion of individual behavior, we talked about how managing one's identity in the digital age is not as clear cut and under one's control as it used to be.

The social Internet has allowed us to seek out and find a "long tail" of online communities where we can share and explore all kinds of tiny parts of our identity. But thanks to Google, all that carefully controlled participation ends up being aggregated by anyone who does a search. Suddenly your expression of politics, religion, hobby, family, work, education, and more will all show up (in 0.13 seconds) when someone Googles you.

This has changed the nature of authenticity, particularly when it comes to creating trustworthy organizations. In the old days, authenticity might have been determined by a perceived match between behavior and identity, but that was often measured in more circumscribed ways—we expected only to see a sliver of someone at any given moment. Today, a much more diverse identity is expected thanks to the Internet. We led a workshop at a conference a couple of years ago and asked participants in the room to Google themselves and report any surprises. One marketing professional noted that although she was an avid marathoner, the Google results on her name did not show anything related to her passion for running—and this concerned her because it reflected a disconnect between who she was and what others were seeing about her.

It is a small example, and not directly related to her professional identity at all. But in the digital age, if there are gaps in your online identity, it is more likely to be noticed—not in the sense that people are searching to find the bad things you have done. They are searching to find the whole you, and when they discover less—when they only find your resume or other sources of information that have been carefully crafted by you, they are likely to trust you less. Just like organizations that try to spread the truth like pollen in an ecosystem, individuals maintain their authenticity by expecting a more complete and varied identity to be shared online.

To create a trustworthy organization, we expect authenticity, in all its complexity. This has important implications for individual behavior, both in terms of knowledge and skills.

Knowledge: Know Thyself

The first step in authenticity is to know who you are. Authenticity is demonstrated through the consistency of a person's behavior and identity. So you can't be authentic unless you know what it means to really be you. And because we're talking about authentic behavior in the context of organizations, self-knowledge really has two components: organizational and individual.

For organizational self-knowledge, we simply refer you back to the section on ownership in Chapter 6. The knowledge section there talks about the important nuances of understanding the nature of your organization so you can generate more ownership on the part of all the employees in the organization, including ensuring a true orientation that allows employees to really understand the true nature of the organization and ensuring that strategy is made real for employees, rather than living in a binder up on a shelf. For employees to behave authentically on behalf of an organization, it stands to reason that they must know the identity of the organization beyond what is said in the "about us" page of the website.

For organizations to support truly authentic behavior, though, the individuals in your company must possess some self knowledge of their own. They need to know what they are good at and what they are not. They need to know what is important to them and what they value. It helps if they know a little about what makes them tick, so, for example, they might be aware of when someone pushes one of their "hot buttons" so they can manage the situation without flying off the handle. They should know what gives them energy in the work place and what tires them out. They should know what they want to do when they grow up, and if you really want to see the power of authenticity truly shine, they should know what their real gift is.

They should know what the world needs delivered through them. And if you haven't already figured it out, "they" also means "you" in this case. It is all of us. In human organizations, the humans who work there get to show up as their full selves, because that is what unlocks the power that they bring to the enterprise.

We fully expect some push-back on this one. It's hard enough to hire and support all your employees without having to worry about how well they "know themselves." At the very least it sounds like a lot of work, and it certainly will appear to be a little "out there" to some, or it might even seem to be overstepping some privacy boundaries (how far should we go in asking our people to share themselves at work?). True, it won't be easy. But if you find yourself resisting this idea, then here's your first test: What is the source of the resistance? Because if it is only some discomfort because you've never managed that way or looked at your job that way, we encourage you to put that aside. Human organizations are trustworthy, and trust is much more easily generated when people can be their whole selves.

More than ten years ago Marcus Buckingham and Curt Coffman from Gallup, Inc. presented some interesting conclusions about management based on extensive survey efforts in corporations. They drew the conclusion that one of the four keys to successful people management was to focus on strengths and manage around weaknesses. This is not the conventional wisdom. Conventional wisdom would have you assess your people for strengths and weaknesses and then develop action plans designed to improve their weaknesses. Buckingham and Coffman's research indicated the opposite—that catering to people's strengths and actually managing around the weaknesses led to better performance. They told stories of managers who pay careful attention to the performance of their employees over time in ways that uncovered opportunities for greater performance, even if it wasn't in their current positions. They treated people differently on the same team (even though this might not appear fair) simply because they *were* different and responded to different things.

Underlying their view was an important conclusion about the individuals who work in our organizations:

> Each person has a unique set of talents, a unique pattern of behaviors, of passions, of yearnings. Each person's pattern of talents is enduring, resistant to change. Each person, therefore, has a unique destiny.[9]

Again, we can feel the push-back. Destiny? I thought this was a business book, not self help?!

---

9. Buckingham, Marcus, and Curt Coffman. First, Break All the Rules: What the World's Greatest Managers Do Differently. New York, NY.: Simon & Schuster, 1999. 141.

Yes. Destiny. We are not apologetic about talking about things like destiny and purpose and meaning. As authors, we have a history of talking about those things, and it would not be authentic for us to change our tune now. But beyond that, creating human organizations means letting your people actually be human. The human experience is not just about productivity, measurement, engineering, analysis, and putting in the hours. Being human is equally about relationships, emotions, passion, meaning, purpose, and, yes, destiny. Dan Pink has written two best-selling books that address issues of human motivation. *A Whole New Mind* and *Drive* make compelling and logical cases that the next economy is going to be driven by more right-brained factors, such as meaning, story, design, and purpose. And the growth of social media is evidence of this, where networks and platforms have achieved astonishing growth based on things such as relationships, sharing, fun, and connection.

We don't care if you call it business or self-help, but creating trustworthy organizations is facilitated by the presence of authentic human beings, so the work you do to support that in your organization will make a difference. Authentic individuals are more effective when they participate in social media. Authentic individuals are more comfortable speaking the truth, even if their voice shakes. Authentic individuals fear transparency less. Human organizations do what it takes to support authenticity.

Skills: Equip for Exploration

If authenticity requires a deeper level of self-knowledge, then the skills we need are just means for exploring that more effectively. They are skills like curiosity or emotional intelligence—they reflect the capacity for individuals to explore more of who they are and how they need to show up and interact in a given situation. These are not the skills that you typically find in the skills-training catalogue, such as interpersonal communication or project management, but they are important to develop.

Take curiosity, for example. We don't normally think of curiosity as a skill, but the ability to be curious is critical for developing a stronger self-awareness. Becoming more aware requires initiative—it doesn't just happen by itself—and those who lack curiosity end up being more reactive. Curiosity is what drives us to not accept the first answer and not turn back at the first roadblock. Without it, we never actually take the time to clarify what is important to us or understand our motivation. But as we develop the skill, we end up pursuing more of these paths and increasing our capacity to be authentic.

The easiest way to develop curiosity is to ask questions. It sounds simple, but asking questions is not something that comes naturally to everyone. Our society is answer-focused. We are rewarded for providing answers and providing them quickly. It is not always natural to explore, ask more questions, and challenge answers that seem right. As employees, we need to learn to have the courage to ask more questions, even if they appear to challenge what is being told to us by people in positions of more authority. And as supervisors we need to learn how to encourage more questions, which typically goes hand in hand with asking more questions yourself.

Here's a simple exercise to develop this skill. Find someone who would be willing to let you help him solve a relatively simple problem. He describes what the problem is and why he is stuck with it, and your job is to coach him in a way that the problem gets solved. But here's the catch: You are only allowed to ask questions. This is harder than you might think, because you're not allowed to ask leading questions like "So, have you tried talking to the other party?" That is actually a statement ("You should try talking to the other party"). You have to ask something more open ended ("What have you tried?"). Try it and you will likely discover a strong desire to come up with answers for the other person. We are not used to staying open to letting the other person solve the problem. To actually stay in that place where we ask open-ended questions (where we ourselves don't know the answer) requires us (you guessed it) to be curious. When we are curious, we are comfortable in letting the answer emerge, and that is precisely what is required to support authenticity.

Of course, even if you don't find training programs in "curiosity," there are several options for developing self-awareness, no matter where you are in the organizational hierarchy. For example:

- **Emotional intelligence.** The popular champion for emotional intelligence is Daniel Goleman, and our favorite of his books (this one written with Annie McKee and Richard Boyatzis) is *Primal Leadership*, though many have developed their own emotional intelligence models (and tests and training programs). Goleman divides emotional intelligence into four areas: self-awareness, self-management, social awareness, and relationship management.

- **Myers-Briggs Type Indicator.** Perhaps the most popular of all personality type systems, the MBTI is based on significant research and has its roots in Jungian psychology. Individuals are typed along four dimensions: introvert-extrovert, intuitive-sensing, thinking-feeling, and judging-perceiving. The way the different preferences are combined leads to fairly distinct personality types. Teams often go through MBTI training together so they can use it to help manage interpersonal issues on the team that could be exacerbated by people with different preferences approaching the same issue through two different lenses.

- **DISC.** Another popular typing system also from the field of psychology is the DISC assessment. This one tests word preferences to provide a score along four variables: dominance, influence, steadiness, and conscientious. Dominance and influence scores represent the more extroverted side of a personality, and steadiness and conscientious are introverted. Influence and steadiness focus on relationships, where dominance and conscientious focus on tasks. This system is also used popularly in team-building.

- **HBDI.** Yet another instrument is the Herrmann Brain Dominance Instrument. It was created by a man named Ned Herrmann while he was working in the management education department at General Electric, and it looks at functions in the brain (left-brain, right-brain on the one hand, and rational, emotional on the other) to come up with four modes of thinking: analytical, sequential, interpersonal, and imaginative. Individuals tend to be dominant in one or two of the thinking styles, though everyone has the opportunity, according to Herrmann, to practice "whole brain thinking" as well.

These are just examples, but there are plenty of structured programs for individuals and groups to develop their self-knowledge. You should be careful when pursuing training in these areas to find providers who understand the complexity and nuances of the systems—too many people oversimplify it to the detriment of those trying to apply it.

Making New Meaning

Organizational strategist C. V. Harquail has a post on her Authentic Organizations blog that resonates here. In it, she describes how every individual speaking through social media on behalf of his or her organization creates new meaning.

> We both have to take a big picture message, and convey a big picture intent, in specific communication acts. We have to understand, translate, embellish, exemplify, recreate, rewrite, from general to specific. We have to create new meaning each time, in each blog post and each tweet. And so it is with each of us who, through social media, puts into words and into interactions the values, the attributes, the goals, the meaning of what we are part of, who we are speaking for, and what we are speaking about.[10]

---

10. Harquail, C. V. "How Social Media Create Organizational Meaning." Authentic Organizations. 18 Jan. 20011. Web. 25 Apr. 2011. http://authenticorganizations.com/harquail/2011/01/18/how-social-media-creates-organizational-meaning/.

If we want our organizations to be more trustworthy, because we're embracing transparency, because we're changing our processes so that there's more truth spoken, and because we're encouraging authenticity in our employees not just as they go about their jobs but as they start more and more to speak for the organization through social media, then we have to get used to the idea that this organic system made up of human individuals will be (if we're lucky) evolving and mutating in ways we could not have imagined just a few years ago.

We talk about how to manage and embrace that kind of change in the next chapter.

Must Read

A host of resources cover the issues of transparency of culture, speaking the truth, and being authentic. When your challenge is creating organizations that embrace these three concepts, we recommend three above others. The first is *Transparency: Building A Culture of Candor*, by Warren Bennis, et al. Bennis and his colleagues are leaders in the management and leadership field, and they do a good job of outlining the recent move toward transparency, including a discussion of the role of social media. For speaking the truth, our favorite is *Why Leaders Don't Take Yes for an Answer*, by Michael Roberto. Roberto is an expert in decision making, and his book covers the importance of bringing out conflict in teams to prevent group think and creating false consensus. And for authenticity, it simply doesn't make sense to refer you to words that someone else has written, so we simply request that you go out and get a journal. There are, actually, plenty of books that can inspire self-reflection and exploration, but nothing beats taking the time to write in a journal. The best leaders we've ever met all keep journals, so we think it is a good habit to develop.

> Warren Bennis, Daniel Goleman, James O'Toole, with Patricia Ward Biederman. *Transparency: How Leaders Create a Culture of Candor*. San Francisco: Jossey-Bass, 2008.

> Michael A. Roberto. Why Great Leaders Don't Take Yes for an Answer: Managing for Conflict and Consensus. New Jersey: Wharton School Publishing, 2005.

> Writing journal. We prefer ones without lines, but it's your choice.

Get Started Today: Worksheet

Enough reading, let's get started!

You can download and print the worksheets associated with this chapter at www.humanizebook.com.

All four worksheets are formatted in the same way. The first section helps you assess how trustworthy your organization is and includes a quiz and some open-ended questions. In the second section, we guide you through conversations with others in your organization about trust. And the last section gets you going on an action plan.

We ask you to take a hard look at how trustworthy your organization is. How transparent is your organization, and does information really flow freely? Do you trust others there and can you handle conflict and differences of opinion? Do you let employees speak for the organization? Are your organizational values clear? Can people express their full, authentic selves?

After the quiz, we provide some guidance for having conversations with others in your organization about these issues, which will vary depending on your level in the organizational hierarchy:

- **Executives.** This one may be the most challenging for the top of the organization. Issues of transparency are tough because people at the top always feel the most responsible, and that makes sharing and being transparent harder. Take the time you need working on this issue as a senior team, dig into issues like your transparency architecture, ensuring more conflict in the ranks, and getting rid of "spin." It will help your broader conversations to have worked through some of these issues yourself first. And frankly, there is no more important topic for a senior team than trust, so you could spend a fair amount of time just dealing with that.

  In conversations with other levels, try to find out what information *they* want shared—you might be surprised. But when you do get together with others to talk about transparency, don't hold back! As soon as you start hesitating and telling them you'll have to get back to them, they'll realize it's the same old same old and stop participating. Go into meetings to talk about this with other levels of the organization with the clear intention of being authentic and telling it like it is. If you don't think you can do that—at least at a basic level—then hold off on the conversations for a while and focus within the senior team.

- **Middle Managers.** For people in the middle, this is also a good place to start the conversation just with your colleagues, because being trustworthy (transparent, truthful, authentic) is a lot about giving up control. Letting people be themselves, tell the truth, engage in conflict. Supporting that (when you're in the middle) often means getting out of the way, so it would be good to talk about how you're going to do that.

Then start talking to the people above and below you in the system about what information they need from you, so you can get clear about whether you're the ones to share it, or if others have better access.

- **Front Line Employees.** Be careful as you talk to people above you in the system about this topic. We are going to guess that if you are on the front lines of the organization, you might be at least a little frustrated by lack of transparency and feeling like you are being kept in the dark. But if that frustration gets through, the people higher up tend to react badly, feeling like you're making unwarranted demands. So don't make demands. Work hard to be curious to ask questions about what it's like for those who are supposedly keeping you in the dark. This is one conversation where the way you approach it has a big impact on how the conversation progresses. Also, don't forget that authenticity is a two-way street. You have to show up at these conversations willing to share your whole experience. So take the time (maybe in a few conversations with just your peers) to get clear about what transparency you really need and why.

Ultimately the changes we advice in this book are necessary, they are possible, and they start with you. Don't wait for permission or the perfect timing. Are *you* ready? Go.

How to Be Generative

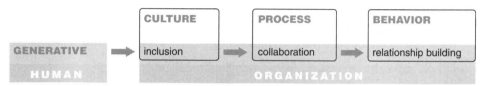

GENERATIVE	CULTURE	PROCESS	BEHAVIOR
HUMAN	inclusion	collaboration	relationship building
	ORGANIZATION		

Yesterday, prosperity's great question was: how much more value than your nearest rival could you, over time, create? Today, prosperity's great question is: compared with your fiercest competitor, how much more meaningful, authentic, enduring value can you, over time, create?

—Umair Haque, The New Capitalist Manifesto

"Generative" is not a word commonly associated with business or organizations. It means, quite simply, to be capable of producing or creating. On the surface, the term does have apparent relevance to the business world. After all, most organizations are designed to produce or create something. But the word generative is not about the single act of production or the creation of a single thing. Being generative implies an ongoing capacity to generate and produce and create. Being generative is ultimately a sustainable capacity, not a one-off event. It is perpetual, like a species' ability to propagate and sustain life.

Organizations, on the other hand, typically don't view themselves that way. They certainly long for sustainability. People rarely create a business with the intention of it failing. (Even though most do, in fact, fail.) But even when we strive for sustainability in organizations, we tend not to think about it in holistic terms. More specifically, we don't think about it in systemic terms (remember systems thinking in Chapter 6, "How to be Open"?). We tend to define sustainability in terms of our organization's bottom line, regardless of what is going on in the rest of the system. We measure costs and revenue, and we track investments in capital to see their return. And our fundamental measurement of growth is that the owners of the company receive more money than they did the year before (or, for nonprofits, that the institution was able to implement more programs or raise more money). Our view of growth in organizations is fundamentally linear and self-centered. We want the line on our particular graph to move, over time, in an upward direction, and our chart never has to end, as long as the line is trending upward.

This self-centered and two-dimensional understanding of growth is now starting to fail us. Social media has demonstrated this through its remarkable growth. Twitter was not designed to be the revolutionary cultural phenomenon it is today. It started out as a way for people in the same organization to send group text messages to each other. No one sat down with a plan to create a global infrastructure for information sharing, learning, and relationship building that would scoop the established news media and actually support revolutions. But that is what has happened. Twitter accomplished its growth by being generative—by building into its own operating system the ability to grow, evolve, change, and move in a decentralized way. By building off the work of independent users and software developers, Twitter's growth wasn't just linear. Twitter isn't bragging about being the best and biggest intra-organizational text messaging platform in the world, which was the linear extension of where the company started. Twitter's growth was more of a spiral, generating new iterations of Twitter, recreating itself based on a variety of inputs. And the future of Twitter may not even be in Twitter. Generative growth is more than a two-dimensional line going up, rather than down. Being generative is multidimensional.

For human organizations, this means taking a different approach to goals such as value, growth, and success. At one level, you can define success in terms of getting people to value your product enough that they buy it at a profitable price. That approach is fine, but doesn't go far enough in today's world. We also must ask questions about the broader value your product delivers to society, or whether the process of creating the product destroys the environment, or further mires communities in poverty, or can help the users themselves become more generative—teach them to fish, so to speak, instead of just giving them a fish. In fact, you are not solely responsible for defining the value proposition of your product, as we indicated in Chapter 6 about being open. The entire value conversation emerges in a more decentralized way through conversations with users and other stakeholders.

Growth can no longer be only about growth in our individual bottom lines. If you view your organization as completely independent from the rest of the system, then an exclusive focus on bottom line growth is fine. That one graph looks great, all by itself, with the line trending up. But human organizations understand systems better than that, and they know that their growth is not independent from the growth and development of others in the system, from employees to consumers, to whole communities, and even to competitors. Securing growth for yourself at the expense of others in the system is frequently not sustainable. Generative organizations recognize this.

Success can no longer be understood in purely financial terms either. It's not only the quantity of profit that matters (that requires beating your competitors). It is also the quality of profit (that helps expand the pool of profit available to all). Even a company like Walmart, which for years has been the target of activists who were concerned that the cost-focused retailer was destroying communities and the environment through its ruthless focus on efficiency, has made a significant shift. Walmart is working toward three goals that are just as focused on social good as the bottom line: using 100% renewable energy, achieving zero waste, and selling only products that benefit the environment.[1] Again, it is no longer good enough to create advantages for your company while simultaneously generating losses for the rest of the system. Today's imperative for organizations is to become more generative, producing and creating value for themselves and the whole system as they grow.

Becoming a generative organization is no easy task. It simply wasn't part of the equation when nearly all of today's organizations were created. The fact that the behemoth Walmart can make a change, however, should be enough inspiration to get you started. That doesn't mean that you need to adopt Walmart's three goals around renewable energy, waste elimination, and eco-friendly products (though feel free to run with those ideas). The challenge internally revolves around the ideas of inclusion, collaboration, and relationship building. Inclusion shows up at the level of culture.

Generative organizations have cultures that go beyond tolerating diversity—they live and breathe inclusion. They grow and create based on the power of including difference in all that they do. Collaboration exists at the process level. Generative organizations understand that collaboration goes beyond liberal use of the cc: field in email. It requires a deeper capacity to collaborate (which is greatly enhanced these days through online tools) in ways that break down traditional barriers between departments or among stakeholders. And building relationships is how

---

1. Haque, Umair. The New Capitalist Manifesto: Building a Disruptively Better Business. Boston, MA: Harvard Business, 2011. 44.

being generative shows up in individual behavior. The people in generative organizations know how to build relationships—both offline and online—because those relationships are integral to the creation, change, and growth of generative organizations.

Generative Culture: Inclusion

A sure path to inhibit your own creativity is to seek out environments where people are just like you.

—Frans Johansson, *The Medici Effect*

In organizational settings, "inclusion" is a word rarely used without its slightly more controversial cousin, "diversity." Diversity and inclusion have quite a presence in organizational life. There are vice presidents of diversity and inclusion, diversity and inclusion have their own programs and even departments, and if we dig hard enough I am sure we can find some diversity and inclusion best practices. This makes inclusion slightly more difficult to talk about in the context of creating more human organizations. It's like the idea of "leadership." When an entire industry of speakers, consultants, and change programs has emerged, the words tend to take on lives of their own. You may hear plenty of organizations claim to have inclusive cultures, but watch them squirm when you ask them to define inclusion. That doesn't cut it in human organizations.

As management-speak terms, however, "diversity" and "inclusion" have additional challenges, not faced by terms like "leadership" or "management," because they open up a piece of our organizations and our society that we are not always comfortable facing: a long history of inequity and injustice. We hope the fact that inequity and injustice have both existed in the past and exist today does not surprise anyone. Pretty much every modern society was built upon some kind of rather large, enduring injustice performed by one group against another, and although we've come a long way in our societies compared to 100, 25, or even 10 years ago, we have not solved our diversity issues by any stretch of the imagination.

But here's where the diversity and inclusion conversation gets hard. Yes, it is about issues of oppression and injustice. In the United States this means you'll be digging into issues of race, gender, sexual identity, and more. But diversity and inclusion are also about thinking styles, personality difference, learning styles, generations, and other differences that are not based in a history of oppression. For some, the issues of race, gender, and so on are simply too difficult to face, and diversity and inclusion get ignored. For others, talking about thinking style or generation in the context of diversity and inclusion makes it too "watered down" and not serious enough. It all gets down to those basic definitions of diversity and inclusion that we tend to overlook. By not defining them, we let them mean different things to different people. That often leads to frustrations when one person wants to talk about race relations, and the other is discussing the difference between Generation X and Baby Boomers. This frustration is unnecessary because the definitions of diversity and inclusion are both simple and clear. Diversity and inclusion consultant Joe Gerstandt actually nails the diversity definition in only three words:

> Diversity means difference.

That may sound too simple, but it's not. Diversity simply means difference. It doesn't mean affirmative action or race relations or employee engagement programs. Those ideas are all important, and they are certainly related to difference, but they all have their own definitions. Let's not confuse things unnecessarily. The definition of diversity is, simply, difference. And inclusion, it turns out, has an equally simple definition according to Gerstandt:

> Inclusion is the capacity to include difference.

Again, we are sorry if you were expecting a definition that was more pithy or somehow "politically correct" (or incorrect for that matter) that we could then tie to a nice two-by-two matrix you could use to develop your diversity and inclusion program. But these concepts are, at their heart, simple. They are by no means easy, but they are simple. Diversity means difference, and an organization that truly has a culture of inclusion is one with a strong capacity to include difference in everything it does.

Of course, defining diversity and inclusion doesn't tell us why they are important to organizations, and that brings us right back to the notion of being generative. Today's imperative for organizations is to become more generative, producing and creating value for themselves and the whole system as they grow. This requires innovation. As we said in Chapter 3, "We're Not Moving Forward," innovation is more than just change or doing things differently. It is about creating new dimensions of value. Innovation is inherently creative—it is about ideas that are new, valuable, and (just as importantly) realized so that they have an actual impact on the system.[2]

It turns out that diversity (difference) is a critical factor in innovation. In the research for his book, *The Medici Effect*, innovation expert Frans Johansson discovered that the opportunity for innovation increased at what he called the "intersection" between different fields and cultures. His term, the Medici Effect, referred to the wealthy De Medici family that lived in Florence during the Renaissance who

---

2. Johansson, Frans. The Medici Effect. Boston: Harvard Business School, 2004. 14–15.

sponsored a variety of artists and scientists to work together in their court, generating an impressive amount of creativity and innovation as a result of this diverse group working together. When you and the people you work with are all in the same "field," broadly defined, then there is a tendency to all move in the same direction. By introducing concepts and ideas from other fields, you increase the chances of generating real innovation. Johansson cites examples of architects innovating heating and cooling systems based on learning from termite ecologists, and telecommunication companies increasing the efficiency of their signals based on learning about the behavior of social insects. In general, groups who possess difference have the potential for greater innovation:

> Diversity in teams allows different viewpoints, approaches, and frames of mind to emerge. Diversity is also a proven way to increase the randomness of concept combinations. It is often said that one of the reasons for the United States' unparalleled innovation rate is its very diverse population.[3]

To be generative, then, requires innovation, and innovation is fueled by difference. That is why generative organizations have cultures of inclusion. They walk the walk of an inclusive culture by building a strong infrastructure to support difference in the organization. They talk the talk of inclusion by making difference visible. And they embrace a key set of paradoxes in their underlying thinking and assumptions about inclusion.

Walking the Walk: An Infrastructure for Inclusion

Inclusive cultures do not happen by accident, and unfortunately they don't tend to develop organically. As human beings, we are drawn to people like ourselves and to ideas with which we basically already agree. The familiarity is comforting to us. It feels "right." Scientists have studied and documented this phenomenon as the similar-attraction effect. With mathematical precision, people will predictably be more attracted to people who are similar to them. So inclusive cultures do not emerge simply from everyone agreeing on the idea that diversity is good for innovation, for instance. Walking the walk of an inclusive culture means actively building an infrastructure that will support difference. You need to have this infrastructure in place, in fact, before you start to actually include more difference in your organization. We see a lot of organizations push right away for attracting more "diversity" to their staff, only to eventually measure a high turnover rate among the people who are different from the mainstream in the culture because they never feel truly supported. Creating a culture of inclusion requires hard work to allow difference to thrive.

---

3. Johansson, Frans. The Medici Effect. 79.

Here are some ways this infrastructure is built.

Inclusive cultures are proactive in seeking out difference. This is one reason why inclusive cultures often have integrated into their hiring processes an active search outside the traditional sources for employees. Simply expecting that you'll "know the right person when you see him" is not being proactive enough. You have to work to seek out sources for potential hires who are different in a variety of ways from the people you already have. But it goes beyond hiring. Organizations with inclusive cultures look for opportunities for people on different internal teams to work together. They create cross-departmental task forces. They are proactive in creating opportunities for younger employees to work together with older employees. They want people at different levels of the hierarchy to work together, so they create structures for that to happen. For example, at W. L. Gore and Associates, a new employee is assigned a "sponsor" who takes that person around to see where she best fits and to support her in her long-term growth within the organization. The point is, new hires are not automatically assigned to the group that shares their background. They are given the opportunity to see a variety of areas before they settle in.

On the other hand, inclusive cultures can also support sameness. Many large corporations with a reputation for focusing on diversity issues have created a structure of affinity groups where people who are similar can come together within the organizational context to support each other. This goes back to having a support system in place before you seek to increase the level of difference in your staff. Remember that the existence of difference in and of itself does not create innovation or make the organization generative. It requires a system where the diverse elements can thrive, both apart and together. You have to demonstrate to your people that you are supporting them both by welcoming them into the fold and by allowing them to exist independent from the fold.

In that same vein, inclusive cultures almost always pay attention to building what have traditionally been called "soft" skills in organizations—dealing with conflict, communicating effectively, and managing relationships—because capitalizing on diversity is no easy task. If you convene a diverse team, but don't pay attention to the way the team members work together, then the diverse team will actually perform worse than a homogenous team. But the diverse team that develops its capacity to work together, despite differences, will outperform homogenous teams. This capacity is an important part of the infrastructure that generative organizations put in place to support inclusion.

These skills are not only relevant for dealing with people who are different than you—they are also critical within your own network. It is perhaps more obvious to us that we would need conflict resolution skills when dealing with people who are different. Two people who want different things are by definition in conflict. But the less obvious (and maybe more important) application of conflict resolution, when it comes to inclusion, is in managing conflict between people within the same network. We create and join networks because we are supported by them. People in the same network connect around the same issue and in general are headed in the same direction. When that alignment is created, everyone in the network can be supportive of each other, and that's a good thing.

But when it comes to being generative, innovating, and leveraging a culture of inclusion, a point will come when people will need to move in a different direction than their network. That is the whole point of leveraging inclusion. We can discover new directions, new ways of doing things, and create new value in the process. Networks, however, resist this. Networks form around a particular direction, and when individuals within the network move in a different direction, it is considered counterproductive by the network. This is precisely where conflict resolution skills are required to negotiate flexibility within the network. Inclusive cultures have their radar up for these kinds of conflict. They provide support to employees to resolve conflict in ways that preserves the support network without denying the flexibility, change, and new directions that emerge from access to diversity.

Another important part of an inclusion infrastructure actually relates to the decentralized culture we talked about in Chapter 6. Centralized cultures tend to weaken an inclusion infrastructure. When control of decision making rests in the hands of a few, it becomes harder for a diverse group to be involved in decision making. It is a numbers game. It may not be intentional—the leaders in a centralized culture may have a firm desire to create an inclusive culture. But by consolidating the decision making to a small number of people—even if that small number appears "diverse"—the effect is a culture where the majority of people in the system realize they are left out (excluded) from decision making. Diversity may exist in the system, but it is not leveraged. In decentralized cultures where decision making is pushed closer to where the problems are actually being solved, the opportunity to make decisions is afforded to more and more people. That helps build an environment where diversity is expected, sought out, and valued.

Talking the Talk: Making Difference Visible

Inclusive cultures are not shy about the stand they take on inclusion. Because effective inclusion requires an infrastructure and proactive measures to ensure difference is welcomed and leveraged, it is not the type of thing one does on the sly. Unfortunately, too many organizations seem to focus on this one aspect of an inclusive culture. They bend over backward to make it clear both internally and externally that their culture values diversity and inclusion. This has created a steady stream of work for the attractive and multicultural models who populate the stock photography in the category we like to call "smiling rainbow," where that ideal

group of white, African American, Asian, and Latino employees are all having a rau-
cously good time overlooking that slide deck or those sales projection documents.
We see these photos on nearly every website and in every brochure, trying to con-
firm (convince us?) that they are committed to diversity.

At one level, this is a good thing. We do need to be conscious about what we present to the outside world so that it accurately reflects the diversity within our systems and communities. Everyone who is in our system wants to look at what we are
presenting to the outside world and see at least a part of themselves there. For
decades, we did not pay attention to this and ended up painting a picture that was
not accurate and was a piece of a system that excluded difference at every level.
Generative organizations intentionally reverse that trend.

On the other hand, the near obsession with appearing diverse can be a problem. It's
the same issue as when organizations work hard to hire a visibly diverse workforce
without putting in the support mechanisms to handle that kind of diversity, resulting in high turnover. If all you do is create diverse images, you are not going to har-
vest the bounty of diversity's potential. Inclusive cultures learn to walk this fine line.
They clearly speak about and make visible their commitment to inclusion, without
sounding like they are desperately trying to be politically correct.

This means going beyond the "smiling rainbow" photos on the website. (Though
you can still keep those; they're fine.) It means ensuring that a wider variety of people end up in the front row when you present to both internal and external audiences. Think about your internal meetings, particularly when a large number of the
people in the department or the whole organization is present. Who's in the front of
the room? Is it the same people each time?

In cultures that value inclusion, it's not the same people every time. If you are
infused with difference, you need to demonstrate that you value something other
than hierarchy, and that means putting different faces and voices in front of the
room at important meetings. Yes, sometimes it is important to have the head of the
company up in front of everyone. That's fine. But if that's all you do, you need to
create more opportunities, because you also need other departments up in front of
everyone, different generations, different accents, different approaches, different
solutions. Talking the talk of an inclusive culture requires an intentional broadcast
of difference. It has to not only exist; it must also be visible.

There is an important social media component to this as well. Many companies
struggle with the online and social media presence of their employees. A lot of fear
surrounds people saying and doing inappropriate things. Many "about" pages in
blogs and Twitter profiles stress that the views are those of the author and not any
affiliated company. Okay, that person is not speaking for her company, but is she
even allowed to note that she works for the company? Inclusion requires at least a
basic acceptance of the diverse group of individuals who work for the organization,

and that means a tolerance of who they are. Fully. Which means allowing them to be visible in online spaces. We talked in the previous chapter about the individual challenge of actually knowing yourself and choosing how to represent yourself in online spaces in authentic ways. It is important for generative organizations to consciously provide support to their employees to be seen and heard.

Thought: Assumptions Behind an Inclusive Culture

When you think about inclusion, you often think about having an "open mind." It is the closed minded people, after all, who are not tolerant of diversity, right? So it should be no surprise that the series of broad assumptions that underpin inclusive cultures require an advanced level of open-mindedness—open to the point of being able to entertain paradoxes. That is what is required of the thinking that goes into inclusive cultures: embracing a series of paradoxes that help us truly take advantage of difference. The three paradoxes we have identified are proud humility, aggressive sensitivity, and dynamic stability.

Proud Humility

Management consultant Jim Collins identified this paradox in his book *Good to Great,* and he called it the Stockdale Paradox, named after a U.S. soldier who was captured in the Vietnam War and survived years in a prison camp, partially by maintaining both an unwavering determination to make it home and a brutally honest understanding that this outcome was likely a long way off. Those who didn't make it were the ones who become overly hopeful or overly pessimistic. For inclusion there is a similar paradox that has to do with pride and humility.

Part of the power of difference is in each different person or group maintaining a distinct pride about who they are and where they come from. This applies to individuals and their ethnic background as much as it applies to different departments or units. That pride is important for accessing the energy and drive groups need to excel. The strong connection that individuals feel about the group identity is a good thing. But it must be balanced with humility for inclusion to really take hold. When individuals or groups become too prideful, they end up too easily dismissing the input or accomplishments of others in the system. You end up with a more competitive system, with each prideful group trying to outdo the other. And perhaps more importantly, without humility, individuals and groups become unable to acknowledge their shortcomings or their contributions to the system's problems.

This happens frequently as organizations struggle to manage relationships between groups that have a history of oppression, a big sticking point when it comes to an inclusive culture. People, particularly in groups who have been historically dominant (white, male, heterosexual, and so on) often have a hard time embracing the paradox of proud humility. It is uncomfortable facing the reality that your group has oppressed others in the past and is currently enjoying certain unearned privileges, simply because you belong to that group. In that discomfort, people tend to reject both the pride and the humility. They tend to deny that there are any privileges, and they disassociate themselves from the acts of their group in history ("slavery wasn't *my* idea…").

Proud humility is an alternative. Through humility you can acknowledge wrongdoings more easily, both historical and current. Humility recognizes that you and your group(s) are not perfect. You make mistakes. You're willing to explore that side of your identity. But you don't give up the pride to embrace the humility. You still maintain a proud connection to your group, even though you are not perfect. If you try to distance yourself from your group, it only looks like you are trying to escape responsibility or deflect the situation. Proud humility puts you in a place where you can actually move forward. This concept is equally true for racial and ethnic groups as it is for the accounting department or specific stakeholder groups in an organization.

Aggressive Sensitivity

One of the common knocks against diversity and inclusion is its overemphasis on sensitivity. In the early days, employees were forced to go through "sensitivity training" to make the workplace more comfortable with diversity. Some of those training programs were done better than others, but enough were ineffective that the whole thing has been cast in a negative light. Whether they were intended this way, the popular belief was that the goal of the training was to learn how not to offend anyone. As in, "Let's all learn how *not* to offend women, people of color, the disabled, and so on." The result is an office full of employees who are afraid to talk to each other for fear of offending or choosing the wrong word. That's not real inclusion.

True, the goal in an inclusive culture is not rampant offensiveness. That would be obviously counterproductive. People are sensitive. People do make an effort to understand the people in other groups so they know what would offend and why. This is even true among departments—there are plenty of opportunities to offend if you are not aware of the culture, history, or values of a particular discipline within an organization. In short, the more you know about the other group—what makes its members tick, what they value, what they notice—then the less you will offend them. But remember that lack of offense is not the actual goal here. The goal is to create a relationship where communication can be more open, frank, and even aggressive—rather than polite, hushed, or tentative. When being offended is taken off the table (because of appropriate sensitivity), the people involved have freedom in their conversation. They can challenge each other, joke with each other, and take more risks with each other. By knowing each other better, they are not trapped by fear of offending. They are let loose to push each other more. So we don't mean "aggressive" as in attacking; we mean it more in the sense of being a fierce opponent in a game. It is this fierceness that we respect and appreciate because we know it brings out more in us. Inclusive cultures are known for this kind of fierce or aggressive sensitivity—a passionate pursuit of understanding of others to open up the opportunity for a higher level of interaction, learning, and performance.

Dynamic Stability

Inclusive cultures embrace the underlying premise that change is the new normal. Since a key goal of inclusion is innovation, organizations that actively work to be inclusive must also be ready for continual change. As you embrace diversity and provide opportunities for different teams to innovate at the "intersection" of their fields, you will end up with an organization that moves in different directions, leverages emerging trends, displays different faces, and speaks in diverse voices. But remember that organizational culture is also relied on as a unifier. It is somewhat of an anchor in a turbulent world—something that lets us know that among all the chaos around us, we are, in fact, part of this unique organization. So the culture cannot embrace change to the point where the organization's identity is lost. That is the paradox of dynamic stability.

Inclusive cultures understand how to compose a consistent narrative about who they are and where they are going, despite implementing nearly continuous change. They tell a story that makes sense of all the diversity, innovation, and change. The story provides some stability, even though on the ground things are changing at a fast pace. Look at Apple. Apple makes computers but also sells music, publishes books (sort of), and sells personal media consumption, creation, and display devices (iPods and iPads). Apple clearly is a company that embraces innovation and has changed radically, but still manages to maintain a narrative that identifies it as uniquely and distinctly Apple. That is the hallmark of an inclusive culture, one that can withstand change without it threatening who it is, and one that is willing to even change who it is (taking "computer" out of its name) to become something that is even more connected to their essence.

Generative Process: Collaboration

People don't connect with other people to accomplish less. Behind all our organizing is the desire to accomplish, to create something more.
　　　　　—Margaret Wheatley and Myron Kellner-Rogers, *A Simpler Way*

If generative culture is about including a broader, more diverse set of people and groups in the enterprise, it makes sense that the process focuses on how those people are going to work together effectively: through collaboration. To be generative is to be creative and productive. Raw numbers of people won't do you any good in that regard unless they can find a way to collaborate effectively and be productive.

We do run into a bit of a problem, however, with the word "collaboration," because it is so broad. It fundamentally means to work together, which means it could cover just about anything, from two people collaborating by not running into each other as they cross the street, to two multinational corporations collaborating in a joint, global manufacturing and distribution project. When the meaning is that broad, it's fairly useless.

Harvard Business professor Morten Hansen has studied collaboration for decades and includes some important qualifiers in his definition of collaboration.[4] First, when people or work teams collaborate, they must provide "significant help to each other" on a common project. Sometimes it can be one-way (one team providing consulting assistance to another team), but it has to be significant help. You getting out of my way in the crosswalk does not count as true collaboration. The second qualifier is that it must involve people. People collaborate with other people. Data and information don't collaborate. They simply get shifted from one computer to another. Sending me the numbers on this quarter's book sales isn't really collaboration. Helping me to market my book (including giving me data I need to solve a problem) is.

Although this definition of collaboration is a bit clearer, it ultimately doesn't go far enough, at least not for us. The premise of this book is that (a) our world is changing radically and quickly and (b) the mechanical models on which our organizations are built are not providing us with an adequate response. Collaboration is logically an important part of dealing with this kind of change, but we have to be careful not to settle for the outdated, mechanical understanding of collaboration. That kind of collaboration, as Hansen's definition reflects, is fundamentally focused on problem solving—it is for groups working together on a common project. As such, that definition is fairly linear. People come together and collaborate to get a particular problem solved. Start, middle, end.

Today's collaboration needs to go further. Today's collaboration is generative. Yes, it includes solving the tough problems we face in our organizational contexts—none of us can do that alone, so we need to ensure that the right people in our organizations work together on problem solving. But to really be generative, today's collaboration must go beyond solving problems and into generating new value both today

---

4. Hansen, Morten T. Collaboration: How Leaders Avoid the Traps, Create Unity, and Reap Big Results. Boston, MA: Harvard Business, 2009. 14-15.

and into the future. Collaboration (at the risk of turning our readers off with a buzzword) must achieve synergy. It's not enough to provide valuable help to a colleague in another department to solve that particular problem. That's a good start, but we also need to be building that colleague's capacity along the way (or the capacity of others in the system) so that at the end of the project, the whole system is able to solve future problems more easily. That is generative collaboration. We need that kind of collaboration to get out of the mess we've created with today's organizations.

Given this less linear definition of collaboration, we want to be careful not to be too linear in the way we discuss organizational process. In the preceding two chapters we talked about process in terms of three levels: structural, internal, and external. In our discussion of open organizations (in Chapter 6), this translated into a focus on creating silos that work (structural); on processes for strategy that worked continuously rather than on a scheduled basis (internal); and engaging broader stakeholder communities in developing products and services (external). For trustworthy organizations (see Chapter 7, "How to Be Trustworthy"), our conversation about truth brought us into issues of whistle blowing and reporting relationships (structural); dealing with conflict and performance reviews (internal); and speaking the truth in PR and online (external).

For the exploration of collaboration, we want to simultaneously cover the structural, internal, and external elements, rather than examining them separately. This will help us avoid falling back to the default, linear understanding of collaboration and push us to better understand how collaboration can truly simultaneously solve problems and build system capacity. So instead of covering separately the different types of internal, external, and structural collaboration found in generative organizations, we will explore two different major organizational process areas—brand and strategy—and articulate how collaboration is infused into these processes to make them more generative.

Collaborative Brand

Social media technologies are having a greater impact on collaboration than any other aspects of openness and trustworthiness. Here more than anywhere else, we're seeing some great proactive (as opposed to reactive) examples of collaboration that begin with building a website to support it. Companies all over the Web are building and nurturing online communities, whether on Facebook, LinkedIn, or other community sites like Google Groups, Groupsite, or Ning. New interdepartmental teams are emerging simply to deal with multifaceted social communications—and these new ways of collaborating need to spread through the entire organization. Let's take a look.

We discussed MyStarbucksIdea.com in Chapter 6 as systems thinking applied externally. Starbucks built a site to collect product ideas for the company from customers. The key, though, is that Starbucks had what Alexandra Wheeler, director of digital strategies, calls a "philosophical commitment" to becoming a social, collaborative company. Starbucks' "idea partners" who moderate the site are responsible for being the voice of the customer inside the company, looking for ideas that hit the zeitgeist of customers, going to bat for the right ideas, and being transparent about what won't work. She says this site has changed the culture of the company by helping it create what she calls a "listening culture"—more than just marketing strategy—which ultimately has reflected positively on the brand.[5]

Marketing professionals are realizing that "brand" is not the same animal that it was in the early days of advertising (think *Mad Men*). Traditional branding is control-based (mechanical, in fact). We gather information from the consumers to craft the perfect branding messages and images, and then we deliver them to the market with machinelike efficiency and consistency to "build" the brand." Messages and images are still a part of it, but as the Starbucks example illustrates, brand is equally created by the consumers and their engagement with the company in a variety of settings.

But this kind of collaboration on brand creation goes beyond consumers. Nokia, the mobile telephone manufacturer, has a site called IdeasProject (http://www.ideasproject.com), which provides a space for users and developers to exchange ideas. Like Starbucks drinkers, the users of Nokia's products have a voice in what gets developed. But in this case the collaboration goes beyond simply between the headquarters and the consumers, which is representative of what Nokia calls the "manufacturer-centric innovation development systems that have been the mainstay of commerce for hundreds of years." Participation extends to other companies and other developers, knowing that collaboration with such a broad network helps realize ideas. Nokia actually shares ideas from within the company that are not being used with the public, including application developers and startups.

IdeasProject is designed to be collaborative and generative in every sense. You can submit an idea using a simple form that connects and categorizes your idea in relation to other ideas on the site. Anyone can review and provide feedback on the idea as well as vote on its value. People are encouraged to share their ideas through social media channels, too. Nokia reviewers then give each idea a "status":

- **Open for Voting.** Idea has been shared and is open for voting, commenting, and any contribution.

---

5. Warner, Bernhard. "Starbucks' Alexandra Wheeler: Forget Social Strategy, Think Social Philosophy | SMI." Social Media Influence: Intelligence, News & Analysis. 16 July 2010. Web. 20 May 2011. <http://socialmediainfluence.com/2010/07/16/starbucks-alexandra-wheeler-forget-social-strategy-think-social-philosophy/>.

- **Needs Community Input.** Idea has potential and should be taken further, for example, by making a prototype of it.

- **Reviewed.** Idea has been reviewed and did not lead to immediate action. However, if idea receives a lot of new votes, it will be reconsidered.

- **Put into Action.** Idea is in progress and taken up by a business unit or team for implementation.

Nokia is committed to open innovation, so all ideas are shared for the benefit of the community. They warn openly on the FAQ page that by participating, you invite open collaboration and building upon your ideas, with the risk that others may take those ideas forward without further permission.

OpenIDEO (www.openideo.com), started by the design agency IDEO, is a similar collaboration site with a twist. The site presents a "challenge" to help society in some way, and people essentially compete for the best idea to solve problems—such as how to better connect food production and consumption, how to increase the number of registered bone marrow donors to help save more lives, or how to improve maternal health using mobile technologies in low-income countries. Nonprofits have also made huge strides in this area. In Chapter 2, "We Can't Go Back," we mentioned Ushaidi, the open source platform that allows people to collaborate during crisis situations in real-time using SMS, MMS, Twitter, email, and the Web.

When the idea of generative collaboration is applied to brand, a new picture emerges. Companies engage people across traditional boundaries (both internal and external) not only to create products, services, and experiences, but to create meaning. Doing social good is no longer a buried section of your website where you brag about donating to charity as part of your corporate social responsibility program. Doing social good means collaborating with people directly to activate social good on the ground, and that becomes integrated with the rest of your efforts. Brand becomes enhanced, not because people read your marketing messages, but because they themselves are able to do more, be more, and make change all while collaborating with you, your company, your people, or your ideas. Your brand lives and grows through the collaboration. It exists within your customers, and it exists within your employees—and not just the ones in the marketing department. Generative collaboration becomes essential to brand development because in today's world, it is no longer enough to simply have a good product or receive good customer service. That is the "left-brained" world in which we have been entrenched for decades.[6] Today's more whole-brained economy is driven by things

---

6. Pink, Daniel H. A Whole New Mind: Why Right-brainers Will Rule the Future. New York: Riverhead, 2006.

like meaning and story and design. Thanks to automation and outsourcing, our left brain needs are met more easily. That is why collaboration has to be generative now, particularly when it comes to brand. Like it or not, we've raised the bar on what brand means, and by collaborating effectively—and deeply—both inside and outside your organization, you can create a brand that has an impact.

Collaborative Strategy

Like brand, strategy has traditionally been viewed as something created by a small group of people, and then brought forth into the world in a relatively linear fashion. We challenged traditional strategic planning in Chapter 3, pointing out serious flaws in its inherent assumptions that (a) you can predict the future, (b) you can separate thought from action, and (c) you can successfully script and schedule the formation of strategy. In Chapter 6, we talked a bit about how to apply systems thinking to strategy processes. We suggested that strategy conversations need to cut across different levels in organizations, and while you can schedule periodic conversations as part of your process, unscheduled conversations also need to be integrated into strategy formation to be successful.

In other words, developing a strategy needs to be collaborative—and not the old-fashioned, linear collaboration. (Traditional strategic planners love that kind of collaboration, actually.) Strategy requires generative collaboration (just like brand), where boundaries are crossed and people are allowed to engage in real value creation together. Where strategy and implementation are intertwined, and where strategic solutions lay the foundation for a growing system, rather than merely the platform for tomorrow's problems to be solved— or, worse, simply the outline for your organization's version of a TPS report.

We have a simplified framework for understanding strategy that can be boiled down to four actions: understand, choose, do, learn. Although they are not always done in that order, these are the building blocks of strategic action. We have to *understand* who we are, what we are trying to accomplish, and what is happening in the environment. We have to make clear *choices* about what we will do, what we will not do, and how we are doing it. Of course, we actually have to *do* something (strategy without action is pointless), and if we're not *learning* throughout the process, there is no hope of it being generative. Sounds good so far, but if you pursue strategy formation with this framework in mind—and don't include true, generative collaboration—then you often end up with the traditional (and weak) strategic planning processes with which we are all too familiar. Those linear collaborations produce the binders that sit on the shelf collecting dust.

Here is what it looks like with generative collaboration infused into the process.

Understand

Traditionally, the processes we use to develop understanding are linear. First, we crunch numbers. We analyze our past performance, and we measure everything we can get our hands on—costs, profits, margins, hours, markets, opinions, preferences, sales, leads, and so on. We get as much analysis as our army of PowerPoint designers can handle. With that in hand, we do what all good managers do: We hold meetings. We hold departmental meetings, interdepartmental meetings, cross-functional team meetings, and finally senior management meetings. In those meetings we debate and discuss until a final version of our reality is agreed on (and wordsmithed) by the powers that be.

Yes, you are correct in reading our sarcastic tone. Perhaps we shouldn't be so sarcastic. These activities do generate insightful analysis, and with that in hand, it is possible to make some good choices. But in comparison, look at the understanding that companies like Starbucks, Dell, and Nokia are getting by actually engaging, in real time, their employees, partners, and customers in ongoing conversations. Ideas build upon each other and don't necessarily end up in the place envisioned when the conversation started. That is developing real understanding through a more collaborative and generative process.

So how can we generate those kinds of conversations internally when we are developing the shared understanding that forms the base of our strategy? How would we need to conduct our meetings differently to create that kind of result? This would challenge our traditional notions of hierarchy, because we know that when senior people are in the room, the junior people don't speak up. So get ready for a more decentralized approach to developing the understanding. This would challenge our traditional meeting agendas, filled with boring PowerPoint presentations that are all about conclusions, rather than encouraging inquiry. It would challenge our budgeting and operational schedules, because we would realize that this shared understanding is changing constantly. We would need to change our standard measurements so that we could read changes in the middle of our processes, rather than at the end of them, because sometimes that is when we need to learn. To be generative in these processes, we need to shake them up. Remember that the progress here is three-dimensional, changing in ways that we cannot control—nor would we want to. We intentionally cut across traditional boundaries, including involving customers or even competitors, because it allows for this kind of generative progress.

Choose

The traditional process for making strategic choices is not particularly collaborative. This tends to be the domain of the top of the organizational chart. Analysis is fed to senior people, they make the choices, and that strategy is then communicated down the chain. Every organization uses a seemingly different process for identifying and making the choices. Often the quality of the choices depends on the workings of the senior management team. Those who are afraid to really engage in conflict are the ones who end up with fairly watered down strategic choices. (Let's do what we did last year, but with 2% better results.) Sometimes you get a long list of strategic priorities and options, where everything seems important. (And no one knows what, exactly, to do next.) Sometimes you get a list of strategic objectives that come with a subsequent list of specific tactics you are supposed to employ to achieve the objectives. This is fine until you start the work and realize the tactics are not going to work, or you hand The Plan over to lower level execs who had no part in deciding the tactics and eventually end up shelving the plan because they are not invested in either the process or the outcome.

These ways of choosing are failing us because they are neither collaborative nor generative. First, we separate the choices around high-level strategy (or "where we want to compete," using the language of business strategist Nilofer Merchant) from the important questions of "how we will compete."[7] Senior decision makers either restrict their decisions to the high level, or they try to bind the executives and the implementers together; again, this leaves the implementers scratching their heads because they are being ordered to do things in specific ways, when they usually know better approaches. We need choice processes that bring both sides together when making both sets of important choices. We need to have the discipline to rule out ideas that are good, but not good enough. We need to build the capacity to make choices on-the-fly, based on clear principles because we cannot predict the future. To do that, however, we need to bring people together to make choices together, which has not traditionally been allowed ("they" don't know enough to make the choices, we don't have enough time, it's too expensive to bring people together, I can't take them away from their job to do this, and so on). We have seemingly built into our processes an avoidance of collaboration, and we need to reverse that.

Do

If there is any piece of this simple strategy model where we would not require assistance, it would be the doing part. We don't usually complain that our organizations are not doing anything. We may worry that our activities are not strategic enough, that we do things because we've always done them, or that we do them because of politics and ego, but there is usually little doubt that we are getting things done. Of course action, in and of itself, is not necessarily strategic, nor collaborative. In

---

7. Merchant, Nilofer. The New How: Building Business Solutions through Collaborative Strategy. Sebastopol, CA: O'Reilly, 2010. 13.

Chapter 3, you recall that one of the inherent flaws of strategic planning is its separation of thought and action. It happens on the front end as we assign strengths and weaknesses outside the context in which we are applying them, during our SWOT analysis. And it happens on the implementation end as we do things without considering how the ever-changing landscape might require a different set of actions. We plan the work, and then work the plan—but apparently thinking is somewhat secondary.

This is where a collaborative mindset can help. In Chapter 6, we talked about the role of "middle-level thinking" in strategy. It is the part that is typically missing that connects the high-level strategic objectives with the everyday tasks that need to get done. But not enough organizations have processes in place that allow for people at all levels of the organization to collaboratively fill that gap. It is similar to the challenge in making collaborative choices. As we take action, we need to bring the right people together to infuse thinking into the action. In this sense, collaboration allows the choosing and the doing to become more of an integrated and iterative step.

Learn

Learning is the glue that holds your strategy process together, so it needs to be collaborative. Plenty of organizations regularly follow the U.S. military model of an "after action review," where project teams get together to analyze what happened so the learning can be applied to the next project. Those types of collaborative efforts can be expanded upon to serve the same function for an organization's strategy. You have to ensure, however, that the learning is truly strategic. It must generate insight beyond what tactically worked or did not work into a deeper understanding of who you are as an organization and how you will be able to create enduring value within the current and emerging system. It's not just what strategies would be good ideas— it's what strategies are the right ones for your unique company to pursue, strategies that contribute to your flourishing as a company and contribute to the overall growth of the system. You won't be able to get at those generative answers unless you create opportunities for people at all levels of the system to have conversations about it.

Brand and strategy are just two areas where you need to be more collaborative in your processes if you want a generative organization. This kind of collaboration requires proactive discussion among groups of people who typically do not collaborate in these areas, and it likely stretches the comfort zone of those involved. We welcome this. We believe that being generative is becoming less of a luxury and more of a necessity. There is no way we are going to shift into a more generative mode by making a series of minor adjustments to the way we do things.

Generative Behavior: Relationship Building

Digital channels break down the notion of "it's who you know" because we all now live in a world where we can know everyone—and everyone can know us.

—Mitch Joel, Six *Pixels of Separation*

Inclusion and collaboration are obviously based in relationships. So it makes sense that relationship building is the focus for creating generative organizations at the level of individual behavior. It is not new information that relationships are important in business, but if we are going to create generative organizations—ones that create enduring value and help the system grow in the process—we are going to have to elevate the importance of relationship building. Relationship building is not just a part of the sales process, and it isn't something that the extroverts in your organization do to enhance their career. Building relationships is a core competency. For everyone. Strong relationships enable better collaboration across departments. To be genuinely inclusive, you must build relationships across traditional boundaries to take advantage of Johansson's "intersections." The quality of relationships you have with others in the system positively impacts your efforts to be open and trustworthy as well. Healthy relationships are a central part of our existence as human beings, and they certainly play a role in social media's power. Relationships are a big deal.

Yet building relationships has not received much attention in the business world. Most people wouldn't really know where to start if they wanted to build this capacity at an individual level, outside maybe taking some courses on interpersonal skills. That could be a good start, but it goes beyond that. In today's social world, relationship building goes beyond the one-on-one of relationships with individuals in your life. It now also includes relationships with the networks in your life.

Yes, you need good relationships with other individuals in your system. They can be supervisors, direct reports, peers, customers, suppliers, vendors—you name it. This is where the interpersonal skills help. Social media, by its nature, helps with that, of course, and many of us (though not all of us) find it relatively easy to make true connections online before we ever meet those new people face to face (if we do at all). Strengthening your ability to build relationships at an individual level helps you to be more generative. But it doesn't stop there. You also have to factor in certain skills that help you build your relationship with your network. This facet has grown in importance with the growth of social media, though it has always been there. Each of us is part of several networks, and while the individual relationships are important, there is a quality of our relationship with the network as a whole that also requires attention and its own set of knowledge and skills.

As we look at the knowledge and skills needed to support more generative relationship building in organizations, we address each type of relationship building—interpersonal and network—separately.

Interpersonal Relationship Building

We look at interpersonal relationship building in terms of both knowledge and skills.

The knowledge piece is straightforward. In all relationships, you need to know about three things: you, the other, and the context. In Chapter 7, we discussed self-knowledge in the context of authenticity. To create more trustworthy organizations, individuals must know who they are, what their real strengths are, and what their emotional states are. The more you know about yourself, the more easily you can engage in authentic behavior, which is critical for building trust. That is helpful for relationship building as well. Trust and authenticity are helpful for smoothing out bumps in any relationship building process. But when you think specifically about that process, other elements of self-knowledge support your building relationships with individuals in your system.

The self knowledge that is integral to generative relationship building, however, is not as much knowing who you are or what your talents are. It's knowing what you want. We are talking about work and professional relationships, and the reason we have professional relationships is because each party gets some kind of benefit from the relationship. We interact with other employees, external partners, vendors, and even customers because by working together in a relationship we can actually accomplish something (get a project done, save money, complete a sale, and so on). Professional relationships are by their nature somewhat transactional. They have a certain element of negotiation in them. So to make it work, you need to be clear on what you want out of it.

So from a negotiation perspective, knowing "what you want" is really about understanding your interests. In negotiations, two parties come to the table with conflicting positions. That is, they each have a different answer to a problem, and the answers are incompatible. The marketing director thinks she should be in charge of the organizational Facebook page, and the IT director thinks he should be the one to control that. Those are their positions. To break the deadlock, a mediator would work with each party to identify the interests that lie behind the positions. The marketing director may have concerns about the timing and consistency of messages sent out through that channel and needs to ensure they flow well with other marketing efforts. The IT director may have concerns about security and which web pages are exposed to the public. So their positions are incompatible (only one of them could be officially in control of the Facebook site), but the underlying interests are in different areas. This allows for some kind of proverbial win/win solution when they come to an agreement about how to protect both the brand consistency and IT security of the organization.

Professional relationship building involves negotiation like this all the time. To avoid the deadlocks and impasses, you have to understand your own interests—not just your positions. Knowing what you want can include understanding your desired solutions to particular problems, but it requires going beyond that to knowing *why* you want them. Some of this may be uncomfortable. What if you want control of the Facebook page because you're making a power play in your internal hierarchy to secure more budget for other projects? Not all of our interests are pure and noble. We have to be honest with ourselves about those things (which also helps with authenticity) because that kind of self-knowledge will direct us in the way we build our interpersonal relationships in work settings. What do you want in your relationships with other members of the senior management team? What are your true interests when it comes to developing customer relationships? What are you hoping to get out of a relationship with a direct report? The more you know yourself and can answer questions like these, the more effective you will be in building professional relationships.

Of course, the other side of self-knowledge in building relationships is knowledge of the other. Just as knowing your interests helps in choosing actions that build relationships, when you know the needs or interests of the other person, you are more likely to engage him in ways that strengthen the relationship. If you know that the IT director is always concerned about security, you would probably start the conversation about the security issues when it comes to figuring out how to manage that Facebook page.

But beyond simply understanding the interests of the other party, what is really needed for effective interpersonal relationship building is empathy. As branding expert Tom Asacker says in his book *A Little Less Conversation*, "the marketplace is as much about identity and community as it is about stuff and money. Nearly all of our action and interactions are in some way an expression of how we think about ourselves relative to how we think others like us feel and act in similar situations." Empathy goes beyond the rational understanding of the other person. It reflects a deeper and more nuanced connection to the other person's feelings, attitudes, and thoughts. This is typically what we mean when we say someone "gets" us, and it is critical to our ability to "connect" with others. This makes it critical in relationship building. Sometimes knowing that the IT director keeps security concerns at the top of his mind isn't quite enough when managing that relationship. You have to get a better sense of what is on the line for him, how a security breach would impact him personally, or perhaps how he sees IT security as contributing to the mission of the organization. Knowing people at this level helps you respond and reach out more appropriately and effectively.

The third piece of knowledge required for effective relationship building is knowing the context. All relationships exist within a context, and the context determines the nature of the relationship just as much as the uniqueness of the individuals does. How the marketing director and the IT director relate to each other in some work contexts, such as a specific project that has a marketing focus, will be different from how they relate to each other as peers on the senior management team. Think back to the conversation about systems thinking in Chapter 6. Your relationships with that individual coworker, vendor, or customer are always connected to a broader system of relationships, and your knowledge about that system, the interrelationships, and the dynamics occurring in the background will help you be more effective in your one-on-one interactions.

Communication is the single most important skill for interpersonal relationship building. We talked in Chapter 6 about managing conflict as a skill for creating more ownership, and we talked in Chapter 7 about curiosity and asking questions as a skill where the focus was on authenticity. Those are obviously also helpful to the general task of building solid interpersonal relationships. But they will never be enough if you don't have a solid foundation of communication skills. A relationship between two people exists in the interaction between them, and the overwhelming majority of interaction will be in the form of communication.

We cannot tell you everything you need to know about communication here. There is simply too much good material out there. But we point briefly to two important concepts in communication that can help tremendously in building relationships.

The first is about giving feedback, which we will define here as constructive criticism, as opposed to praise. This is feedback that is designed to improve something, solve a problem, or correct a mistake. We all give feedback at one point or another in our relationships, and it is not always welcomed. When is the last time you reacted warmly when someone started the conversation with "Hey, can I give you some feedback?" Feedback is a communication when the current situation involving you and the other is not working optimally. When that happens, you have to give feedback to the other person about the negative impact so the two of you can solve the problem.

Feedback is usually handled poorly. The marketing director gives the IT director feedback by telling him that his obsessive need for control is generating unnecessary roadblocks to the marketing efforts and is ruining the project. We won't say out loud how the IT director would respond to that "feedback." The problem with that feedback is one we see all the time: It is overly judgmental. The speaker is presenting both the problem and the cause of the problem in one fell swoop—the cause being the other person and his inadequacy. This type of feedback never actually helps the two people in question solve the problem.

What you need in your feedback is the discipline to stay focused on two things: behavior and impact. Start the feedback by identifying the specific, observable behavior of the other person, and then link that behavior to the impact it is having on you or the system. This helps keep the feedback from being judgmental. The marketing director could instead tell the IT director about the two times last week when marketing messages were delayed because they were waiting for approval from the IT department. She could explain the volume of messages going out in this campaign and how even a week delay in the schedule, over the long run, could impact their reach and, in the end, sales volume. Notice that any suggestion about the IT director's need for control was left out of it this time. And frankly, the IT director may, in fact, be a control freak. Either way, however, it's best to leave the judgment out of the communication. The feedback has simply identified the problem, and now the two of them are poised to do problem solving. This kind of effective communication is the foundation for good interpersonal relationship building.

Network Relationship Building

Building relationships with other individuals, as important as that is, is not enough these days. Yes, our organizations are collections of individuals, but individuals don't operate in vacuums. Each individual is simultaneously connected to a number of different networks as she goes about her work day. These networks all overlap with each other, and the strength and reach of the networks vary wildly. They are a critical factor in how work gets done and whether entire organizations (and individuals) succeed. We have obvious internal networks within our organizations, sometimes defined by hierarchical boundaries, and sometimes outside of those boundaries. We have our broader professional networks, consisting of people with whom we have developed relationships throughout our career from a variety of different organizations or even industries. If we are active in our professional associations, we have even broader networks from those communities. Of course we also have our network of personal acquaintances.

In the world of our parents, where networks were fairly well defined and not terribly overlapping, those personal connections didn't necessarily have an impact on our work lives, though there were occasional exceptions. Some individuals might have developed extensive networks (typically the sales folks), and they might have that "golden rolodex," but everyone else made it through life with a smaller number of isolated networks. What kept those networks limited was simply time—they didn't have time to meet more people than they were already interacting with in their normal routine.

Social media has completely revolutionized the network. You don't use a rolodex any more. You log on to your social networks to broadcast a request for information or a resource that you need. The people who you know, who themselves have their own disparate networks, can reproduce your request with a few clicks; now you are reaching well beyond the group of people that you could get to know personally and are much more likely to get the answer you seek. And because the person who has the answer or the resource is responding to a request that comes from someone in his trusted network, he is happy to provide it, even though he may never have heard of you. We now spend time liking Facebook pages, following Twitter hashtags, and starting Linked In discussions, all as part of building and maintaining our networks.

This is network relationship building. Just like the interpersonal level, where we develop strong relationships to get more done and be more effective in a generative organization, building strong networks can be equally powerful in creating effective, generative organizations. The knowledge and skills you need to build strong networks overlap with those at the interpersonal level. You're still dealing with individuals as you network, so it will help to master the communication skills and the knowledge of yourself, the other, and the context that we discussed. But for network relationship building, some additional knowledge sets and skill sets are needed in today's social world.

On the knowledge side, you have to understand your network. It's not just a count of how many contacts are in your database or your number of friends, followers, or connections in the social media tools. That is part of it. Those are all connections, or ties, that you have in your overlapping networks. But some ties are stronger than others, and you need a mix of both strong and weak ties. You can typically rely on your strong ties to help you out in ways that require more effort, but the weak ties are critical for expanding your network outside your closest community. You need to nurture both types of ties. You also want to identify the people in your network who are at the center of other networks (also called nodes). They are the most active and most well connected, so obviously they are key when you are trying to activate your extended network. The overall picture of your connections, the strength of ties, and the location of network nodes is called your social graph (see one example of a visualization of author Maddie Grant's social graph in Figure 8.1), and you need to know how strongly or weakly you are connected to others, just like you need self-knowledge to build interpersonal relationships.

Networks are more than just connections among individuals. What makes them actual networks is the exchange of value among those individuals. That value can take many different forms. For personal networks it can be as simple as sharing information about your life with your friends. Your network derives value from staying up to date on your life. For professional networks the value is more often in the form of content of some kind. You share information, insight, or access to resources that your network might not otherwise see. Or maybe you can connect people in your network to other organizations or other networks that can help them get their job done.

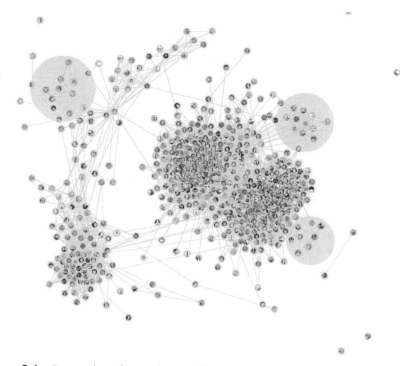

Figure 8.1 *A snapshot of co-author Maddie Grant's Facebook social graph, generated by the SocialGraph Facebook application.*

It is critical to really understand what is of value to your networks because that is how you build relationships—by sharing that value. This has been central to the growth of social media, particularly in professional circles. The connections and exchanges among members in social media networks are driven by the sharing of "social objects," a phrase coined by sociologist and entrepreneur Jyri Engstrom.[8] A social object is simply something of value to people in the network that can be shared using online tools. A specific blog post can be a social object, because it can be shared (and re-shared) easily through a post on Facebook, Linked In, or Twitter. All kinds of online content, including podcasts, videos, and photos, can be shared as social objects. Social objects could even be invitations to in-person events, so it doesn't all have to be virtual. But these objects are the currency in the social networking economy, so you have to know what they are and have access to them if you are going to build an effective network. In *Open Community*,[9] co-author Maddie Grant defines social objects thus:

8. Engstrom, Jyri. "Why Some Social Network Services Work and Others Don't—Or: the Case for Object-centered Sociality :: Zengestrom." Zengestrom. 13 Apr. 2005. Web. 21 May 2011. <http://www.zengestrom.com/blog/2005/04/why-some-social-network-services-work-and-others-dont-or-the-case-for-object-centered-sociality.html>.

9. Dreyer, Lindy, and Maddie Grant. Open Community: a Little Book of Big Ideas for Associations Navigating the Social Web. Madison, WI: Omnipress, 2010. 139.

> Social objects are what your [online] community revolves around, the content that will inspire your community members to have a social interaction with each other and not someone else. To figure out your social objects, answer the "now what?" question: "OK, so someone has logged in to the site, *now what*? What are they here for?

On the skill side of the equation, building relationships in networks has a foundation in competency with social media tools. At one level this is obvious simply because of the ubiquity of social media these days. Facebook grabs everyone's attention when the site gains 200 million users in nine months. But skill in social media does not stop at setting up a Facebook page and a Twitter account simply as new channels for broadcasting your organization's message. Using social media is still about relationships. So before you become a "power user" in any of these tools, you have to master one critical social media skill: listening.

Using a variety of search tools, you need to listen to what people both inside and outside your network are talking about. You certainly want to set up automatic alerts that identify when people are talking about you or your organization. This is one way to expand your network because it helps you find people who you are not already connected to engaged in conversations about your company. But it's critical to listen carefully to what the people you already know are talking about, because that is the key to understanding what they value.

We know you are listening online already. But listening is actually more than just monitoring what others are saying. The same is true interpersonally, actually. The communication skills trainers call it "active listening," where in addition to actually paying attention to what the other person is saying, you indicate your understanding by reflecting back what he is saying or asking clarifying questions. You have to do the same thing online to build relationships. When you hear people in your network saying things about a topic relevant to you, you have to chime in, respond, and maybe ask some questions. This does not mean responding with a marketing message about how your product will solve their problem. It means responding to what they are saying in ways that are relevant to their experience (not necessarily your needs). These kinds of social media skills need to be developed at all levels of the organization to be effective.

And listening and responding are not limited to interactions with public social networks—they are also critical for developing strong networks inside your organization. That is why some of the same social media technologies are now being applied more broadly to internal interactions. Deloitte Australia, for example, uses the tool Yammer to engage employees more broadly and solve problems more efficiently. Yammer is something like Twitter, but used privately within an organization's network. Deloitte Australia needed a tagline for an ad campaign and could have hired an agency to come up with one. Instead they posted the challenge internally through Yammer and got 1,500 suggestions in a 24-hour period, from which they chose their tagline, engaging employees and saving time and money in the process.[10] The popular customer relationship management (CRM) software, Salesforce, also now has a Twitter-like function called Chatter that can enable people in the same organization to collaborate, communicate, and share information in a more social and networked way.

Finally, a skill that is not always connected with network relationship building but should be is work-life balance. Many organizations are thrown for a loop by social media because it evolved such that the personal and the professional are both shared in the same channel. In Chapter 7, we discussed how the way we share our identity online has changed. This now requires some skills. We need to have an awareness of how we share information online and how the many different ways we share things can be pulled together (via Google) to create a picture of who we are. And the challenge isn't really about controlling the information so only the "right" people can see the "right" information about you. That was how we managed our identity in previous eras. In a social world we don't have control like that. It's more difficult to limit who has access to information put online. But we can manage it by being intentional about what we put online. Individuals can share activities from their different networks and even different parts of their personal life, to enhance the connections they can make in their networks. It's similar to what people do with basic search engine optimization for websites. You include the terms in the text of the pages that you want people to find. Similarly, your activity on social networks helps determine how you are found.

Another aspect of work-life balance is time management. Many people who don't use social media often wonder where people find the time to do it (which is a somewhat puzzling question, given the ludicrous amount of time we spend, as a society, watching television). But time spent on social media can be a factor to consider. Participation is unstructured, so there is no end to the ways in which you can participate, and that can translate to many hours spent in social media activities that do not necessarily translate to personal or business results. You need to be able to understand what you are doing in social media, and why—knowing how you want to build your network and how that will help you get things done. It's not always easy to make a direct cause and effect relationship, but you can manage your effort by looking at results. This is one reason why the measurement component of social media needs to be understood better.

---

10. "Yammer: Success Stories." Yammer: The Enterprise Social Network. Web. 21 May 2011.
   <https://www.yammer.com/about/case_studies#deloitte-story>.

Accomplishing More, Better

Remember the Margaret Wheatley quote earlier in this chapter in which she says organizing is about "the desire to accomplish, to create something more"? We're going to read into her words a bit, because we don't think she means just more, as in more quantity. She's talking about quality, too. More and better. This is the essence of being generative.

Our organizations need to be more generative—more inclusive, valuing different voices; more internally and externally collaborative, with systems and processes and technologies that allow for ideas and innovation. They need to improve the inter- and intra-personal skills necessary to ramp up our networked relationship-building abilities. If we start to bake this in to how we work, then accomplishing more better will become second nature.

One human element is essential to doing this, though, that we have not talked about yet. We can't truly be collaborative and generative until we address the "fear factor." That's for the next chapter.

Must Read

Our three "must read" recommendations for this chapter each illustrate a key aspect of generative culture, process, and behavior. *The Medici Effect* by Frans Johansson is a book that integrates inclusion and innovation, which is one of the critical lessons around inclusion: It brings change. Nilofer Merchant's *The New How* is about collaborative strategy and beautifully illustrates how collaboration has been absent from that important process. And Beth Kanter and Allison Fine's *The Networked Nonprofit* is a great resource for understanding how behavior needs to change for our employees and organizations to build relationships in a more networked world. And, by the way, if you work in the corporate world and are surprised to see a nonprofit book in the list, then go back and reread the section about inclusion. This could be a great opportunity for you to find some ideas at "the intersection."

Johansson, Frans. *The Medici Effect*. Boston: Harvard Business School, 2004.

Kanter, Beth, and Allison H. Fine. *The Networked Nonprofit: Connecting with Social Media to Drive Change*. San Francisco: Jossey-Bass, 2010.

Merchant, Nilofer. *The New How: Building Business Solutions through Collaborative Strategy*. Sebastopol, CA: O'Reilly, 2010.

Get Started Today: Worksheet

Enough reading. Let's get started!

Download and print the worksheet accompanying this chapter at www.humanize-book.com.

All four worksheets accompanying this book are structured in the same way. The first section helps you assess how generative your organization is and includes a quiz and some open-ended questions. In the second section, we guide you through conversations with others in your organization about generativity. And the last section gets you going on an action plan.

We ask you to take a hard look at how generative your organization is. Do you really see different people making decisions? Does everyone in your organization freak out when there is change? Can people in your organization put it all out on the table? These are things to look for in cultures that value inclusion. At the process level you probe into issues of collaboration. Our favorite question is about whether people in your organization argue about which department "owns" certain processes. We also ask about how much you include people outside organizational lines in your processes. At the behavior level we have you examine how well your people build relationships, including their skill in doing that using social media tools.

The next step is to have some conversations with others in your organization about these topics. As usual, we include in the worksheets some advice about how to approach these conversations based on where you are in your organization's hierarchy:

Executives. As was the case with "Open," the executive level can get some benefit from exploring their own commitment to being generative (think inclusion, collaboration, and relationship building), without anyone else in the room. For these topics (particularly inclusion) you might also benefit from securing the assistance of an external facilitator, or else you run the risk of a substantial amount of awkward silence.

But because this is about including others and collaborating, you obviously don't want to have all these conversations behind closed doors. Still, we don't recommend running out and inviting in the managers and line employees for an all-staff meeting about inclusion and collaboration. Being generative is about creation and productivity, so give some time to the other groups to start some conversations and actually invite *you* to attend, rather than the other way around. Don't wait forever, but don't rush in to control it. The same advice from the "Open" worksheet applies: Be curious and don't dominate the conversations.

Middle managers. Of the four elements in the book, generative might be the one where the middle level should really take the lead in the conversations. As a manager, you're a connector, which is critical to being generative. It's sometimes easier for you to make the connections for collaboration or to facilitate new relationship building. Spend extra time thinking about who you want to include in these conversations so that you get good content in the conversation and start making connections that help build the capacity for being generative. And brush up on your facilitation skills!

Front line employees. You have a lot to bring to the table in the conversation about being generative. Make sure you get to some of those conversations with managers and senior executives so you can share your experience as someone who is implementing on a daily basis. Don't fall into the trap of "nothing will ever change about inclusion, collaboration, or relationship building," and don't fall into the "there's nothing I can do about it anyway" trap either. Step up and share your perspective about where you can create new and exciting things—and where those efforts are thwarted. This is also a great topic for engaging your coworkers who are more active in social media (or if that's you, making sure you share your insight and experience with others). That's a critical piece for generative action.

Ultimately, the changes we advise throughout this book are necessary, they are possible, and they start with you. Don't wait for permission or the perfect timing. Are *you* ready? Go.

9

How to Be Courageous

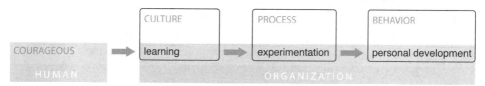

	CULTURE	PROCESS	BEHAVIOR
COURAGEOUS	learning	experimentation	personal development
HUMAN		ORGANIZATION	

The world knows how to grow and change. It has been doing so for billions of years. Life knows how to create systems. Life knows how to create greater capacity. Life knows how to discover meaning. The motions that we sought to wrestle from life's control are available to us to support our desires if we can stop being so afraid.
　　　　—Margaret Wheatley and Myron Kellner-Rogers, *A Simpler Way*

We made being courageous the last of the four human elements for organizations on purpose. Fear is arguably the most important source of dysfunction in organizations today. Fear drives senior executives to share only the bare minimum about what happens in those conversations in the boardroom. Fear causes middle managers to try to do too much themselves, burning themselves out and leaving the groups they serve frustrated. Fear lets front line employees take the safe route and not confront people when things aren't working, resulting in frustrated employees, present but not engaged. Fear keeps us out of vibrant online conversations because we don't trust our employees to respond or we worry what people outside the organization will say about us. Fear keeps us from taking risks. Fear keeps us from doing what we need to do. Fear keeps us from living a whole life.

We have been decrying fear in organizations for a long time. Peter Drucker and W. Edwards Deming, arguably the fathers of the management and quality fields, respectively, both wrote about driving fear out of organizations to improve performance.[1] More recently, Jeffrey Pfeffer and Robert Sutton, authors of *The Knowing-Doing Gap*, which we listed in our Must Read section in Chapter 6, "How to Be Open," documented fear's negative impact on performance in organizations, arguing that it prevents people from taking action that they know they should take.[2] Their research indicates clearly that the presence of fear has a negative impact on performance, despite the popular belief that fear can be a good motivator in organizations. For example, fear of the boss typically prevents people from sharing bad news, which results in leaders not getting the information they need to make the right decisions (the "emperor has no clothes" phenomenon). Even worse, when managers demand high performance no matter what, people will even lie about their performance or their achievements to please the demanding boss. Being afraid generates behavior that we don't want.

And even in actual cases of life and death, fear has been shown to be a poor motivator. A group of heart patients who had already undergone bypass surgery were told by their doctors that they needed to change their behaviors that were contributing to the problem (unhealthy eating, smoking, lack of exercise, and so on) or they would die. You would think that a literal fear of death might motivate them to change. But nine out of ten did not make lasting changes in their behavior.[3] Even the fear of death, it seems, is not enough to get people to engage in the right behavior.

Despite the problem with fear, we need to be careful about our desire to drive it out of organizations. The problem really isn't fear. Fear is a natural part of the human condition. Unless you live in a world where everything is known and there are no bad results—ever—then you will have fear in your life. Fear is like conflict in that regard—you can't wish for it to go away; you have to develop strategies for dealing with it. The problem is how we react to fear. That is where the idea of courage comes in.

1. Allan, Kelly. "Driving Out Fear and Other Similarities Between Drucker and Deming by Kelly Allan." BPM, Lean Six Sigma & Continuous Process Improvement | Process Excellence Network. 21 Feb. 2011. Web. 03 June 2011. <http://www.processexcellencenetwork.com/process-management/columns/peter-f-drucker-and-w-edwards-deming-intersections/>.

2. Pfeffer, Jeffrey, and Robert I. Sutton. The Knowing-doing Gap: How Smart Companies Turn Knowledge into Action. Boston, MA: Harvard Business School, 2000. 109–137.

3. Deutschman, Alan. "Change or Die | Fast Company." FastCompany.com - Where Ideas and People Meet | Fast Company. 1 May 2005. Web. 03 June 2011. <http://www.fastcompany.com/magazine/94/open_change-or-die.html>.

Courage is not the absence of fear. Being courageous is taking action, despite the presence of fear. Courage causes you to do what you need to do even though you are afraid. It is about facing difficulty and moving forward. It is about speaking the truth, being yourself, taking ownership, embracing difference, revealing who you are, and letting go of control, which is exactly what we have been talking about in the previous three chapters. Courage is at the heart of what it means to be human. And it is also at the heart of human organizations.

But we have to be careful not to overromanticize this. Courage is not some quality that only brave heroes and heroines possess, to be admired by the rest of us who settle for an ordinary existence. Courage, like leadership, is something that by definition needs to be accessible to everyone. So if we want to create a courageous organization, we cannot start from the place that courage requires some kind of superhuman effort. In fact, it starts in a simple and humble place: Courage starts with admitting that you don't know.

You don't know how it's going to end. You don't know if it is truly a best practice. You don't know if she will say yes. You don't know if the relationship will benefit their group more than yours. You don't know if the strategy will be successful. You don't know, because you can't know. The future is not knowable in that sense. Yes, you can do your homework and you can make informed choices (moving forward randomly isn't particularly courageous), but you cannot know the future, and because of that, there is going to be fear. So to be courageous, you have to actually embrace the not knowing part. You start by being comfortable that you don't know exactly where you are going to end up. And then you take action anyway.

That is the second part of courage. Being courageous starts by admitting you don't know and is completed by taking bold and confident action. Being courageous means you move forward based on that paradoxical clarity of confidently knowing what you are going to do, even though you admit you don't know exactly how it's going to end. Bold moves require that clarity—that ownership of what is being done. Otherwise you might simply be reacting because of fear. We have all seen action just for action's sake. That is not courage.

So for an organization, being courageous requires the capacity to take bold action in the face of not knowing. A famous example is that of Netflix, the DVD-rental-by-mail company that shifted its business model several times in the company's short history. First, it discarded late fees for DVD rentals and introduced a monthly flat fee subscription model. Then it developed personalized ratings and reviews. Most recently, it introduced its Watch Instantly video-streaming over the Internet, first with restricted viewing hours then switching to unlimited streaming. At the same time, Netflix has always listened to its customers—a 2008 decision to eliminate customer profiles (for example, different users such as a husband and wife with different movies in their profile queues under one subscription) was reversed when users complained. The percentage of subscribers using this feature was small, but it was essential enough to their experience of the service that it turned out to be worth keeping. The company is now exploring the delivery of original programming.[4] Each of these moves has been risky and has positioned Netflix as forward-thinking and customer-centric, even over industry teeth-gnashing. And so far it's paid off (remember Blockbuster?). But the Netflix story sounds a lot easier in retrospect. As it made these twists and turns in its business model, there wasn't a clear understanding that the moves would pay off, particularly because Netflix was breaking new ground. This kind of management requires real courage.

Taking action in the face of not knowing is something that social media has embraced in a myriad of large and small ways. Experimenting publicly with new ideas is baked into how businesses learned to use social media in the first place. In the beginning at least, the cost of failure was low or nonexistent, so companies simply launched their forays into setting up Facebook pages, LinkedIn groups, or Twitter accounts in public. They didn't work in a laboratory to figure out what kind of content works best in those spaces to achieve engagement of some kind—retweets, likes, discussions, comments—they did it all in public, because these spaces rely on being public to get people to notice the organization's efforts. Obviously, it doesn't always work, and the failures are noticed as much as the successes. Examples of the good, the bad, and the ugly are shared all over the social web every day as more and more businesses start experimenting and look for "best practices" to help them along the way. A Google search for "best Facebook pages" provides hundreds of links to examples of brands and businesses experimenting in public—the same goes for "worst Facebook pages." (And the brands listed on both change all the time). Courage comes hand in hand with the use of social media, although more by necessity than by choice.

Courageous organizations tap into the same kind of power that social technologies demonstrated over the last several years. They do more and they are more effective because they have built the capacity to take action in the face of not knowing what the results will be. We see this in our three levels of culture, process, and behavior. Courageous organizations have cultures based in *learning*. The only way to move forward when you don't know is if you can learn as you go along; otherwise, you are just moving forward blindly. On the process side, this requires strength in *experimentation*. Moving forward is an ongoing process of trying, failing, and learning before you hit the answer that works. This needs to be baked into processes. In terms of behavior, courageous organizations emphasize *personal development*. Being courageous means not settling, not staying in that safe and comfortable zone of repetitive consistency. Courageous organizations constantly seek new growth opportunities, new challenges, and new skills.

---

4. "Netflix." Wikipedia, the Free Encyclopedia. Web. 03 June 2011. <http://en.wikipedia.org/wiki/Netflix>.

Courageous Culture: Learning

A learning organization is a place where people are continually discovering how they create their reality.

—Peter Senge, *The Fifth Discipline*

Learning in organizations is not a new concept. Peter Senge's *The Fifth Discipline*, is subtitled "The Art and Practice of the Learning Organization," and it was published more than 20 years ago. In fact, the phrase "learning organization," which was popular in management circles in the 1990s, is really almost passé now. Still, relatively few organizations have achieved anywhere close to what Senge was talking about in terms of learning in organizations. We get by, year after year, hoping to gain enough insight from what we have been doing to improve our performance for the next year, but we are not getting to that proverbial next level in our learning. Our learning and improvement are typically incremental, at best.

This is what Senge and his colleagues refer to as "reactive learning."[5] Learning, at its most basic, is simply an iterative integration of thought and action. We do things or observe things being done, and then we think about that, and then we do new things based on our thinking, and think about that some more. That's the learning process. Reactive learning is the kind of learning we do when the learning stays on the surface. We don't think too deeply about what we're observing or doing—we base our thinking on our existing view of the world, the context, the organization, and so on. This is where we learn how best to react to current circumstances. This learning is limited, and it can actually get us in trouble because it can reinforce the habits that we have already developed. We don't challenge our basic thinking, so the things that we've already done appear first in our mind as the logical options. Interestingly, Senge and his colleagues point out that in situations of anxiety and fear, we naturally default to our habits.

Courageous organizations, of course, rise above the default settings. Learning goes deeper. This sometimes takes longer, but this is the kind of learning we expect in courageous organizations. They spend more effort to develop a deeper sense of what is and an understanding of how the organization's behavior impacts the broader system. They are comfortable letting their learning actually change the organization, even the organization's basic identity. Individuals in courageous organizations even take time to explore a deeper understanding of self as part of the learning. Courageous organizations take learning seriously, because they know it is critical to their competitive advantage. It has the power to be generative, in fact, so the larger system benefits from the learning, not just the organization.

---

5. Senge, Peter M. Presence: Human Purpose and the Field of the Future. Cambridge, MA: SoL, 2004. 8.

In *Leadership Without Easy Answers*, Ronald Heifetz, a professor of leadership at Harvard's Kennedy School of Government, frames the issue in terms of technical work versus adaptive work when it comes to leadership.[6] In technical situations, the definition of the problem is clear, as is the solution that is required. The leadership required in those situations is oriented around a competent implementation of the solution and applying the right expertise. Although that can certainly be hard work, it's easier than the situations that are more complex and require adaptive leadership, because those require learning. In adaptive situations, either the problem or the solution is unclear (or both), and the only way the system will succeed is through learning. This challenges some of our traditional notions of leadership (particularly in the old, hierarchical model) in which we expect the "leaders" to provide the answers and solutions for us. In adaptive situations, leadership (from everywhere in the system) is employed in ways that facilitate problem solving by all the people who are involved in the situation. And an integral part of all problem solving is learning.

But as we said, organizations with a strong learning culture are the exception rather than the rule. To create a learning organization, you will need to evolve your culture significantly. While most culture change is difficult, building a learning culture can be particularly difficult because people tend to be overly optimistic about their own organization's commitment to learning. To create a learning culture, you need to make adjustments to walk, talk, and thought, even if some people in the organization think it is unnecessary.

Walking the Walk: The Power of Conversations and Failure

It may sound too simple, but the one single distinguishing characteristic between organizations that value learning and those that don't is the ability to have conversations. Not meetings, not memos, not communications, not lectures, not email exchanges, not PowerPoint presentations—those are fine (when done well) and important, but they do not necessarily provide the opportunity for actual conversations. We are talking about serious conversations in which learning is valued and expected. People can challenge each other's thinking and actually explore new ideas, and you don't necessarily have to find the answer in an hour. Learning cultures value these kinds of conversations, and they do whatever it takes to make sure they happen regularly. But this requires attention to several different components at the same time.

It starts with data. We are not the first people to ever suggest that data are helpful to organizations. It's almost a no-brainer. If you want good learning conversations, you

---

6. Heifetz, Ronald A. Leadership Without Easy Answers. Cambridge, MA: Belknap of Harvard UP, 1994. 69–100.

need good data as the foundation. So human organizations have a fondness for data, and the really good ones flat out love data. They love to analyze it and slice it and dice it in the learning process to make better decisions. They get data from many different sources, at different times, with an almost insatiable curiosity. The richness and diversity of data is a key factor in the quality of the conversation. It is similar to the impact of having a diverse team when it comes to innovation, including the variety fuels the creativity and capacity for problem solving.

At the same time, human organizations do not obsess over the data. A strong contingent of managers and leaders out there love the data maybe a little too much. Under the banner of "what matters is measured," they focus on analyzing the data in ways that lean too much toward providing answers, rather than sparking good conversation. Here's the real story: If it matters, then measurement is only half the battle. The data rarely give you the answer. If they do, then the problem was so ridiculously simple, most people could figure it out without the data. For complex problems (you know, the ones that occupy 90% of your time), the data are rarely conclusive. They may be clear and helpful and generate insight, but they won't tell you what to do. It is similar to a maxim from the conflict resolution field: Getting the facts straight rarely resolves the conflict, at least not the tough ones. Facts are important, but they can never tell the whole story, and true resolution comes when the parties get beyond the facts and address broader relationship issues. True learning cultures know this, and they are sure to manage their data obsession. They can be relentless in gathering and analyzing, but always in service of the conversations that generate deeper learning and never in discovering the data that solve the problem in and of themselves.

And that is one of our big problems: wanting answers. We frequently treat our learning conversations as a drive to find answers, but that actually degrades the conversation. That is why we have so many meetings with PowerPoint presentations or overly simplistic discussions of what we should be doing. We want to skip as quickly as possible to the part with the answer so we can get out of the meeting and get back to work. But these meetings *are* our work, or at least they should be. These are the conversations where we have the opportunity to engage in genuine inquiry and learn from what we have done. But because we lack the skills to have real learning conversations, we end up settling for the overly simplified answer-driven ones.

Answers (and data) should be the beginning of the conversation, not the end. We should use answers to prompt more questions that push our conversation (including maybe gathering more data) and, ultimately challenge our assumptions. When we start connecting the data, the insight, and the underlying assumptions, then we are starting to get at the deeper learning we need in our organizations. This is not a new idea. Again, Senge wrote decades ago about the power (both positive and negative) of our mental models.[7] Mental models are simply the collection of assumptions, stories, and generalizations we have about the world or, more specifically, about our own little corner of the world. Our brains like complete pictures of things, so even though we don't have a complete set of data (nor could we), we do have relatively complete models of ourselves, our organizations, our industries, and so on. Each one of us has these models in our heads, so when we create cultures that value learning, we bring people together with the express intention of shining light on these often conflicting mental models.

It requires courage to take the learning conversations to the level of challenging assumptions and mental models. That is probably why the idea of mental models has not caught on more in organizations—we often don't want to challenge our own mental models. It is uncomfortable and scary, because we might discover that we do not know as much as we thought we did or at least as much as other people think we know. Learning cultures are aware of this fear factor and create structures and processes to support it.

Perhaps the primary thing you can do to encourage better learning conversations in your culture is to address the issue of failure. It is counterintuitive to feel good about failure. As human beings, we don't like to make mistakes, so we don't like to draw attention to them. Unfortunately, it is only through paying attention to our failures that we can actually learn from them. So learning cultures (and courageous organizations) find a way to make failure an acceptable part of how they do business.

Google seems to be the poster child for companies that do failure right. Known for its "fail fast, fail smart" slogan, Google provides plenty of evidence that it values failure (and, more important, learning from failure). Many stories and quotes from Google's founders and managers all stress the value of failure. Founder Larry Page said "I want to run a company where we are moving too quickly and doing too much—not being too cautions and doing too little. If we don't have any of these mistakes, we're just not taking enough risk."[8] Google even seems to be willing to tolerate mistakes that cost a lot of money, because the company leverages the learning from the mistakes.

But it is difficult to hold Google up as the gold standard here. By the time anybody started studying its culture, Google already had a virtual monopoly on search and the kind of revenue that allows skeptics to say, "Well, if I had the resources Google

7. Senge, Peter M. The Fifth Discipline: The Art and Practice of the Learning Organization. New York: Doubleday/Currency, 2006. 174–204.

8. Lashinsky, Adam. "Chaos by Design - October 2, 2006." Business, Financial, Personal Finance News - CNNMoney. 02 Oct. 2006. Web. 03 June 2011. <http://money.cnn.com/magazines/fortune/fortune_archive/2006/10/02/8387489>.

has, then I could embrace failure too." We're not convinced. It's not about the amount of resources you have. Sure, you won't be able to make bets as large as Google can, but when Google had fewer resources, it simply made smaller bets. But you can be sure that Google still made bets and still allowed people to fail in implementing them.

One of the key tricks is a clearer understanding of the definition of failure (and success). In most organizations today, success and failure are personalized. They are often presented as primarily about the individual involved. That director of IT couldn't make the technology upgrade happen. That CEO could not turn around the organization. That meeting planner blew that meeting. That team member derailed the project. Failure is something that people do (or a term that describes someone specifically). As long as we keep failure defined personally, it will never be embraced in our organizations.

So look at your culture. Are the conversations about failure always about the people involved? Or are they more broadly about the project, the initiative, the organization, or the strategy? Separating the people from the project is critical for the conversations to really be about learning. When you frame the conversation in terms of an individual's failure, the learning is either moot (that person is a failure, and there's nothing we can do about it), or it's something specific to that individual (she needs to work on her time management skills). But it shuts down any conversation about the capacity in the system or dynamics within the team, and that's where the learning lies. In the conflict resolution field this has been described as being "hard on the problem, but soft on the people," because it enables better problem solving.

Talking the Talk: Actions Speak Louder

In trying to communicate a learning culture to stakeholders, remember that the ultimate goal here is building the capacity to be courageous. You want people in your system to step up and take action even though they feel fear. With that goal in mind, the talk about a learning culture should be somewhat downplayed. When the situation demands courage from your people, then the last thing they need is someone ordering them to be courageous or telling them that they work in a learning culture where courage is supported. You don't support people or alleviate fear by overemphasizing that point.

But having a learning culture should not be a secret, either. Saying nothing would be a mistake, because it would simply give employees some empty space that they could fill with assumptions, like the general fear many employees have of organizations—that you will punish them if they make a mistake. So it is important to be proactive in communicating a learning culture. The way to do it is by focusing your communication on the actions of learning, rather than the ideas or principles that stand behind it.

In short, you need to make the actions of a learning culture more visible by narrating them as you go along. Talk less about the culture and more about the learning itself. Make it clear that it is happening and that it is valued. This typically involves three types of communication: admitting mistakes, letting things die (visibly), and talking about what is different.

Admitting mistakes is probably the most significant thing you can do to support a learning culture. Failure is a key source of the power of learning, so it is important that failure be both visible and, essentially, "approved" at all levels, including the top. That means if you are a person with authority in your organization, you are going to have to admit to mistakes. A few years ago when Facebook changed its terms of service in ways that frustrated and angered many of its users, Mark Zuckerberg quickly posted a message admitting that what they had done (and the way they did it) was wrong, and he laid out a new plan for developing new terms of service with input from the users. It was quick, clear, and did not mince words about having made a mistake. They got feedback from their users, and they reversed their decision while they worked to address the issues raised. Facebook is now well known for making decisions that annoy people, but we as consumers know that it is watching the reactions and sticking to its guns anyway, which is something we can (mostly) live with, knowing from that original experience that we're being heard.

Contrast that with the traditional PR spin session, in which a spokesperson apologizes for anything the company "may have done" that "might have caused harm" to anyone else. (Remember BP's handling of the 2010 oil spill?) Granted, by the time you need a spokesperson to face the press, you might have some criminal charges developing in the wing, so maybe that is not the best scenario for owning up to a mistake. But those kinds of statements are not limited to press room scenarios. Plenty of leaders stand in front of their staff and choose not to own up to mistakes, to diffuse blame, and to refocus on the positive. In human organizations where learning is valued, leaders choose a different course. Mistakes are acknowledged in a matter-of-fact way, because it is understood that human beings (and human organizations) cannot be perfect.

Admitting mistakes is not the sole responsibility of the people in authority positions, however. For it to be a deep part of the culture, everyone has to feel comfortable doing it. That means if you are not in a position of authority, you have to actually look for ways to admit mistakes. We know this sounds odd. But frankly, in most organizations it is way too easy to slide through without ever having to stand up and say "I goofed on this, I'm sorry." We create many ways for the meeting to just move on to the next agenda item. But courageous organizations don't settle for that. They (you) stop the meeting so you get a chance to admit the mistake. And then the people with authority have the opportunity to welcome that news (as opposed to punishing you for it). All this is part of talking the talk around learning because you are making visible your commitment to supporting failure.

Beyond failure, it is important to simply give voice to what is different. Many organizations have developed a habit of moving from one project to the next, one strategy to the next, even one CEO to the next, without actually telling people within their organization why they are starting new projects or ending old ones. We value action so much (and learning not enough) that we focus on the next steps and where we are heading, rather than understanding what led to our choices and why we made the choices we did. We also skip the conversations that discuss why we are doing things because we are often afraid that our employees or other stakeholders will push back and challenge our decisions. That's why a learning culture is part of being a courageous organization. We must have the collective courage to present our decisions for all to see. We must be willing to hear the challenges and answer them honestly.

When you cut a program to free up budget resources for activities that are of a higher strategic priority, you need to have the conversation with all the people who were working on that project about why it was cut. Share the highlights of the learning process that led to the decision. Express your concerns. Be honest about your doubts. But have the conversation so you can make visible the actual progress that is made when organizations learn. It is a critical story that needs telling in your organization. If you don't tell that story, then your people will invent their own story, which is usually not as good as the truth:

- They cut the project because they had a vendetta against that manager.

- They cut the project because they are stubborn and don't see the value of it.

- They cut the project because they wanted to show the higher ups that they are "proactive."

Not everyone in every organization will welcome a learning culture. It challenges the status quo. That is one reason why, despite being an obviously good idea that just about everyone can support in theory (who could argue that learning is a bad idea?), we don't see a lot of true learning organizations. People like learning, just as long as it doesn't disrupt their comfortable pattern at work. So when it comes to building a true learning culture, talking the talk means making visible the change that is a normal part of learning organizations. It means welcoming challenges and explaining why you are moving in the direction you are moving. This is how we can make learning more visible and reinforce the learning culture.

Cultural Assumptions: Free Your Mind

Of all the cultural imperatives that we present in this book, a learning culture is the one most highly dependent on its cultural assumptions. Learning begins with a state of mind. If you go into a situation already knowing the answer, you are guaranteed not to learn anything. Our organizations have a "state of mind." They have underlying cultural assumptions that guide how we learn and what kind of courageousness is really permitted. For most organizations, these assumptions obstruct real learning and courage. They prevent us from questioning, they encourage us to keep silent, and they allow us to feel complacent when we blame others for problems. To turn this around, we need to infuse our organizations with a new set of assumptions.

Change Is Good

Learning and change go hand in hand. There is no point in learning anything new if nothing changes, so a learning culture assumes from the beginning that what we have now is not going to stay the same. It assumes that change is not only a given, but part of the path to better performance and a stronger system. So in building a learning culture, try to facilitate ongoing conversations about change, in addition to addressing learning specifically. We're not talking standard "change management" conversations. Change management is an unfortunate field that is more aptly described as "change enforcement." It comes from the control mindset, where your job is to make other people do what you want (but what they might not want). Change is more than that, and in human organizations, change is not viewed as something you enforce. Yes, sometimes part of change requires people to do new things—things they may not want to do initially. But the methods for getting that to happen acknowledge that change is something that emerges and is connected to growth and development of everyone in the system, including the ones who might be resistant to the change.

In their book *Switch*, Chip and Dan Heath outline a clear process for understanding change that addresses reason, emotion, and systems. At the end of the book, they point out the important fact that change, like learning, takes time and repetition. In their research, they examined how animal trainers teach animals to do tricks such as jump through hoops and ride skateboards. It is a long process that requires repetitive praise and reward for small behavior changes.

> Change isn't an event; it's a process. There is no moment when a monkey learns to skateboard; there's a process. There is no moment when a child learns to walk; there's a process. And there won't be a moment when your community starts to invest more in a school system, or starts recycling more or starts to beautify its public spaces; there will be a process. To lead a process requires persistence.[9]

---

9. Heath, Chip, and Dan Heath. Switch: How to Change Things When Change Is Hard. New York: Broadway, 2010. 253–254.

Learning, like change, is not an event that you manage. It is a process that you facilitate and nurture. Organizations with learning cultures understand this at their core.

Look Under the Rocks

Organizations with learning cultures understand that what you see is most certainly not what you get. Real learning doesn't happen by observing the surface and drawing conclusions. That is reactive learning. To have a learning culture means that your people know from the get-go that when they engage in an activity, they are going to need to turn over some stones to see what's underneath them. Learning requires constant curiosity. Organizations with learning cultures ask more questions, challenge more assumptions, and question more data. Inclusive cultures look in out of the way places to ensure they have a diverse workforce. Decentralized cultures expect to find answers and insight from every level of the organization, not only those anointed as managers. Transparent cultures understand the value of revealing what is underneath those stones. All of this is in the service of learning.

Stay Through the Hard Places

Courageous organizations know that learning is not all fun and games. It is hard sometimes, even frustrating. Anyone who has achieved mastery of a musical instrument, sport, or martial art understands the frustration of not being able to do something that you think you should be able to do. Of course, the only way to get past that frustration is to keep working and practicing. You stay through the hard places. Learning cultures know that this frustration is par for the course. Insight is never achieved instantly and without hard work. So people in these organizations are not thrown for a loop when it gets hard, or they have to struggle, or there isn't agreement on what to do next. People in learning cultures are not content with the quick answers or the shortcuts, and they continue to do the work they need to do to emerge on the other side.

Free Your Mind

There is a moment in *The Matrix* when Morpheus (the teacher) explains to Neo (the student) that the limits of the digital Matrix world are, in fact, enforced by his own mind. "You have to let it all go, Neo. Fear. Doubt. Disbelief. Free your mind." In the film, this allowed Morpheus to leap from one tall building to the next, seemingly defying the laws of gravity. In organizations, freeing your mind allows for innovation, creativity, new solutions, and learning. Freeing your mind means you are not willing to be constrained by the conventional wisdom, best practices, and dogmas of current organizational life. It's not that you get to disregard realities like accounting, revenue, the law, or policies. It's not extreme freedom. It's actually letting go of preconceived notions or thoughts that are comforting but not based in fact. It's refusing to be limited by the "that's not the way things are done around here" mindset. Free minds form the foundation of a learning culture, because more opportunities are opened.

Courageous Process: Experimentation

Cheap failure, valuable as it is on its own, is also a key part of a more complex advantage: the exploration of multiple possibilities.
—Clay Shirky, *Here Comes Everybody*

Courage starts with admitting that you don't know the answer and finishes with you taking action anyway. This definition of courage also happens to be a good definition of an experiment. Experiments start with a guess—a hypothesis—and then a plan of action designed to shed light on whether the guess is right or not. So from a process perspective, courageous organizations build experimentation into their organizations at every level. Experimentation is a critical component of learning where assumptions can be tested, new data can be generated to push the learning conversations, and new options can be generated for problem solving.

Experimentation is also critical to innovation. Courage, learning, and experimentation are all at the heart of innovation. Innovation is not merely change or doing things differently. Innovation is about creating new value. It is generative, leaving more behind than when you started. In that regard, innovation is deeply human. The demands of innovation are similar to the demands of courageous organizations. They both need learning. They both fail in cultures dominated by fear. They both are comfortable with mistakes. And they both are supported by the building block of experimentation.

Unfortunately, they also face a big obstacle: today's "best practices." The processes and systems that you find in today's organizations are designed specifically to avoid making mistakes. Our quality initiatives are all designed to reduce the number of errors. Our legal counsels are there to ensure we don't take unnecessary risks. Our performance management systems are designed to identify and reward people for doing things that work, not things that fail. There is nothing wrong with quality, risk management, and project successes, but this is not where the learning happens, and an excessive focus on those things can end up unintentionally thwarting innovation. As Stefan Thomke points out in *Experimentation Matters*, "A relentless organizational focus on success makes true experimentation all too rare."[10] All those traditional process solutions (which come from the traditional command and control

---

10. Thomke, Stefan H. Experimentation Matters: Unlocking the Potential of New Technologies for Innovation. Boston, MA: Harvard Business School, 2003. 2.

approach) need to be balanced with the risk taking, experimentation, and learning that both innovation and courageous organizations embrace.

Human organizations know they must change the way they do things to embrace more experimentation. At the structural level, this requires an intentional effort to create more space for experimentation. Internally, the focus is on reexamining measurement, and externally the challenge is translating the technology-focused concepts of beta release and open innovation to management.

Structural: Creating Space for Experimentation

Because the deck seems to be generally stacked against risk, experimenting, and innovation in today's organizations, it is important to recognize that experimentation is not likely to erupt spontaneously in your organization. It won't work to send out a memo indicating that you just read a nice book that stressed the value of experimentation, so from now on you would like your people to experiment more. It's not enough that experimentation is a good idea. It needs structural support if it is going to happen. And in this case, when we say structure, we really do mean a "space" for experimentation in an organization.

This doesn't mean a literal space, as in a room or building where experiments happen. That can work, of course, but it tends to be associated with the luxurious foosball and entertainment spaces of the dot-com era that were designed to unleash creativity. That's not what we're talking about. Physical spaces may help, but they may also get in the way, because having a special room for creative thinking, for example, can create the false expectation that the only place you can do an experiment is outside of your normal working environment. That is most decidedly not true.

The space we are talking about is more virtual or conceptual. Perhaps the most famous example is one that we have already mentioned: Google's 20% time. By giving employees the freedom to spend 20% of their time on projects that are not necessarily related to their job description, Google creates space for experimentation. It's not necessarily tangible, in that it is about managing time, but it is still a structural solution that encourages experimentation. Because that 20% of time can be spent on things unrelated to Google's core business, there is more freedom to make mistakes and fail. And Google has repeatedly reaped the rewards, as many successful programs (like Gmail) were created during 20% time.

We are almost reluctant to mention Google's solution, however, because it seems to be one that everyone talks about but few organizations actually implement. The common complaint we hear is that people are too busy to take a day every week for experimenting. If that's the case, don't create the space by blocking off time. Simply add experimentation to the job description of everyone in your organization. A nonprofit trade association, the Society of American Florists—whose 15,000 members are the retailers, growers, wholesalers, importers, manufacturers, suppliers, educators, students and allied organizations in the floral industry—did something like this in the area of social media. It was frustrated that employees were not getting engaged in the social media efforts that the association had launched, so it added social media activities to selected employees' job descriptions. The result was a noticeable increase in staff participation in social media activities. Sometimes all people need is permission; the SAF's employees needed the tasks to be officially part of what they were supposed to be doing—not because of lack of interest, but because they were busy and needed to prioritize. Putting social media activities in writing gave them that priority weighting.

What would happen if you gave your people the written permission to experiment? It doesn't mean they have to spend 20% of their time on it, but if most job descriptions included language that indicated a responsibility to experiment with new ways of getting the job done, more people would do it. Museum 2.0 blogger Nina Simon frames this issue beyond job descriptions as an issue of matching "space makers" with "risk takers" in organizations:[11]

> Risk-takers need "space-makers" to provide them with the support, the creative license, and the encouragement to try new things, fail, and get up again.
>
> Beck beautifully described her entry into museum work. She was told from day one that her director would be disappointed in her if she "didn't fall flat on her face." At first, she was excited, but it took time and trust for her to really believe her supervisors and start to pursue challenging goals. Over time, she transitioned from being a risk-taker to also being a space-maker for others in her organization, holding their hands and cheerleading them through the beginning of a process that would eventually end with a hand-off in which the new risk-takers would take total ownership of their new projects.

Adding specific responsibilities for experimentation to a job description is one way to create space. Something as simple as a manager "taking the heat" for an employee whose experiment didn't work out or for you to include other staff people in an experiment that you are working on in your own organization are also ways to create more space for experimentation.

Space making is not always about adding or expanding—sometimes it can be done with constraints. Software company NFi Studios employs a technique on some of its projects called "extreme programming." On these projects, programming teams

---

11. Simon, Nina. "Empowering Staff to Take Creative Risks." Museum 2.0. 31 May 2011. Web. 03 June 2011. <http://museumtwo.blogspot.com/2011/05/empowering-staff-to-take-creative-risks.html>.

are specifically limited to one-day cycles in developing some of the most important parts of the product. The time constraints actually encourage experimentation under the concept of "aim small, miss small." Rapid feedback allows them to try new things and still stay on track with the project focus. In this case, they are taking perfection off the table (at least in the short term), which allows for more experimentation. Had they been given more time on the project, there might have been more pressure to get it exactly "right," and experimentation would have felt too risky. You can apply this concept in a variety of contexts, even in the way you run team meetings. You can radically change the format of a single team meeting without throwing off the overall project. The parts of the new meeting structure that work can be kept and you can continue to experiment. By limiting yourself to a single meeting, you can free up more creativity in the experimentation.

Internal: Experimentation and Measurement

When thinking about how to support more experimentation internally, one area of internal processes that requires attention is measurement. In our previous discussion of learning, we warned against an over-obsession with measurement in organizations. Although an important part of management, the metrics are never going to solve the problems for you. Still, there is some truth to the notion that what we measure drives our attention. So if your goal is to support more experimentation in your internal processes, you should see whether (a) any of your existing metrics help put attention where it needs to be to support that goal or (b) you should develop some new metrics to do that.

Frankly, we are guessing that your organization does not have in place widely shared measurements related to experimentation. When we look at what most organizations measure, we more often than not are looking for results—and positive ones to boot. We measure sales, page views, attendance, hours, leads generated, email addresses captured, engagement, likes, and so on. We look for something that shows us our successes. So it would probably be a hard sell to go to your bosses and suggest that we start measuring how many times our teams did an experiment that didn't work.

But this is precisely why experimentation is so hard to come by. If no one is looking to see whether we're doing it, then it doesn't get done. Yes, some gets done whether we measure it or not. But the fact remains that establishing measurements is a relatively easy way to start to shift organizational attention and resources to experimentation. It is not good enough, though, just to measure failed experiments. You would want the metrics to capture not only the number of experiment attempts, but also (and more important) what was learned from doing the experiments. The point here is the learning, not the experimentation for its own sake. Imagine if your department head came to the all-staff meeting with a report on last quarter's experiments. This report documented how four key internal processes were all radically altered for short periods of time to see whether results could be improved. Only one change resulted in improvements, but in the other three you identified the stumbling blocks and are designing some new experiments that are more tightly focused on those parts of the process. This kind of report is rare. Instead we hear departments describing what they have done, how great they are, how impressive their accomplishments are. That is actually good, but if all we measure is what we have done, experimentation will continue to take the back seat.

In some areas, people are already doing this. In email marketing, for instance, it is common for people to develop multiple subject lines for a single campaign, using the click-through and open-rate results they get on the early emails to help make decisions on the subject lines used in later emails. Courageous organizations do not have a problem with taking those risks. Obviously the subject lines that have lower open rates were "failures," but because they contribute to learning that is nearly immediately applicable, it is deemed to be worth it.

And even if the measuring and reporting is not all positive, we still tend to report on measurements that are taken at the end of a process. We like to measure results. It is, of course, easier to measure results because the things we are doing are all (ostensibly) tied to predetermined outcomes that we desire. But waiting until everything is done squanders many opportunities for learning. An alternative is to develop and pay more attention to in-process measures (as opposed to measuring only at the end of the process). This is not a new concept, of course. In-process measures have been integrated into the Baldridge Quality Awards (which recognize U.S. organizations for performance excellence) for some time. In-process measures obviously make sense in complex manufacturing processes where parts of the process can be singled out and examined.

But there is also value in applying this concept in nonmanufacturing contexts, because it can actually open up the door to experimentation. The challenge is to find logical ways to break up the process in internal conversations so the team can create somewhat distinct areas where experimentation can take place. It may be one thread of the process that stretches the length of the project but can be treated separately enough to allow for experimental approaches to be tried. Or it may be a phase of the work that has enough down time before and after where new approaches can be developed and then measured. This act of breaking down larger processes into parts is not done in an attempt to perfect their mechanical combination. On the contrary, it is designed to bring in the more human element of play—the "sandbox." It's like marking off the boundaries of a playground and making it clear that within those boundaries, you're allowed to run and jump and use your outside voice. You can actually use measurement as a way to define those boundaries and draw people's attention to the opportunity to experiment with existing processes and practices. This is where people can get excited about trying things in new ways and solving their own problems.

External: Shifting from Technology Experimentation to Management Experimentation

In Chapter 6 we talked about how Dell and Starbucks engaged their customers online and let them have input into decisions about their product line or store setups. In Chapter 8 we talked about how Nokia expanded that idea to include partners and developers in a process like that, as well as consumers. To some extent these are all examples of external experimentation—engaging people outside the walls of your organization to develop experimental ideas about products and services. These examples are well known. It is no longer a new idea to involve people outside your organization's walls to get the work done.

Just look at the tradition of the "beta" release in software development. In the software development life cycle, there comes a time when the product is still not finished but is good enough for the consumers to give it a try. It is put out as a "beta release," and either an open or closed group of consumers gets to use the product, knowing full well that the product is basically unfinished. Their access to the product (for free usually) is given in exchange for feedback they give to the authors of the software about its performance, any glitches, and so on. This is also a good example of external experimentation—trying things out in ways that provide feedback that contributes to learning. Beta testing is becoming more and more commonplace with social software, which by the time the average online user signs in to a new application he or she might have read about in Mashable or TechCrunch, it already has a user base of hundreds or thousands of people who have been testing it.

Even the idea of product innovation has taken on an external twist in recent years with the rise of "open innovation." In 2006, consumer product giant Procter & Gamble got a lot of attention for its "connect and develop" strategy that incorporated open innovation as opposed to a closed research and development department. As a $70 billion company, it had already developed an impressive internal research and development team of 7,500 scientists but realized it wasn't enough. By the company's estimates, for every one of its people, there were 200 more out there who were just as good, doing good work. P&G wanted a way to connect to these 1.5 million other sources for innovation to grow the company, so it created the Connect and Develop program to do that—and 35% of its new products in 2006 came from research ideas that originated outside Procter & Gamble.[12]

---

12. Huston, Larry, and Nabil Sakkab. "Connect and Develop: Inside Procter & Gamble's New Model for Innovation - Harvard Business Review." Harvard Business Review Case Studies, Articles, Books. 01 Mar. 2006. Web. 03 June 2011. <http://hbr.org/product/connect-and-develop-inside-procter-gam-ble-s-new-mo/an/R0603C-PDF-ENG>.

InnoCentive is another example. A company started with seed money from Eli Lilly and Company, InnoCentive provides a marketplace for innovation, where "seekers" (large companies, including Procter & Gamble) can post problems that need to be solved, and then a network of "solvers" from all over the world receive payment for solving the problems. It has even received funding from nonprofit organizations to use the network to address challenges in disease research and science and technology issues in the developing world.[13]

But all these examples are about either technology or product development. We don't think the idea of external experimentation needs to be limited to these areas. In fact, some of the biggest opportunities that organizations have to do more experimentation outside the walls of the organization are not about technology—they are about marketing, branding, and customer service. They do involve technology, however, because the opportunities for experimentation typically involve social media.

One way to experiment is with content creation and information sharing as part of marketing and branding. Organizations building their brand presence using social media usually concentrate on the "big three"—Facebook, LinkedIn, and Twitter. Each of these spaces has a different culture of its own: The kind of content that works best on one doesn't necessarily work so well for another. The only way brands can figure out what works where is by testing different kinds of posts and seeing what gets comments, what gets linked to, what gets reviewed or rated, and what gets shared. Another experiment option is with customer service. Organizations are monitoring social media spaces for brand mentions. Then when they spot someone in need of a response, they can figure out whether to answer the question right then and there or point the person to the customer service department or some other kind of appropriate action. Companies can experiment with evangelists, finding those people passionate about an organization, and making it easy (in a variety of ways) to encourage them to spread word of mouth love on your behalf.

Many organizations are building online communities for their customers, members, users, or other stakeholders to accomplish a variety of organizational goals. Once again, there is no simple playbook for doing this; building online communities takes a lot of time, nurturing, and experimentation. What works for sponsors and business partners may not work for the most powerful influencers in your community, and you could end up with a feature-rich community with few people participating. People are unpredictable. Cause and effect relationships will be tenuous at best, and shifting quickly as new technologies and cultures emerge on the social web. With the rules changing constantly, it is critical for an organization to build a more advanced competency with experimentation (and learning) to ensure success in these types of ventures.

13. "InnoCentive." Wikipedia, the Free Encyclopedia. 31 May 2011. Web. 03 June 2011. <http://en.wikipedia.org/wiki/InnoCentive>.

Courageous Behavior: Personal Development

Without a better understanding of human development—what it is, how it is enabled, how it is constrained—what passes for "leadership development" will...be like new files and programs brought to the existing operating system. They may have certain value—new files and programs do give you greater range and versatility—but your ability to use them will still be limited by your current operating system. True development is about transforming the operating system itself, not just increasing your fund of knowledge or your behavioral repertoire.

— Robert Kegan and Lisa Laskow Lahey, *Immunity to Change*

Courageous organizations have cultures that understand deep learning and have developed processes that incorporate experimentation and risk taking. That's a big deal, actually. We don't throw those terms around loosely. Relatively few organizations are truly committed to deep learning or have found ways to build experimentation into everything they do. It is hard work to do these things, and many companies today will survive and even make some profit without working that hard. But that success won't last, and those companies should not be our models. The path of the human organization offers great potential, and as the pace of change increases, it is becoming the only viable path forward. But for those disciplined few that choose the hard (and more rewarding) path, there is another important fact that must be faced: Deep learning, experimentation, and risk taking, quite frankly, are not for everyone.

Courageous organizations need a critical mass of people who can handle risk and change and deep learning, and human beings do not acquire that capacity automatically. So the individual behavior needed most in courageous organizations is personal development. The individuals in courageous organizations are well aware that the world is changing faster than before, and they respond by holding themselves to a high standard of personal development. They embody a learning culture by constantly seeking to increase their knowledge. They are unafraid of going through personal changes to do their job better. They can handle risk. They will challenge their own assumptions. They are certainly not perfect, nor are they superheroes. They are regular people who make mistakes, but also have the courage to learn from them and not settle in their personal and professional lives.

You might think that we have already covered this topic. After all, in the preceding three chapters we covered the different types of knowledge and skills that individuals need to develop to be effective in human organizations. In open organizations we talked about ownership, including deeper knowledge of how the organization works and the skills of conflict management, communicating across media, and managing your ego. For trustworthy organizations, we talked about authenticity, knowing yourself, the skill of curiosity, and knowledge of personality typing systems. Generative behavior covered relationship building, both at the interpersonal level and at the systemic level. This sounds like enough for people to work on in terms of personal development, doesn't it?

Yes, those sets of knowledge and skills are important, but they are not enough. Remember how central fear is to organizational dysfunction. Getting past fear requires more than competency, particularly in today's fast-paced, social world. Developing skills will only help so much. Earlier in this chapter we made reference to the distinction that Ron Heifetz makes between technical leadership challenges (it is known how to solve the problem; you just need the relevant technical competence) and adaptive challenges, where a clear definition of the problem and the solution are not known as you begin to tackle them. Adaptive challenges can be anxiety producing, because so much is unknown. The skills themselves don't reduce the anxiety. What is required is a stronger capacity to deal with complexity. The personal development we need to develop courageous behavior, therefore, is in managing complexity.

Unfortunately, that is not something typically included in the agendas of our leadership or management training programs. Fortunately, the research in the field of adult development is starting to show us some methods for increasing this capacity in individuals. Robert Kegan and Lisa Lahey have been doing research in this arena for 20 years with the goal of busting the myth that our brains stop developing once we become adults. We have no problem understanding that our brains go through different developmental stages all through childhood, but there is a common perception that once we hit adulthood, the only thing that changes in our brains over the rest of our lives is how much we use them.

Kegan and Lahey's research has shown otherwise. They identified three distinct phases of development in an adult's capacity to handle mental complexity.[14] The first is the "socialized mind," where people define themselves mostly in their relationships to other people or to ideas. They assess what is going on in their environment and choose behaviors related to the role expectations in that environment. People at this level of complexity capacity are good team players because they identify so strongly with specific groups or ideas. The down side is that they often have trouble filtering information properly if it conflicts with their existing ideas or connections (groupthink). Kegan and Lahey call the second level the "self-authoring mind," where individuals can step back a bit from their environment and see themselves more clearly. Individuals here have found their voice and are more comfortable being in the driver's seat, though the clearer understanding of self can get them

14. Kegan, Robert, and Lisa Laskow Lahey. Immunity to Change: How to Overcome It and Unlock the Potential in Yourself and Your Organization. Boston, MA: Harvard Business, 2009.

into trouble if they end up off-course. The third and more elusive level is called the "self-transforming mind." At this stage, individuals can actually step back and get some perspective on their own agenda and approach to see systems more completely. They are more comfortable with paradox and are more skilled at seeing their own, inner contradictions (which is a critical step in achieving this level of development in the first place).

Think, for a moment, about how this applies to much of what we have been writing about in this book. We are suggesting that human organizations are marked by individuals who can take ownership, be authentic, and build relationships both interpersonally and within systems. Although we provide guidance on how to develop relevant knowledge and skills in those areas, it still seems obvious that they are areas that are becoming increasingly difficult to master for people who are stuck at the "socialized mind" level. Nathaniel Branden wrote about this 15 years ago in a book about self-esteem. Even then he could see the business world changing in ways that demand a greater capacity for innovation, self-management, and self-direction at all levels of the organization:

> Today, organizations need not only an unprecedentedly higher level of knowledge and skill among all those who participate, but also a higher level of independence, self-reliance, self trust, and the capacity to exercise initiative.[15]

He's talking about having more people in your organization at the levels of self-authoring or self-transformation. That is where you can not only be independent and exercise initiative, but you can also have a little perspective about yourself so you can be more effective within, between, and among different systems.

Unfortunately, according to Kegan and Lahey, only a small percentage of people have made it fully to the self-transformation level. So we have our work cut out for us in the realm of personal development if we want this kind of capacity in our organizations. There is clearly not one single path to developing our capacity to deal with complexity. Note, though, that this challenge is not limited to the executive level. Personal development is needed at every level and every department. This is how we develop the capacity of the whole system to have more of an impact on its environment. That, in fact, is the real definition of leadership development—improving system capacity to shape the future. Even though we can't give you a simple checklist of instructions to follow for moving up the complexity scale, we do have some broad guidelines for going about the work of personal development.

---

15. Branden, Nathaniel. The Six Pillars of Self-Esteem. New York, NY: Bantam, 1995. 22–23.

Make Time

People need time to do this work. You cannot fit personal development in at the end of the day on Friday, at an occasional two-hour senior staff meeting, or during an annual performance review. Like any kind of deep learning, it takes serious, repetitive effort. Human organizations take a stand here and grant time for their staff to develop themselves—beyond letting them go to a conference once a year, or stopping by their office now and again to ask how it's going. You must do more than use your commute time to think about where you want to be in five years. Organizations also need to find ways for line employees to get the job done without them being on the line all the time. Maybe not everyone on the line needs to be operating at the self-transformational level, but look for the ones with promise and support them in getting there, because the sooner they hit that level the more effective they will be. Of course managers and executives also need time for this, but we rarely give it to them. We might schedule an "off-site retreat" now and again, but frequently no more than once a year. We like Patrick Lencioni's suggestion of quarterly one- or two-day retreats for senior management teams.[16] And even that will be tight, because so much of those retreats needs to be focused on strategy, planning, financial management, and so on. Senior management teams also need specific time devoted to helping each other develop personally. It's a critical part of developing leadership.

Get Personal

It's not called "personal development" by accident. Human organizations are comfortable with their employees examining issues that are personal as part of the process of becoming better employees. There is an obvious line between personal and professional in everyone's life, and we are not advocating the elimination of that line. But the line has never been as sharp as it has historically been made out to be, and the fuzziness is only increasing in today's social world. When you take the time to work on increasing your capacity to deal with complexity, you'll want to get feedback from your coworkers, but you'll also benefit from feedback from your spouse, partner, or close friends. If you want to be a more effective CEO, you'll likely address issues of control, identity, and personal meaning. This is just part of the process, and as "touchy-feely" as it might seem to traditionalists who insist on remaining "strictly professional" during the off-site, the most powerful human organizations recognize it as part of what must be done.

---

16. Lencioni, Patrick. Death by Meeting: A Leadership Fable—about Solving the Most Painful Problem in Business. San Francisco, CA: Jossey-Bass, 2004.

Say Good-Bye

As you explore personal development in your organization, you are likely to discover that not everyone in your organization is "the right person on the bus," to borrow a phrase from Jim Collins' *Good to Great*. Sometimes in the process of personal development, you may realize that your current job does not support you in becoming the person and professional you are called to become. And on the other side, as a boss or an employer, you might realize that some of the people in your employment are either not where they need to be in terms of development or not likely to get there anytime soon.

In those cases we need to say good-bye. Now, obviously we cannot give generic advice about quitting or firing people (nor would our lawyers let us). But this is an important issue that needs attention in most organizations when it comes to personal development. Maybe it's just the independent Generation X in us, but we feel like organizations sometimes take the whole employer/employee relationship a little too seriously. We are afraid to fire people, not only because of potential lawsuits but also because of the costs of retraining people or even the genuinely caring desire to not see anyone hurt or unhappy. Yet we will absorb the costs of underperformance for years, hurting our results and weakening our capacity over the long term. And we are also afraid to quit, worried we won't find as good a job or one with the right benefits and culture, so we stick it out (for years) in a toxic workplace.

Just the Beginning

Trinity: *Neo... nobody has ever done this before.*
Neo: *That's why it's going to work.*

—*The Matrix*, 1999

Almost everyone fears change, to some extent. That's human, as much as is courage in the face of that fear. The key when it comes to organizations is that a mechanistic view of progress—and of success—has created a business environment where all our processes are meant to minimize the risks involved with change. The pace of change is accelerating and becoming less predictable, but the solution is *not* to figure out different ways to minimize the effects of that change. The solution is to embrace learning, to bake experimentation into our processes, and to make each individual responsible for striving to continue their own personal development in ways that will help our organizations roll with those changes.

Must Read

This chapter is about courage, so we thought it would be fitting to suggest a few books that might make you a bit uncomfortable. The following three books are not "easy read" leadership books that give you encouraging stories about successful leaders that leave you feeling inspired. These are books that challenge your thinking, push your assumptions, and actually make you do the work of figuring out what to do next. That is what is required of leaders at all levels in courageous organizations.

Our choice related to the topic of learning cultures is *Presence*, by Peter Senge et al. We recommend Senge's classic *The Fifth Discipline* for systems thinking, and this book goes further. It is based on a series of interviews with both leading edge scientists and entrepreneurs and represents a level of thinking not found in most business books. For experimentation, we suggest *Open Community* by Lindy Dreyer and Maddie Grant. This is the shortest book on our "must read" lists, but by no means the easiest. It is a social media book, which makes sense for experimentation, but it's not a how-to. It lays out the key issues that nonprofit organizations need to face when building community on the Web and then makes them figure out themselves how to do it. (Because that's the only way that really works.) For personal development, we present Kegan and Lahey's *Immunity to Change*. Based on a generation of research, the authors finally present a serious "self-help" book for leaders that explains how people and organizations can build a capacity for dealing with complexity.

Dreyer, Lindy and Maddie Grant, CAE. *Open Community: A Little Book of Big Ideas for Associations Navigating the Social Web*. Madison, WI: Omnipress, 2010.

Kegan, Robert, and Lisa Laskow Lahey. *Immunity to Change: How to Overcome It and Unlock the Potential in Yourself and Your Organization*. Boston, MA: Harvard Business, 2009.

Senge, Peter M. *Presence: Human Purpose and the Field of the Future*. Cambridge, MA: SoL, 2004.

Get Started Today: Worksheet

Enough reading. Let's get started!

Download and print the worksheet accompanying this chapter at www.humanize-book.com.

All four worksheets accompanying this book are structured in the same way. The first section helps you assess how courageous your organization is and includes a quiz and some open-ended questions. In the second section, we guide you through conversations with others in your organization about courage. And the last section gets you going on an action plan.

We ask you to take a hard look at how courageous your organization is. Do people admit mistakes? Do all of your data and measurements actually generate conversations that lead to real change? Do you give learning the time it needs and deserves? These are things to look for in cultures that value learning. At the process level you examine how good you are at experimentation. This includes assessing your organization's comfort with innovation and how much space you give people to experiment and try new things. At the behavior level the focus is on personal development. Is your organization truly committed to developing people beyond the simple acquisition of new skills?

The next step is to have some conversations with others in your organization about these topics. As we said at the beginning of this chapter, we put being courageous as the last chapter on purpose. This topic is a bit more challenging, and we think it will be more difficult to talk about. So we actually recommend you have conversations about the other worksheets first, so people will already be more comfortable with these types of conversations when they start to dig into learning, admitting mistakes, trying new things, and confronting personal growth. We include in the worksheets some advice about how to approach these conversations based on where you are in your organization's hierarchy.

Executives. Start with a conversation just among the senior management. Because we're talking about fear here, if you get everybody together too quickly, you're likely to end up with a lot of awkward silence. When you have those first conversations, hold yourselves accountable to a responsible conversation. That is, own up to where *you* at your level are getting in the way of learning, experimentation, or personal development. This topic lends itself more to "blaming" others in the system for the problem. You need to identify your responsibility here.

When you do get together with other groups, you want to start by acknowledging your own responsibility. That's the best way to ensure that people will open and up and share in a multilevel conversation about these issues. And when you get people together, also start by making it clear that not all the problems will be solved in one conversation. Do everything you can to create a safe space for people to talk openly.

Middle managers. Like the senior managers, we recommend starting this conversation with a group of people at your same level in the organization. The conversation about overcoming fear needs to start with you (and others) taking responsibility for your role in the issue, which is easier to do with just middle managers in the room. And you might want to focus first on the experimentation issue, as that one might be playing out in several different ways for you. (In one context you might wish you could experiment more, and in another you might find other people think *you* are the ones blocking experimentation.) When you start meeting with people from other levels, move on to learning more broadly. As connectors, people in the middle play a key role in learning.

Front line employees. Again, we recommend you start this conversation with people at your same level. Start with the learning topic, particularly opportunities to learn from failure. That's obviously a topic that is easier to address without the higher-ups in the room. But you want to clarify that value, because it will be an important part of the conversations you'll have as a whole organization. Also, because you're closer to customers or external partners, you might have good insight to share about ways to increase external experimentation.

Ultimately, the changes we advise throughout this book are necessary, they are possible, and they start with you. Don't wait for permission or the perfect timing. Are *you* ready? Go.

10

What Now?

I don't know the future. I didn't come here to tell you how this is going to end. I came here to tell you how it's going to begin.

—Neo, in *The Matrix*, 1999

Humanizing your organization is hard work. Thank you for bearing with us to this point, even though, as you have by now realized, this is only the beginning. We all need to act, now.

We need to create organizations that inspire us and bring out the best in us. We need to create organizations that people are eager to join and where people want to go to work on Mondays. We need to create organizations where people will invest the same kind of energy, time, and passion, quite frankly, that they put into interacting through social media. It is not enough to aspire to create organizations that are merely tolerated, where our employees stick around because they do not have a better offer. We should not celebrate simply because our employees do not post Dilbert cartoons on their cube walls. Much as we love Dilbert, let's work together (or, heck, each on our own, to start with) to make that kind of truth a thing of a bygone era.

Social Media Challenges Are Organizational Challenges

In practical terms, let's see how far we've come. Let's go back for a minute to some of the social media challenges we explored as questions in Chapter 4, "Challenges to Socializing Business." At a cultural level, we have the following hurdles (among others):

- Some people in my office are gung ho about starting social media initiatives, but I think we don't have a strategy; I want to know more about why this is important for me or for my department or for my company as a whole.

- How do we respond if someone wants to know more than we want to share about something related to our company?

- We have some smart younger folks in our company who we'd love to get doing some social media management for us because they find it easy and they're tech savvy, but we're not sure we can trust them to act professionally.

Can you see how these questions appear to be about social media implementation issues, but they are really asking how this organization could be more trustworthy? More open and decentralized, more clear about strategic objectives? More collaborative? Employees in an open organization have a clear understanding of what they can share and why they can share it, and that allows them to be more responsive to customers. Even if they have to say no to a customer, they know *why* they have to say no. Open organizations give each person the knowledge he needs to take ownership, and that decentralizes decision making as a matter of course. They trust their employees (at every level), and in doing so they enable the organization as a whole to be trustworthy. They listen to different voices and incorporate learning into the way they do things. Examining and removing the cultural hurdles that create these questions will build the capacity for growth and progress, starting with social media work but extending through everything an organization does.

And what about at the process level? Here are some of the challenges:

- The PR department insists that we clear every tweet and Facebook post through them first. We can't work like this.

- I just heard of Quora and I want to start answering questions about our industry. Can I just go for it? Whom do I ask?

- I'm in charge of our brand monitoring and I use some good tools, but it's really hard to be the only one. What if I got hit by a bus?

- The education department got really annoyed that we responded to a post asking about the date of our conference. That made no sense! We knew the answer, so we should be able to respond!

Once again, these questions are not, in fact, about social media tactics and implementation, but about how employees inside an organization must be able to collaborate, share information, have space to experiment, and trust each other. These kinds of problems appear time and again in working through the details of social media management, but they illuminate deeper structural issues.

And finally, on the behavior side:

- My boss doesn't get that interacting online with people is good for work. If they know me, they will keep coming back.

- I don't know enough about the big picture. Why is this particular initiative important? What are we trying to achieve?

- I want to be able to respond to someone online on behalf of my organization, but I'm not sure if that's okay.

- We need a community manager for our private site, but we don't have anyone on staff who really knows how to nurture a community.

We hate the word "empowered" because that's like some gift bestowed from the C-suite on high, as opposed to something that comes from within. But it's clear that all these individual behavior challenges would be solved if people felt supported by their organizations. If they had the access to the training, the knowledge, and the skills they need to be able to play their individual parts to nurture connections and relationships, they would be able to help their organizations flourish. And growing and developing their personal interests would also create a vibrant, creative, experimental, diverse environment for people to work in and learn from each other. In the end, how open, trustworthy, generative, and courageous your organization is will be just as relevant to the previous questions as will be individual tactical skills in social media.

These questions and challenges were all spoken by people implementing social media for their organizations, but, as we warned you at the beginning, this book hasn't actually been about social media. This is a book about leadership. It's a book about the definition of leadership that is woven into the fabric of human organizations, which comes from Peter Senge, the champion of both systems thinking and learning organizations:

> Leadership is the capacity within the human community to shape its future.

That definition can be scaled down, of course, to focus just on your organization. Organizations that have leadership are the ones that shape their future, that actually work to create the outcomes they seek. They won't have complete control (as a mechanical system might demand), but they are more effective at shaping the future. Systems in which the leadership capacity is weak simply have the future happen to them. Their energy tends to become dissipated or scattered, and it's harder for them to count on positive results. And notice that within this definition, leadership is not something that exists only at the top of the organization. It is a system capacity. So, yes, individuals who hold positions of authority are key figures in determining the system capacity, but they are not the only ones. That is why when we developed the downloadable worksheets at the end of each of our chapters on the four human elements, we wrote specific instructions for executives, middle managers, and front line employees. Leadership exists simultaneously at all three levels.

So take another look at your social media implementation issues. Are these roadblocks you're running up against actually tactical, or is this a broader leadership issue? By all means, keep working on the tactical issues. Leadership capacity does include the ability to master tactical challenges. You should continue to push through the good social media implementation books and leverage your networks to bring in more capacity to build community in your organization. But don't stop there. We need more than better tactics and better band-aids. We need to fix the root of the problem. We need more human organizations.

We attempted to break up the hard work of determining how and where to start pushing your organization to be more human by giving you many angles and perspectives from which you can look at the four elements. If you haven't already done so, make sure you download at least one of the worksheets and complete it. Do your own assessment of your organization's capacity for embracing that human element, and have a few conversations with your colleagues about it. Take the time to develop even a small action plan, and then start implementing it. And as you put ideas into action, of course, you need to keep learning. Then you can start to weave in work on some of the other human elements.

As you get into this work, you will find that the elements are inextricably linked. You can't become more trustworthy, as an organization, without becoming more open. You can't become more generative without becoming more open. You can't become more courageous without becoming more trustworthy, internally and externally. As you move forward with your work on becoming a more human organization, you may find the boundaries between the human elements disappearing, and that's okay. The point here is not to win a trophy for becoming the most generative organization in your industry. The point is to start increasing your capacity to shape the future.

How to Be the Catalyst for Change

We can't talk about building capacity within systems without talking a little bit more about how to spark change. The worksheets we provide are there to help you evaluate where your organization is in terms of its openness, trustworthiness, generativity, and courage. They are meant to be conversation starters for comparing your thoughts with others in your organization. They are one way to start coming up with actionable ideas. But here's the truth you already know: Our systems are built to stop you. We have created structures and put them in place to minimize risk and change. So even as you (individually or in groups) come up with actions you can take, it'll never be as easy as "just do it."

We mentioned Chip and Dan Heath's book *Switch: How To Change Things When Change Is Hard* in an earlier chapter. This book has some essential advice for how to make change happen, and we urge you to read it if you get stuck. The authors suggest three ways to think about how you can change behavior:

1. **Direct the rider.** Sometimes resistance to change is actually simply a lack of clarity of what people are supposed to do. Directing the rider is about giving clear directions and clear objectives. It's also about finding things that are working well and doing *more* of those things.

2. **Motivate the elephant.** Get people's emotional attention. Our argument for humanness is somewhat emotional to begin with, but we need to figure out how to unleash passion about it. Passion means motivation. It's not about facts and figures (even when the data demonstrate clear improvement to the bottom line) but about getting people to feel good about the changes we're trying to push. Use stories about successes, and think of ways people can share experiences and be recognized for those that show positive change.

3. **Shape the path.** Change the situation or the surrounding environment to clear the way for change to happen. A lot of what we talk about in this book, specifically at the internal process level for each of the four human elements, is about shaping the path. When we can see in practical terms how certain internal structural factors (such as performance reviews, our interview process, or who we invite to meetings) create barriers to change, it becomes possible (sometimes easy, sometimes not easy) to change those structures. Doing so can make behavior change easier.

Switch has a lot of examples to clarify what these three motivators look like in real life situations. That book will be extremely helpful when you get ready to start the work of humanizing your organization, at whatever level of the hierarchy you may be.

Another way to think about effecting change is to think about ideas in terms of frequency, reach, and yield (FRY). Olivier Blanchard adapted this FRY method originally from Microsoft and applies it to social media measurement and return on investment in great detail in his book *Social Media ROI*. We love this formula (acronym notwithstanding), and it works great in many different contexts. Here is the concept in terms of sales:

- **Frequency.** Getting customers to buy more often

- **Reach.** Getting more people to become customers

- **Yield.** Getting customers to buy more, either per transaction or buying more products/services

Frequency relates to *time*, reach relates to *how many people*, and yield relates to *how much* they invest. In our worksheets, we ask you to bear this formula in mind when you start coming up with ideas for becoming more human as an organization. So instead of sales, we're talking about how to generate more of the four human elements. Can you find ways to be open *more often*? Can you get *more people* to be transparent in particular circumstances? Can you *expand* the areas where you're already generative? This meshes really well with the idea of finding the bright spots and doing more of those.

The work involved in humanizing your organization is not a feel-good, we all get to be fulfilled humans and sing "Kumbaya" kind of thing. It needs discipline, and we guarantee you will hit the point where you want to go back to the mechanical simplicity of cubicles, strategic plans, and performance reviews. What we're trying to do is parse your thinking and your efforts out into manageable chunks, so anyone can find a chink in the armor and try their hand at chipping away. But we all need to figure out how this will work in each of our individual circumstances. Reading this book is only a start. Everyone is different and has different work circumstances to deal with. We think everyone has a part to play—willingly and passionately—if you make that choice.

Red Pill or Blue Pill?

"Choice" is the operative word. At a key moment in the first *Matrix* movie, the hero Neo is offered a critical choice. He can take the red pill and become unplugged from the Matrix's virtual reality and wake up to the "real" world (which is decidedly more messy and harder work). Or, he can take the blue pill, which will simply erase his more recent memories and place him back into the Matrix, continuing the status quo. It is a critical, adaptive choice, a rare crystallized moment separating one level from the next. Humanizing your organization has a similar feel to it. Like Neo, we're choosing to take the red pill that enables us to unplug ourselves from the

Matrix, even though we know there's no turning back. We choose to move forward into a truly human way of organizations—not back to simpler times before technology. Being human is hard work and messy, but when we start on the path of humanizing our organizations, and enable ourselves and our communities to thrive, we'll start to change the world.

We believe that our four human elements—being trustworthy, generative, open, and courageous—are characteristics that you find in people who fully embrace changing the world. These are not the only four, and we don't pretend to have a grand theory backed by research that proves that the only people capable of changing the world are the ones who possess these four characteristics. But we're not waiting for those research results to come in, either. We are moving forward with our hypothesis, which is that part of our development and growth as human beings is to figure out how to be these things. We see it when we look at the people we respect and admire who are actually changing the world for the better. When we see the people who run away from that challenge, who cannot embrace these elements, we have compassion and provide support; we know that during certain times in our lives, we all were (or are) these people. These people are not evil, bad, or wrong. They (we) are just at that particular point in the journey. If we have the opportunity, we should help them to continue on the path, because being open, trustworthy, generative, and courageous yields returns for those individuals and all who are connected to them.

We are arguing that the same is true for organizations.

Spurred on by the demands of a social, mobile, connected society, growing numbers of consumers, employees, and other stakeholders are starting to make a change. Successful organizations, companies, and brands are starting to be more human, changing not only appearances, but also the way they do things. They are refusing to be stuck within mechanical boundaries. They are also innovating in ways that respect and encourage the individual people at their core. This is what we mean by humanizing the organization—one that flourishes by being more human.

As we become more successful in creating human organizations, we can start to apply these concepts more broadly. What if our government were more human? What if our neighborhoods were more human? What do we need to do to be able to create a healthcare system that is more open, trustworthy, generative, and courageous? How might these human elements change the way we do philanthropy? These conversations will be even more challenging than getting the people from the marketing and product development departments to speak the same language. We need to get entire systems talking to each other. We will challenge assumptions that have literally been institutionalized. There won't be a set of best practices to get us through these problems. It's going to be hard. But these are the areas where we face the real adaptive challenges, and ignoring them in favor of the status quo is becoming less and less tolerable.

It seems that the epic choice between the red pill and blue pill is not a one-time choice. It's like a spiral. As we make one adaptive choice, we break through to a new reality and eventually succumb to the status quo of the new level. It's better than where we were, but there will always be that next level calling to us. So we choose the red pill again to make it to the next level. In today's social world, driven by technology, our spiral seems to be tightening. The framework of open, trustworthy, generative, and courageous doesn't give us all the answers, but it should support us just enough to start answering the call.

Index

Symbols

20% time, 120, 233

A

accomplishing more, 216

actions speak louder than words, 227-229

adaptation, 62

adaptive leadership, 54

admitting mistakes, 228

advocacy organizations, 27

aggregation sites, 27

aggressive sensitivity, 197-198

American Institute of Architects, 143

analog age, 86

Apple, 39

Armano, David, 100

association industry, 26

assumptions
  behind culture of transparency, 165-167
    knowledge, 165
    responsibility, 166
    risk, 165
  behind inclusive culture, 196
    aggressive sensitivity, 197-198
    dynamic stability, 198
    proud humility, 196-197
  courageous culture, 230
    change is good, 230-231
    free your mind, 231
    look under the rocks, 231
    stay through the hard places, 231
  culture, 67

authenticity, 110, 178-179
  knowledge, 179-181
  skills, 181-183

authority, culture and, 71-73

B

balancing loops, 133

Baldridge Quality Awards, 236

Barger, Christopher, 157

beer game, 133

behavior, 82-84
  courage, 239-241
    get personal, 242
    make time, 242
    say good-bye, 243
  culture, 67
  defined, 84-85
  generative behavior, 207-208
    interpersonal relationships, 208-211
    network relationships, 211-215
  identity management, 85-87
  knowledge management, 88-89
  open behavior, 140-142
    knowledge, 142-146
    skills, 146-149
  relationships, 87-88
  social media and, 85
  trustworthy, 178-179
    knowledge, 179-181
    skills, 181-183

Bennis, Warren, 167

Bernoff, Josh, 17

best practices, 34-35
  human resource management, 46-48
    hiring processes, 48-50
    organizational structure, 50-53
  versus innovation, 35-38
  leadership. *See* leadership
  strategic planning, 38-39
    basics of, 40-41
    truth of, 41-43
    you can't predict the future, 43
    you can't script the formation of strategy, 45-46
    you can't separate thought from action, 44-45

Bhargava, Rohit, 24

Blanchard, Olivier, 81, 115

Blogger.com, 20

blogging, 20

Bohr, Neils, 94

Bovatzis, Richard, 54, 182

BP oil spill, 104-105

Branden, Nathaniel, 241

Bryant, Lee, 61

Buckingham, Marcus, 180

Buffet, Warren, 156

C

Callagy, Ms., 103

Carroll, Dave, 101-102, 141

catalysts for change, 251-252

challenges of social media, 63
  behavior, 82-84
    defined, 84-85
    identity management, 85-87
    knowledge management, 88-89
    relationships, 87-88
    social media and, 85
  organizational culture, 64-66
    authority and control, 71-73
    defined, 66-68
    risk, 69-70
    social media and, 68-69
  process, 73-75
    defined, 75-76
    hierarchies, 77-78
    measurements, 80-82
    silos/communication, 78-80
    social media and, 76-77

change, 243
  being a catalyst for, 251-252

Change.org, 106

charitable nonprofits, 27

choice, 252-254

choosing collaborative strategies, 204

Citizen Marketers, 18

citizen-created content, 18

A Civil Disservice, 49

Cluetrain Manifesto, 16

Coffman, Curt, 180

collaboration, 25-27, 199-200
  collaborative brand, 200-202
  collaborative strategy, 203-206

collaborative brand, 200-202

collaborative strategy, 203-206

collective action, 26-27

Collins, Jim, 54, 64, 196, 243

communicating across media, 148-149

communications, processes, 78-80

communities, 25
  Open Community, 28-29

conflict
  managing, 146-147
  truth, 171-174

consistency, 162-164

consumers, becoming producers, 20-21

content creators, teens, 20

content curators, 24

control, culture and, 71-73

convergent thinking, 45

conversations, 224-227

courage, 96, 112-113, 219-222

courageous behavior, 239-241
  get personal, 242
  make time, 242
  say good-bye, 243

courageous culture, 223-224
  assumptions, 230
    change is good, 230-231
    free your mind, 231
    look under the rocks, 231
    stay through the hard places, 231

talk, 227-229
walk, 224-227

courageous process, 232-233
  external process, shifting from technology to management experimentation, 237-238
  internal process, experimentation and measurement, 235-236
  structure, creating space for experimentation, 233-235

Covey, Stephen M. R., 54, 156

Creating Customer Evangelists, 18

CrisisCamp, 27

Culbert, Samuel, 172

cultivating more human organizations, 96-99
  BP oil spill, 104-105
  Etsy's offensive art versus censorship debate, 105-106
  Gap logo reversal, 103-104
  Motrin moms backlash, 99-101
  United Breaks Guitars, 101-102

cultivating truth, 175-177

cultural assumptions, 128
  clarity over control, 130
  leadership is a system capacity, 130
  proceed until apprehended, 130
  protect and serve, 129
  we are not alone, 129

culture
  authority and control, 71-73
  courage. *See* courageous culture
  defined, 66-68
  generative. *See* generative culture
  open culture. *See* open culture
  organizational. *See* organizational culture
  risk, 69-70
  social media and, 68-69
  trustworthy. *See* trustworthy culture

curation, 24

curiosity, 181

D

Davenport, Thomas, 75

decentralization, 107, 117-119

  who steps up

    talk, 125-128

    thought, 128-130

    who acts, 124-125

    who decides, 119-122

    who speaks, 122-124

delays, 133

Dell, IdeaStorm, 139

Deming, W. Edwards, 111, 220

demographics of users of social media, 13-14

destiny, 181

detail complexity, 131

dialogues, 103

differences, making visible, 194-196

Dilbert cartoons, 5

DISC (dominance, influence, steadiness, and conscientious), 182

diverse teams, 193

diversity, 190-191

doing, collaborative strategy, 205

Dolnick, Edward, 93

Drucker, Peter, 220

dynamic complexity, 131-132

dynamic stability, 198

E

ecosystems, cultivating truth, 175-177

egos, managing, 149

Eli Lilly and Company, InnoCentive, 238

emotional intelligence, 182

Enron, 169

environments

  tomorrow's world, 4-6

  world we live in today, 2-4

eras of the social web, 29-30

Etsy's offensive art versus censorship debate, 105-106

experimentation, 232-233

  creating space for, 233-235

  measurement and, 235-236

  shifting from technology to management experimentation, 237-238

external level, 8

external process

  open communities, 138-140

  shifting from technology to management experimentation, 237-238

  truth, cultivating, 175-177

external processes, 76

F

Facebook, 148, 222

  growth of, 12

  terms of service, 228

failure, 224-227

fear, 113, 219-220

filters, 24-25

Fitzpatrick, Brad, 20

Fleet, Dave, 84

Flickr, 21

formalization, 45

free agents, 28

frequency, 252

G

Gap logo reversal, 103-104

generative, 96, 110-112, 187-189

generative behavior, 207-208

  interpersonal relationships, 208-211

  network relationships, 211-215

generative culture, inclusion, 190-192
  talk, 194-196
  thought, 196-198
  walk, 192-194
generative organizations, 189
generative power, 30
generative process, 199-200
  collaborative brand, 200-202
  collaborative strategy, 203-206
George, Bill, 78
Gerstandt, Joe, 191
goals, thematic goals, 145
Godin, Seth, 100
Goleman, Daniel, 54, 182
Google, 87, 112
  20% time, 120, 233
  failure, 226
Gore, William, 51
Gore-Tex, 51
Grant, Maddie, 28, 212
groundswell, 17, 30
Groundswell, 18
growth, 189
  of Facebook, 12
  of LinkedIn, 13
  of Twitter, 12
  of Wikipedia, 13
  of YouTube, 13

H

Hamel, Gary, 37, 52
Hansen, Marka, 103
Hansen, Morten, 199
Haque, Umair, 187
Harquail, C. V., 183
Harte, Beth, 79
HBDI (Herrmann Brain Dominance Instrument), 183

Heath, Chip, 230, 251
Heath, Dan, 230, 251
Heifetz, Ronald, 54, 224
hierarchies, processes and, 77-78
high-speed Internet, 16
hiring processes, human resource management, 48-50
Honesty ROI, 19
Horvath, Mark, 27
Howe, Jeff, 22
Huba, Jackie, 18
human organizations, 4-6
  trellis for cultivating, 96-99
    BP oil spill, 104-105
    Etsy's offensive art versus censorship debate, 105-106
    Gap logo reversal, 103-104
    Motrin moms backlash, 99-101
    United Breaks Guitars, 101-102
human resource management, 46-48
  hiring processes, 48-50
  organizational structure, 50-53

I

IdeasProject, 201
IdeaStorm, 139
identity management, behavior, 85-87
IDEO, 202
inclusion, 111, 190-192
  talk, 194-196
  thought, 196
    aggressive sensitivity, 197-198
    dynamic stability, 198
    proud humility, 196-197
  walk, 192-194
individual behaviors, 64
individualism, 118
information wants to be free, 21-22

InnoCentive, 238

innovation
    best practices versus, 35-38
    open, 237

intelligence, emotional, 182

internal level, 8

internal processes, 76
    experimentation and measurement, 235-236
    perpetual motion, 136-138
    truth, 171-174

Internet, 3
    high-speed, 16

interpersonal relationships, 208-211

intersections, 191, 207

Irlweg, Ms., 141

J

Joel, Mitch, 207

Johansson, Frans, 191

K

Kanter, Beth, 28

Kegan, Robert, 239-240

Kellner-Rogers, Myron, 198, 219

knowledge, 8
    interpersonal relationships, 208
    open behavior, 142-146
    transparency, 165
    trustworthy behavior, 179-181

knowledge archipelago, 138

knowledge management, behavior, 88-89

Kouzes, James, 53

L

Lahey, Lisa Laskow, 239-240

lead users, 25

leadership, 5, 53-57, 249
    adaptive leadership, 54
    system capacity, 130

learning, 223-224
    assumptions, 230
        change is good, 230-231
        free your mind, 231
        look under the rocks, 231
        stay through the hard places, 231
    collaborative strategy, 206
    talk, 227-229
    walk, 224-227

legacy media, 38

Lencioni, Patrick, 135, 242

Levine, Rick, 16

Li, Charlene, 17, 130

LinkedIn, growth of, 13

LiveJournal, 20

Locke, Christopher, 16

M

machine world, 92-94

machines, 2

managing
    egos, 149
    conflict, 146-147

marketing, word of mouth, 18-19

Matrix movies, 1

McCarran International Airport, 62

McConnell, Ben, 18

McKee, Annie, 182

measurements, processes, 80-82

media
  communicating across, 148-149
  legacy media, 38
meetings, 174
message control, 176
micro-collaboration, 89
Microsoft, 39
Mills, Fred, 49
Mintzberg, Henry, 42
mistakes, admitting, 228
mobile phones, 15-16
Motrin moms backlash, 99-101
Myers-Briggs Type Indicator (MBTI), 182

N

Netflix, 221-222
network relationships, 211-215
new meaning, 183-184
newspaper industry, 22
NFi Studios, 234
Nintendo, 39
Nokia, 201-202
noninstitutional groups, 26
nonprofit industry, 27
Nordstrom, talk, 126
Notter, Jamie, 160
NTEN (Nonprofit Technology Network), 123, 177

O

Ogilvy, 103
old world media, 37
online searches, 22-23

open behavior, 140-142
  knowledge, 142-146
  skills, 146
    communicating across media, 148-149
    managing conflict, 146-147
    managing your ego, 149
open communities, open process, 138-140
Open Community, 28-29
open culture, 117-119
  who steps up, 119
    talk, 125-128
    thought, 128-130
    who acts, 124-125
    who decides, 119-122
    who speaks, 122-124
open innovation, 237
open process, 131-132
  external process, open communities, 138-140
  internal process, perpetual motion, 136-138
  silos, 134-136
OpenIDEO, 202
openness, 96, 106-108, 115-117, 150
organizational challenges, 248-250
organizational culture, 63-66
  authority and control, 71-73
  defined, 66-68
  risk, 69-70
  social media and, 68-69
organizational management, best practices. See best practices, 58
organizational silos, 79
  open process, 134-136
organizational structure, human resource management, 50-53
Ormerod, Paul, 42

ownership, 108, 140-142
  knowledge, 142-146
  skills, 146
    communicating across media, 148-149
    managing conflict, 146-147
    managing your ego, 149
Owyang, Jeremiah, 29

P

performance reviews, 172
perpetual motion, open process, 136-138
personal development, 239-241
  get personal, 242
  make time, 242
  say good-bye, 243
Peters, Tom, 155
Pfeffer, Jeffrey, 49, 220
Pink, Dan, 181
Posner, Barry, 53
Prahalad, C. K., 36
predictability, 38-39
Private Client Group of Prudential securities, 161
process, 63, 73-75
  courageous, 232-233
    external process: shifting from technology to management experimentation, 237-238
    internal process: experimentation and measurement, 235-236
    structural: creating space for experimentation, 233-235
  defined, 75-76
  generative. See generative process
  hierarchies, 77-78
  measurements, 80-82
  open process, 131-132
    external: open communities, 138-140
    internal: perpetual motion, 136-138
    silos, 134-136

silos/communication, 78-80
social media and, 76-77
truth, 167-169
  external process: cultivating truth, 175-177
  internal process: conflict, 171-174
  structure, 169-171
Procter & Gamble, 237
producers from consumers, 20-21
professional relationships, 209
project teams, 173
proud humility, 196-197

Q

Quora, 16

R

reach, 252
Red Cross, 27
reinforcing loops, 133
relationships, 207-208
  behavior, 87-88
  interpersonal relationships, 208-211
  network relationships, 211-215
responsibility, transparency, 166
risk
  culture and, 69-70
  transparency, 165
risk-takers, 234

S

salary information, 160-161
Sarbanes-Oxley Act of 2002, 169
Savage, Dan, 27
scenario planning, 41
scientific management, 40

searching, 22-23

Searls, Doc, 16, 91

self-knowledge, 208

Senge, Peter, 57, 130-132, 223

Shaw, George Bernard, 148

Shirky, Clay, 11, 24, 232

silos
    open process, 134-136
    processes, 78-80

Simon, Nina, 234

Simpson, Josh, 104

skills, 8
    open behavior, 146
        communicating across media, 148-149
        managing conflict, 146-147
        managing your ego, 149
    trustworthy behavior, 181-183

social commerce, 30

social media, 3-4
    behavior and, 85
    culture and, 68-69
    defined, 12
    demographics of users, 13-14
    Facebook, growth of, 12
    from consumers to producers, 20-21
    information wants to be free, 21-22
    LinkedIn, growth of, 13
    online searches, 22-23
    process and, 76-77
    Twitter, growth of, 12
    users of, 14-16
    Wikipedia, growth of, 13
    YouTube, growth of, 13

social media challenges, 248-250

social media revolution
    filters, 24-25
    from consumers to producers, 20-21
    information wants to be free, 21-22
    overview, 16-18

searches, 22-23
    word of mouth marketing, 18-19

social webs, eras of, 29-30

Society of American Florists, 234

soft skills, 193

Sony, 39

Southwest Airlines, 145

space-makers, 234

Starbucks, 139, 201

Stetler, Brian, 23

Stockdale Paradox, 196

strategic planning, 38-39
    basics of, 40-41
    truth of, 41-43
    you can't predict the future, 43
    you can't script the formation of strategy, 45-46
    you can't separate thought from action, 44-45

strategic transparency, 159-162

strategy, collaborative, 203-206

Stroup, Jim, 55

structural level, 8

structural processes, 76

structure
    creating space for experimentation, 233-235
    truth, 169-171

Surowiecki, Jim, 139

Sutton, Robert, 49, 220

Switch: How To Change Things When Change Is Hard, 251

SWOT (Strengths, Weaknesses, Opportunities, and Threats), 41, 44

synergy, 200

systems thinking, 131-132
    defined, 132-134
    external process, open communities, 138-140

internal process, perpetual motion, 136-138

structure, silos, 134-136

T

talk, 8

courageous culture, 227-229

generative culture, inclusion, 194-196

open culture, 125-128

trustworthy culture, consistency, 162-164

Tapscott, Don, 160

Taylor, Frederick, 40, 46, 58

teams, diverse teams, 193

teens, content creators, 20

trellis, cultivating more human organizations, 95-99

BP oil spill, 104-105

Etsy's offensive art versus censorship debate, 105-106

Gap logo reversal, 103-104

Motrin moms backlash, 99-101

United Breaks Guitars, 101-102

thematic goals, 145

Thomke, Stefan, 232

thought, 8

generative culture, inclusion, 196-198

open culture, 128

clarity over control, 130

leadership is a system capacity, 130

proceed until apprehended, 130

protect and serve, 129

we are not alone, 129

trustworthy culture, 165

knowledge, 165-167

transparency, 109

trustworthy culture, 158-159

talk, 162-164

thought, 165-167

walk, 159-162

trust, 156-158

trust dividend, 156

trustworthy, 96, 108-110, 155-156

trustworthy behavior, authenticity, 178-179

knowledge, 179-181

skills, 181-183

trustworthy culture, transparency, 158-159

talk, 162-164

thought, 165-167

walk, 159-162

trustworthy processes, 167-169

external process: cultivating truth, 175-177

internal process: conflict, 171-174

structure, 169-171

truth, 167-169

external process: cultivating truth, 175-177

internal process: conflict, 171-174

structure, 169-171

Twitter, 188

growth of, 12

U

understand, collaborative strategy, 204

United Breaks Guitars, 101-102, 141

Users of social media, 13-16

V

voters, younger voters, 23

W

W. L. Gore & Associates, 51-52, 71

Wal-Mart, 156

walk, 8

courageous culture, 224-227

generative culture, inclusion, 192-194

open culture, who steps up, 119-125

trustworthy culture, strategic transparency, 159-162

Weinberger, David, 16

Wheatley, Margaret, 198, 216, 219

White, Leslie, 70

Whole Foods, 160, 164-166

Wikinomics, 25

Wikipedia, growth of, 13

Williams, Evan, 13, 20, 126

WOMMA (Word of Mouth Marketing Association), 19

word of mouth marketing, 18-19

WorldCom, 169

Y

Yammer, 215

yield, 252

younger voters, 23

YouTube, growth of, 13

Z

Zappos, 145

Zuckerberg, Mark, 228

quepublishing.com

Browse by Topic ▼ | Browse by Format ▼ | USING | More ▼

Store | Safari Books Online

QUEPUBLISHING.COM
Your Publisher for Home & Office Computing

Quepublishing.com includes all your favorite—
and some new—Que series and authors to help you
learn about computers and technology for the home,
office, and business.

Looking for tips and tricks, video tutorials, articles and
interviews, podcasts, and resources to make your life
easier? Visit **quepublishing.com**.

- **Read the latest articles and sample chapters**
  by Que's expert authors

- **Free podcasts** provide information on the
  hottest tech topics

- **Register your Que products** and receive updates,
  supplemental content, and a coupon to be used
  on your next purchase

- **Check out promotions and special offers**
  available from Que and our retail partners

- **Join the site** and receive members-only offers
  and benefits

QUE NEWSLETTER
quepublishing.com/newslette

 twitter.com/
quepublishing

 facebook.com/
quepublishing

 youtube.com/
quepublishing

 quepublishing.com/
rss

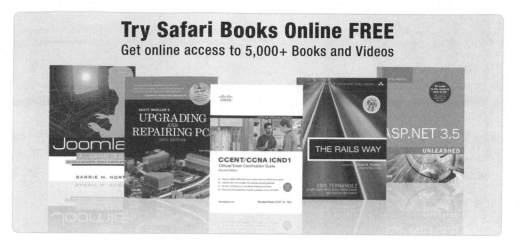

FREE Online Edition

Your purchase of **Humanize!** includes access to a free online edition for 45 days through the Safari Books Online subscription service. Nearly every Que book is available online through Safari Books Online, along with more than 5,000 other technical books and videos from publishers such as Addison-Wesley Professional, Cisco Press, Exam Cram, IBM Press, O'Reilly, Prentice Hall, and Sams.

SAFARI BOOKS ONLINE allows you to search for a specific answer, cut and paste code, download chapters, and stay current with emerging technologies.

Activate your FREE Online Edition at www.informit.com/safarifree

> **STEP 1:** Enter the coupon code: OHGNLCB.

> **STEP 2:** New Safari users, complete the brief registration form. Safari subscribers, just log in.

If you have difficulty registering on Safari or accessing the online edition, please e-mail customer-service@safaribooksonline.com